# A MINUTE of MARGIN

*restoring balance to busy lives*

RICHARD A. SWENSON, M.D.

# NAVPRESS®

Bringing Truth to Life

## OUR GUARANTEE TO YOU

We believe so strongly in the message of our books that we are making this quality guarantee to you. If for any reason you are disappointed with the content of this book, return the title page to us with your name and address and we will refund to you the list price of the book. To help us serve you better, please briefly describe why you were disappointed. Mail your refund request to: NavPress, P.O. Box 35002, Colorado Springs, CO 80935.

NavPress, P.O. Box 35001, Colorado Springs, CO 80935

The Navigators is an international Christian organization. Our mission is to reach, disciple, and equip people to know Christ and to make Him known through successive generations. We envision multitudes of diverse people in the United States and every other nation who have a passionate love for Christ, live a lifestyle of sharing Christ's love, and multiply spiritual laborers among those without Christ.

NavPress is the publishing ministry of The Navigators. NavPress publications help believers learn biblical truth and apply what they learn to their lives and ministries. Our mission is to stimulate spiritual formation among our readers.

ISBN 1-57683-068-3

Cover design by: Ray Moore
Cover photo by: PhotoSpin
Creative Team: Don Simpson, Amy Spencer, Darla Hightower, Pat Miller

Unless otherwise identified, all Scripture quotations in this publication are taken from the HOLY BIBLE: NEW INTERNATIONAL VERSION® (NIV®). Copyright © 1973, 1978, 1984 by International Bible Society. Used by permission of Zondervan Publishing House. All rights reserved. Other versions used include the *Revised Standard Version Bible* (RSV), copyright 1946, 1952, 1971, by the Division of Christian Education of the National Council of the Churches of Christ in the USA, used by permission, all rights reserved; and the *King James Version* (KJV).

Swenson, Richard A.
  A minute of margin : restoring balance to busy lives / Richard A.
Swenson.-- 1st ed.
      p. cm.
Includes bibliographical references and index.
  ISBN 1-57683-068-3
  1. Time management--Religious aspects--Christianity--Meditations. 2.
Stress (Psychology)--Religious aspects--Christianity--Meditations. I.
Title.
BV4598.5.S94 2003
242--dc22
                                        2003014377

Printed in Canada
1 2 3 4 5 6 7 8 9 10 / 08 07 06 05 04 03

FOR A FREE CATALOG OF
NAVPRESS BOOKS & BIBLE STUDIES,
CALL 1-800-366-7788 (USA)
OR 1-416-499-4615 (CANADA)

# TOPICS

(These numbers refer to the reflection number)

# ACKNOWLEDGMENTS

THIS BOOK IS the result of creative work that stretches back two decades. Throughout much of that time, Don Simpson has guided the editorial process with the wise advice of a true literary scholar and the gentle touch of a sensitive human being.

Bill and Gail Thedinga have once again provided literary resources and invaluable practical helps that allow ease of continuation despite other scheduled requirements. Members of our extended family and many close personal friends have provided books, research materials, and exceptional ongoing affirmation and prayer.

Our children, Matt, Adam, and daughter-in-law, Maureen, have provided understanding and support during the weighty distraction of manuscript deadlines. Adam, in particular, has endured significant delays in writing his own novel, portions of which we are working on jointly. I appreciate his patience and now hopefully we can jump back into the flow of fiction with both feet.

My wife, Linda, has once again carried the heavy demands of researcher, copy editor, and literary navigator. As always, she willingly walks step-by-step through this long process: sharing the load, comforting the frustrations, and inspiring the text. It is an honor to co-labor — in writing and in life — with someone whose beliefs and passions so completely mirror my own.

# INTRODUCTION

MARGIN IS LIKE oxygen—everybody needs some. If we have too little, we suffer from the shortage. If we have too much, the excess will not benefit us additionally. But having the right amount permits us to breathe freely.

Margin is a space, specifically the space between our load and our limits. It is this space that enhances vitality and resilience. It is this space that guarantees sustainability. It is in this space where healing occurs, where our batteries are recharged, where our relationships are nourished, and where wisdom is found. Without margin, both rest and contemplation are but theoretical concepts, unaffordable and unrealistic.

We do not follow two inches behind the next car on the interstate—that would leave no margin for error. We do not allow only two minutes to change planes in Chicago—that would be foolish in the extreme. We do not load boats until they are nearly submerged—that would invite disaster. Why then do we insist on leaving no buffer, no space, no reserves in our day-to-day?

Not to romanticize the past, but there was a time when people had some margin in their lives—at least more than we do today. People lingered at the dinner table, helped the kids with homework, visited with the neighbors, took long walks, dug in the garden, and slept full nights. None of this was regarded as unusual but instead represented the normal flow of daily affairs. In our current era of unreasoned hurry, however, such activities are increasingly viewed as rare luxuries.

If we are ever to restore such a margin to overloaded lives, it is first essential to understand what margin is and why it disappeared. In medicine, physicians realize that illness cannot be conquered until it is first identified. All of our therapeutics flow from a correct diagnosis of the disease. If margin is fundamental to healthy living, where did it go and how do we get it back?

That modernity arrived accompanied by so much exhaustion and psychic distress was embarrassingly mispredicted by futurists over the past fifty years. In the previous millennium it was widely believed that education, affluence, time-saving devices, and labor-saving technologies would deliver a world progressively diminished of hurry and tension. The opposite happened, and many are still trying to understand exactly how such a sabotage could broadside an entire culture without warning.

The explanation is fairly straightforward yet still not widely comprehended. Our enemy is also our beneficiary: progress. Progress is helpful but not pure. Even as progress results in many advantages, it is also accompanied by disadvantages. Progress brings blessing, but it also brings pain.

Progress works by differentiating our environment. Thus progress always gives us *more and more of everything, faster and faster*. Always. This differentiation is not a problem—as long as what we need is more. Of everything. Faster and faster. When overloaded, however, *more and more, faster and faster* becomes problematic.

The bottleneck is the established fact of human limits. Limits are both real and universal. If we all have limits, that means we all have thresholds to those limits. If we all have thresholds, that means it is just a matter of time before an escalating progress finds these thresholds and exceeds them. This is now being done with frightening suddenness.

As a result, most of us now live beyond the threshold of our limits. Overload is the new human condition. We have too many choices and decisions, too many activities and commitments, too much change creating too much stress. We have too much speed and hurry. We have too much technology, complexity, traffic, information, possessions, debt, expectations, advertisements, and media. We even have too much work.

When on the unsaturated side of our limits, we can be open and expansive. We can say *Yes* to new opportunities, activities, and obligations. But on the saturated side of our limits, the rules of the game totally change. We cannot say *Yes* to something until we say *No* to something equally time consuming or energy draining.

It is important to notice that these trends are not self-correcting. If progress were to slow or stop, our economy would fall apart. To date, this lacks bipartisan support. Therefore, progress will continue to give us more, axiomatically leading to increasing stress, change, complexity, speed, intensity, and overload. Such a list is not as negative as it might first appear, but it certainly implies that discernment must be used and priorities must be clear when choosing any future course of action.

These issues have special significance for spiritually minded people. We have limits just like everyone else. Once these limits are exceeded, we have no margin for prayer, for caring, for service, for stillness, for community. That I have limits, of course, in no way means that God has limits. His most spectacular work is accomplished in the face of human limits. We are yet secure.

For more than a decade now I have employed various formats to disseminate this message. Several of my books and many of my published articles deal with margin. In addition, I have traveled the world for thousands of speaking presentations and participated in hundreds of broadcast interviews. Several radio producers have remarked that the concepts of margin, overload, and balance would lend themselves well to a daily one-minute radio broadcast. For several reasons I have decided at present against that approach. Instead, I opted for the written reflection rather than spoken commentary.

Many people who perhaps need this teaching most insist they have no time to read. And perhaps with their current levels of busyness, they are right. The format of *A Minute of Margin*, consisting of 180 two-page reflections, is specifically designed to be helpful in such a setting. Everyone, even the desperately time-challenged, can read two pages.

It is my desire that margin will draw you to a new freedom lived on a higher plane, even as it nourishes your life in the direction of things that matter most.

# One September Morning on the 103rd Floor

*If you attempt to talk with a dying man about sports or business,*
*he is no longer interested. He now sees other things as more*
*important. People who are dying recognize what we often forget,*
*that we are standing on the brink of another world.*

William Law, eighteenth-century British theologian

---

THE SKIES WERE partly cloudy, the temperature was 68 degrees, the wind was out of the west at 10 miles per hour. A beautiful day. At 8:45 A.M., people working on the 103rd floor were pouring their morning coffee, straightening their desks, reviewing their Tuesday appointments, bantering with office mates, glancing at the harbor . . .

One minute later, none of that mattered. Twenty floors below, a 757 transected the building, leaving the 103rd cut off, trapped, hopeless. But not yet dead.

When you have ten minutes to live, what are your thoughts? What is important in the last seconds? As a tribute to those nameless faces staring down at us from the smoky inferno, can we stop what we are doing long enough to listen to them? Seeing death from this perspective is not morbid: on the contrary, it can help us see life.

Those who found phones called—not their stockbrokers to check the latest ticker, not their hairstylists to cancel the afternoon's appointment, not even their insurance agents to check coverage levels. They called spouses to say "I love you" one last time, children to say "You are precious" one last time, parents to say "Thank you" one last time. Through tears they called best friends, neighbors, pastors and priests and rabbis. "I just want you to know what you mean to me." And surely those standing on the brink of another world thought of God—of truth and eternity, judgment and redemption, grace and the gospel.

Imminent death has a commanding power to straighten life's priorities with a jolt. At such dramatic moments, people suddenly realize that priorities matter.

Tragically, however, chronic overloading obscures this truth. How we live influences how we die, and misplaced busyness leads to terminal regrets. If we don't move to establish and then guard that which matters most, the breathless pace of daily overload will blind us to eternal priorities, until one day we too stand at such a window and look down. Perhaps with regret.

*R Slow the pace of living until you again remember that day. If that were you on the 103rd floor, what would have been important? Live it. Don't hide behind the excuse of overload. Daily make space in your life for the things that matter most.*

---

The afternoon knows what the morning never dreamed.
<small>SWEDISH PROVERB</small>

# THE DISEASE OF THE NEW MILLENNIUM

*I love a broad margin to my life. Sometimes, in a summer morning,*
*having taken my accustomed bath, I sat in my sunny doorway*
*from sunrise till noon, rapt in a revery.*

HENRY DAVID THOREAU

THE CONDITIONS OF modern-day living devour margin. If you are homeless, we direct you to a shelter. If you are penniless, we offer you food stamps. If you are breathless, we connect you to oxygen. But if you are marginless, we give you yet one more thing to do.

Marginless is being thirty minutes late to the doctor's office because you were twenty minutes late getting out of the hairstylist's because you were ten minutes late dropping the children off at school because the car ran out of gas two blocks from the gas station—and you forgot your wallet.

Margin, on the other hand, is having breath left at the top of the staircase; money left at the end of the month; and sanity left at the end of adolescence. Marginless is the baby crying and the phone ringing at the same time: margin is Grandma taking the baby for the afternoon. Marginless is being asked to carry a load heavier than you can lift: margin is a friend to carry half the burden. Marginless is not having time to finish your stress book: margin is having time to read it twice.

That our age might be described as stressful comes as a discomforting surprise when we have so many advantages.

Progress has given us unprecedented affluence, education, technology, entertainment, and convenience. Why then do so many of us feel like air traffic controllers out of control? Somehow we are not flourishing under the gifts of modernity as one would expect.

The marginless lifestyle is a relatively new invention and one of progress's most unreasonable ideas. No one is immune. It is not limited to a certain socioeconomic group or a certain educational level. Even those with a deep spiritual faith are not spared. Its pain is impartial and nonsectarian—everybody gets to have some.

Marginless living is curable, and a return to health is possible. But the kind of health I speak of will seldom be found in the direction of "progress" or "success." For that reason I'm not sure how many are willing to take the cure. But at least we all deserve a chance to understand the disease.

*R̷ Make an intentional decision about how much marginless-ness—that is, how much overload—is acceptable in your life. Some enjoy a high-stimulus life of continuous multitasking. Others prefer a more controlled, peaceful pace. Once you understand where on this spectrum you function best, attempt to stay within a range of tolerances. Exceeding these parameters will put your productivity and passion at risk, eventually resulting in exhaustion, disorganization, and irritation.*

---

Happiness is a place between too little and too much.
<small>FINNISH PROVERB</small>

# THE ONE-MINUTE MILE

*Much as we long for infinities of power and duration, we have no evidence that these lie within our reach, much less within our responsibility. It is more likely that we will have either to live within our limits, within the human definition, or not live at all. And certainly the knowledge of these limits and of how to live within them is the most comely and graceful knowledge that we have, the most healing and the most whole.*

WENDELL BERRY, WRITER AND FARMER

RECENTLY, I MENTIONED to an athletic friend that humans will never run a one-minute mile. He paused briefly, looked at me with a smile, and said, "Never say never."

Think about this. With whom do you agree? Do you agree with my friend and insist that someone might, *just might*, eventually run the mile in one minute, as unlikely as that seems? Or do you agree with my assertion that it is impossible?

If you paused to consider the possibility of the one-minute mile, I am sympathetic to your pause. But just the fact that we are willing to even *consider* the possibility of a one-minute mile illustrates that we have a problem accepting our limits.

Of course we all wish to be careful making such pronouncements as "the one-minute mile is impossible." In the past, people made predictions only to appear foolish later when the predictions turned out wrong.

But I want to force you into a position here. If you insist on saying that the one-minute mile might eventually be possible, then how about the thirty-second mile? How about the five-second mile? Eventually, you will have to agree that *we have limits.*

The position I am taking is not always popular. We are so accustomed to pushing the limits—even exalting that push— that we often completely skip over the fact that we do, in fact, have limits. We all do. It is undeniable. Everything on earth has limits.

It is true, of course, that many individuals have accomplished stunning feats. One person memorized the nonrepeating number *pi* to thirty thousand digits. Some climb Mount Everest without oxygen. Some run a marathon in Nepal at an average elevation of fourteen thousand feet. Dramatic stuff.

After reading of such accomplishments, we might be tempted to assume that humans have almost unlimited powers. But when we take such an assumption at face value and adopt it as a life motto, we can find ourselves in deep trouble—heart attacks, work dread, ruined relationships, exhaustion, depression, and burnout. Many are already there. And many more are dangerously close.

R Stretch yourself, with my blessing. Dream large. Break records. Accomplish new goals. Perfect your discipline. But *always remember that the race is not a race for records but a race for love. Hear me: You do not wish to come to the finish line and discover you were in the wrong race.*

---

He who opens his heart for ambition closes it for the rest.
CHINESE PROVERB

# REDESIGNING LIFE

*Civilization, in the real sense of the term, consists not in the
multiplication, but in the deliberate and voluntary reduction of
wants. This alone promotes real happiness and contentment, and
increases the capacity for service.*

MAHATMA GANDHI

---

THERE WAS A point in my life when, of necessity, I decided
to investigate a more margined way of living. Everything
seemed out of control. I remember one day in particular—a
Tuesday in 1982. I was finishing an evening meeting across
town and beginning a migraine at the same time. Meanwhile
back home, my wife, Linda, went for a late-evening walk.
Along the dark street, her crying could be in private.

Interestingly, we had no problems: no debt difficulties, no
relational conflicts, no malpractice lawsuits. No problems, but
plenty of symptoms. We looked at each other and scratched
our heads in puzzlement. Where were these migraines and
crying coming from? We made a commitment to remedy
whatever was sabotaging our home.

Once we understood that overload was the problem and
margin the solution, our next question was, How do we start?
Setting aside a special evening, we put the kids to bed early,
built a fire in the fireplace, and settled down on the living
room floor. It was time to make a substantive change. I took
out a pad of paper. "Let's start by pretending everything in our

lives is written on this paper," I said. "Every activity, every belief, every influence.

"Then let's erase it all. Tear up the paper and throw it in the fire. Wipe the slate clean. Erase all our beliefs, hopes, and dreams. Remove all our possessions. Nothing should remain. Then let's give the pencil to God and ask Him to redesign our lives by that which is fully spiritually authentic."

An exhilarating sense of freedom swept over us. As we wrestled control of our lives away from the world, we felt the elephant slipping off our backs. And as we turned and handed control over to God, no spiritualized elephant took its place. We instantly sensed that the Father had in mind much more than our survival. It was an indescribable feeling.

Our redesigned life was simpler. That decision reduced our income significantly, but the freedom, time, rest, and balance have been worth it. We have never looked back.

Today, because of margin, I no longer dread getting up in the morning or looking around the next corner. Today, when I hang out the "Gone Fishing" sign on my door, I don't worry about the opinion of the world. For as I head down the road with my family, I know that the same God who invented both rest and relationship is wishing us a good catch.

> $R_x$ *Ask God to redesign your life. Make a list of changes (our list had twenty-nine)—small or large—and make a plan to implement at least one.*

---

It is not enough to aim; you must hit.

ITALIAN PROVERB

# TIME-SAVING TECHNOLOGY
# THAT DOESN'T

*People are submitting themselves to time-devouring technology.
We're a nerve-racked society where people have difficulty sitting
back and thinking of the purpose of what they do.*

TODD GITLIN, BERKELEY SOCIOLOGIST

---

IT WAS WIDELY assumed that progress would be time gifting,
yet the opposite has been the case. This has caused no small
amount of consternation, and rightly so. As we have seen,
progress gives us more and more of everything faster and
faster. The inevitable result of such a cascading equation is the
automatic consumption of our time.

If we sit back and do nothing about it, next year we will
have less time margin than we do right now. For every hour
progress saves us by organizing and technologizing our time,
it consumes two more hours through the consequences, direct
or indirect, of this activity. Because this fact is counterintuitive
and subtle, we do not notice it happening.

If progress is the train driving us to the land of overload,
technology is the engine. They are coupled. Just as they have
been partners in bringing us benefit, so they have partnered
together in bringing us overload.

Technology plays an integral role in nearly every contemporary form of overload. Similarly, the resisting of technology
plays an equally important role in the suggested prescriptions.

Accessibility overload, for example, is only possible because accessing technologies are now so mobile and miniaturized we have no excuse available for not being on call for the universe. Media overload has exploded precisely because technology has given us a telecommunications revolution unprecedented in human history. There is now even a television set that can be worn on the head. Activity overload is only possible because the technologies of transportation and communication both stimulate and facilitate it. And so on.

These developments are surprising, even shocking. We are now confronted with a new contemporary axiom: time-saving technologies don't. Instead they compress time, consume time, and devour time. All the countries with the most time-saving technologies are the most stressed-out countries, a statement that is easy to prove sociologically. Clocks, watches, alarms, computers, cell phones, pagers, e-mail, beepers, answering machines, voice mail, fax machines—each has a role to play in this important development, and thus each must be used with discernment.

> *R* *Remembering that technology is responsible for a great deal of our time famine and overload, it is helpful to remember where the "off" switch is located. You can use technologies selectively, and you can also turn them off selectively. Try disconnecting from clocks, watches, alarms, beepers, telephones, and faxes for a day, a weekend, or a week.*

---

An inch of time is an inch of gold but you can't buy that
inch of time with an inch of gold.

<small>CHINESE PROVERB</small>

# EXPECTATION OVERLOAD

*The life of people on earth is obviously better now than it has ever been — certainly much better than it was 500 years ago when people beat each other with cats. This may sound silly but now and then when I read old fairy tales and see an illustration of a hunchbacked hag with no teeth and bumps on her nose who lives by herself in the forest, I think: People looked like that once. They lived like that. There were no doctors, no phones, and people lived in the dark in a hole in a tree. It was terrible. It's much better now. But we are not happier. I believe we are just cleaner, more attractive sad people than we used to be.*

PEGGY NOONAN, PRESIDENTIAL SPEECHWRITER, JOURNALIST

A MEDICAL COLLEAGUE bounded up to me, announcing, "I finally discovered the best way to get through the day. In the morning, I say 'This is going to be the worst day of my life.' Then when the day is only half horrible, I'm happy!" It was offered tongue-in-cheek, but along with the humor comes a dose of wisdom: our happiness and contentment are dependent on the expectations we bring to the experience. As progress gives us more and more benefits, it raises expectations. This, in turn, often makes it harder to find the happiness and contentment we seek.

One clear advantage of progress is that we have learned that life *can* be improved. But one clear disadvantage of progress is that we have come to expect that life *will* be improved. The expectation tends to rise faster than the improvement. Happiness versus unhappiness, satisfaction versus dissatisfaction, contentment versus discontentment are all contingent on expectation, not on the actual improvement. If, for example, we expect 10 dollars and receive 1,000, we are ecstatic. But if we expect 100,000 dollars and receive 1,000, we are crushed. In each case, we received the same amount. The emotional result, however, was different.

Expectation overload is one of the most difficult overloads to control. Our affluent, media-saturated age has spawned a rising tide of expectations. We expect health, wealth, and ease—and are discontent if more doesn't come, no matter how well-off we are.

But reining in expectations is a human possibility. Instead of following the "more and more" of progress and the "you deserve the best" of culture, we can follow the "be content with what you have" of Scripture.[1] Our lifestyles can relax, our spirits can rest, our relationships can thrive, and our margin can replenish.

> $R$ *Adjust your expectations. Implicit in the "Expect more and you'll get it"[2] message is that it is always appropriate to expect more. But as you adjust your expectations downward, you'll discover less to be unhappy about. If you always expect success and prosperity, you're destined to be chronically frustrated. But if you give your expectations to God and then accept what the day brings, you'll discover a rare freedom.*

---

Who owns too much, remains unhappy.
TUPURI PROVERB

# A QUANTUM OF ENERGY

*Still another step toward simplicity is to refuse to live beyond our means emotionally. In a culture where whirl is king, we must understand our emotional limits. Ulcers, migraines, nervous tension, and a dozen other symptoms mark our psychic overload. We are concerned not to live beyond our means financially; why do it emotionally?*

RICHARD FOSTER, QUAKER THEOLOGIAN, AUTHOR

---

EACH MORNING WE rise to meet the day with a certain measure of emotional energy, a quantum of stamina. For some this energy reservoir is huge, while for others it is nearly drained empty. Some are buoyant and resilient, filled with a zest and vitality that never seems to change. Others have had their emotional chins on the ground for most of their lives and can't remember what it feels like to smile.

This quantum of emotional energy is not fixed but instead is in constant flux with our daily environment. We are always losing energy into our environment and receiving energy back again. Sometimes the reservoir is being drained, as when we are sad or angry. Other times the reservoir is being filled, perhaps by expressions of encouragement or activities successfully completed.

No matter how large or small the quantum of emotional energy is at the start of the day, and no matter how fast or slow it is exchanging with the environment, one thing is certain: the amount within us is finite. No one has an infinite capacity for emotional discharge. When our reserves are depleted, they are depleted. If we make further withdrawals, we will enter emotional indebtedness. With our margin exhausted, pain will be felt—sometimes at dangerous levels.

It is important to understand our emotional reserves. It is important to understand how much we have at the beginning of each day and which influences drain our emotions dry or recharge our batteries. It is important to learn what our limits are and not to make further withdrawals if we are already maximally depleted. And it is important to respect these limits in others.

We often have trouble accepting the idea of rationing our emotional energy. It is simply too difficult to quantify feelings. We feel ashamed admitting that our spirit is exhausted. But our hesitancy in no way constitutes proof that such limits are only a convenient fiction for the weak. Instead our hesitancy is an obstacle to overcome. Margin gives us permission.

*R℞ First, identify those triggers that drain you disproportionately—financial difficulties, argumentative children, traffic, noise, sleeplessness, work overload, negative people. Perhaps you cannot change the external event itself, but you can either decrease exposure to such events or develop more personal control over your response. Second, identify those activities that enhance emotional resilience—positive people, laughter, rest, music, worship, prayer, Scripture reading, accomplishment, sports, hiking, fishing. Specifically schedule space in your energy budget for this important recharging of your batteries.*

—⦿—

That's too much sand for my truck.
PORTUGUESE PROVERB

# MARGIN IN FINANCES

*The only thing wealth does for some people is to
make them worry about losing it.*

COMTE DE RIVAROL, EIGHTEENTH-CENTURY FRENCH WRITER

---

ANY DISCUSSION OF financial margin would be incomplete
without mentioning the pure joy of it. There are three reasons
this is so.

First, by lowering expenses below income, you live with
far less stress and pressure. If the refrigerator breaks down, you
don't. If your car needs new tires, you simply go out and get
them. Without margin, life struggles and staggers and stum-
bles. But when margin is present, life flows. And flowing is
more enjoyable than staggering.

Second, having financial margin allows beneficence
toward others. This is one of the most rewarding of all human
activities, and I am convinced it is a subset of love. Meeting
the needs of others delivers us from the world of selfishness
and into a world of grace and gratitude.

These two sources of joy are sufficient grounds to recom-
mend margin. But there is yet a third, even greater, source of
joy. It is a transcendent kind of pleasure that comes neither
from within nor without but from above. It comes from the
source of all that is right, and when you approach it you feel
its warmth even from a distance. In giving, you are ushered
into a world where cynicism and hatred have been banished.

You are considering others before yourself. You are choosing heaven as the place you will put your treasure. You are doing what God asked you to do, and what He did Himself. In giving, you are pleasing Him.

"It is more blessed to give than to receive," Jesus taught.[3] These words are not talking about a future-tense, theoretical blessing waiting for us beyond the eternal horizon, reserved there as compensation for the excruciating pain of giving today. Instead, this is a kind of joy that begins with the *thought* of giving, with the declaration of freedom in your soul that, indeed, you belong to God. And the joy culminates in the *act* of giving, often a secret except for the spotlight of heaven.

German existentialist Friedrich Nietzsche once claimed that Christians have no joy. But joy is mentioned over five hundred times in the Scriptures and clearly ought to be a part of the normal Christian life. If you wince because Nietzsche's dagger finds a joyless heart, restore your financial margin and then give it away.

*R͟x Rediscover the joy of using money for transcendent purposes. Always control its power over your attitudes and behaviors. Offering up your wealth for the purposes of sacrifice and love introduces you to a higher realm—one not ruled by advertising, trinkets, discontent, and suffocating debt but instead by the joy of serving.*

---

Money is a good servant but a bad master.
FRENCH PROVERB

# CONFOUNDED SUNDIAL

*Time has no divisions to mark its passage; there is never a thunderstorm or blare of trumpets to announce the beginning of a new month or year. Even when a new century begins, it is only we mortals who ring bells and fire off pistols.*

THOMAS MANN, GERMAN AUTHOR

LONG BEFORE OUR nanosecond culture, frustration with time urgency was apparent. Already in 200 B.C., Plautus was cursing the sundial:

> The gods confound the man who first found out
> How to distinguish hours! Confound him, too,
> Who in this place set up a sun-dial,
> To cut and hack my days so wretchedly
> Into small portions.[4]

Of course time frenzy had barely begun, and were Plautus alive today he might run his chariot off a cliff. What was it like to have no notion of a second or a minute or even an hour? To never be late . . . or early? To not even know what late or early is?

In the first mechanical clocks of the 1200s, only a bell indicated time. In the 1300s, the dial and hour hand were added. "Here was man's declaration of independence from the sun, new proof of his mastery over himself and his surroundings," explains historian Daniel Boorstin. "Only later would it be revealed that he had accomplished this mastery by putting himself under the dominion of a machine with imperious demands all its own."[5]

By the 1600s, the minute and second hands were common. The wristwatch arrived mid-1800s, when Matthew Arnold penned his famous *The Scholar Gypsy*—a coincidence perhaps, but still one wonders.

> O born in days when wits were fresh and clear,
> And life ran gaily as the sparkling Thames;
> Before this strange disease of modern life,
> With its sick hurry, its divided aims.

In 1879 Thomas Edison produced the first electric light. If the clock broke up the day, the light bulb broke up the night. Humanity was flushed with its presumed victory over yet another of nature's limitations. Yet all victories have their associated costs. The clock and the light . . . they gave us time; then they stole it away.

The clock measures one kind of time, but there are other types as well. As it turns out, not all time is created equal. According to time scholar Arthur Dunn, the Bible distinguishes between *chronos* and *kairos*. *Chronos* is clock time: chronological, measurable, quantity time—where we live. *Kairos* is significant time: meaningful, vertical, quality time—where Jesus lived. While *chronos* is occupied with the linear measurement of the past, present, and future, *kairos* is occupied with nonlinear measurements that are event-conscious, life-focused, and meaning-sensitive. Busyness and productivity are usually activities of *chronos*, while spirituality and relationships are usually activities of *kairos*.

R *No matter what the chronos is, determine to live major portions of your life in kairos. The clock is not god: God is.*

———✧———

Life just gives you time and space—it's up to you to fill it.
<small>CHINESE PROVERB</small>

# OVERLOAD AND THE FAMILY

*When we insist on doing too much, we are not only inflicting the damage of this choice on ourselves, we are sharing this damage with those we love the most.*

ANNE WILSON SCHAEF, WRITER AND LECTURER

---

CULTURE IS MOVING. It is flowing. This means that we can't take a snapshot and assume that we have captured anything. By the time the snapshot has been developed, the world has already flowed past, warping into something different.

If it is flowing, in what direction is it flowing? This is, of course, a very important question, yet one we spend too little time assessing. If we are on a boat rushing down a raging river, it is wise to know if the next bend is New Orleans or Niagara Falls.

Culture—and life—are flowing *in the direction of* overload. Culture—and life—are flowing *away from* family, church, and community. More rapidly than we can imagine.

Progress and technology were billed as time-gifting. The opposite has been true. This unexpected madness of modernity has not been kind to relationships, to community, to the church. The busy weariness of our age has not been kind to families, to marriages, to parenting.

Overload is a burden families should not be asked to bear. Most families are far too fragile to carry overload on their weary backs and could easily collapse under the pressure.

We cannot recover all that has been lost, because relationship depends much on the cultural context, and at present much of that context is either wounded or hostile. However, neither are we helpless. Many intentional actions can help to neutralize even an obstacle like overload.

> *R Simplify and slow down. Communicate and care. Listen and love. Unplug the phone, forget the calendar, close the door on the world. Of course you can't do it every day, nor should you. But you can do it far more often than you think. Who has a foot on the accelerator pedal for the family? Throttle back. Who makes spending and scheduling decisions? Leave a buffer.*

---

Children have more need of models than critics.

FRENCH PROVERB

# BREAKING THE SPEED LIMIT OF LIFE

*It is a sprinting, squirting, shoving age.*
NORMAN COUSINS, EDITOR AND WRITER

---

WE ARE A nation on the move and in a hurry, the people of the forward stampede. We eat fast food during rush hour. We ship by FedEx, place calls through Sprint, balance books on Quicken, and diet with SlimFast. We're hyperliving, like field mice on amphetamines at harvest time, moving so fast we're passing up photons.

Our global treadmill is equipped with an automatically advancing speed rheostat, and every year the world spins faster. Gone are the 1930s of *To Kill a Mockingbird:* "People moved slowly then. They ambled across the square, shuffled in and out of the stores around it, took their time about every-thing. A day was twenty-four hours long but seemed longer. There was no hurry, for there was nowhere to go, nothing to buy and no money to buy it with, nothing to see outside the boundaries of Maycomb County."[6] If we were bored in 1930, we are breathless and exhausted now.

The speed phenomenon is not only subjectively true but objectively measurable. Because progress gives us more and more, faster and faster, the escalating pace of daily life is both scientifically verifiable and a permanent feature of the modern age.

Personally, I don't mind going *fast.* I don't even mind going *faster*. But going *too fast* is another issue altogether. It is not wrong to enjoy the pleasure of being efficient and productive. But the anguish of being gasping, resentful, and consumed is real, compliments of excessive speed.

Is there a speed limit to life . . . a pace beyond which the brain, body, and spirit begin to suffer? What happens when we exceed this limit? Clearly there is such a limit, and clearly many of us exceed it routinely.

The increase in ambient speed is one of the most pressing problems of our time. Our lives are nonstop. We walk fast, talk fast, eat fast, and then excuse ourselves by saying, "I must run." This frenzy is responsible for much personal and family dysfunction. Very little of lasting spiritual value happens in the presence of speed.

Speed. Hurry. We pay a price for the pace at which we live.

℞ *Consciously slow the pace of life. Take your foot off the accelerator pedal. Throttle back. Put on the brakes and obey the speed limit of the soul. The green pastures and still waters yet await us — but not in the direction the treadmill is spinning.*

---

Haste manages all things badly.
<small>LATIN PROVERB</small>

# CURBING THE CLUTTERING

*If you own something you cannot give away,
then you don't own it, it owns you.*

ALBERT SCHWEITZER, MISSIONARY DOCTOR

OUR HISTORICALLY UNPRECEDENTED affluence has brought many benefits for which we should be appropriately grateful. There is, however, a downside as well. We bring our wheelbarrows of money to our massive malls to buy mountains of stuff. Then we cart it home and try to figure out where in the world to put it all.

It isn't just the stuff from the malls. It's also the presents from Christmas, birthdays, weddings, and showers. It's the gifts that Grandma and Grandpa keep bringing. It's the garage sales, auctions, and catalogs . . . and everything else that continuously shows up on the nonstop conveyor belts flowing into our homes.

Realizing that such mountains of clutter impede our journey, many now seek to reverse the flow. Intentional deaccumulation results in fewer things to take care of. Life is busy enough, days are interrupted enough, and space is crowded enough. Many of us don't need richer estates; we need richer lives.

In Tolstoy's *War and Peace*, Napoleon is marching on Moscow in 1812. Within a few days the city is doomed to fall, so all the people are busy packing their possessions to evacuate.

One wealthy count has over thirty carts loaded with furniture and valuables in the courtyard of his mansion. But also in the courtyard and lining the streets of the city are wounded soldiers, waiting inevitable death at the hands of Napoleon's advancing army. Suddenly, the count's daughter sees it: possessions on the carts to be rescued; wounded people on the ground left to die. With tears in her eyes, she runs to her father, pleading to put the wounded on the carts. The count, who has a tender heart as well, sees the shame of it. Weeping, he hugs his daughter: "The eggs are teaching the chickens."

The count quickly tells the servants to take the possessions off and put the wounded on. The servants, who one minute before were doing "the only thing there was to do"— loading the possessions—were now doing "the only thing that could be done"—taking possessions off the carts and putting people on.[7]

What is on our carts? Possessions? Things that consume both our time and money? Things that are temporal, perishable, here today and gone tomorrow? May we have the grace to unclutter our carts to make room for that which matters most.

> R℞ *Reverse the tide. One New Yorker discovered a novel way to unclutter by having a different kind of birthday party. "I've proven that I can make what I need to make, buy what I need to buy," said New York writer Liz Perle McKenna. "What I own doesn't say who I am anymore." So for her fortieth birthday party, she asked her guests to come to her home and take one thing.*[8]

—⊶⊷—

Great needs grow from great possessions.
IRANIAN PROVERB

# THE ECONOMICS OF THE RELATIONAL LIFE

*Love is extravagant in the price it is willing to pay, the time it is willing to give, the hardships it is willing to endure, and the strength it is willing to spend.*

JONI EARECKSON TADA, ADVOCATE FOR THE DISABLED, AUTHOR

———————————————

TO HAVE ACCEPTED the love of God is to be armed and disarmed at the same time. No weapon is more powerful. But in using such a weapon it is the user who is broken wide open. This is a love that cannot rightly be kept in—it is a bursting-out love. In its spilling out, it binds to others. And when it binds to others, it heals, it knits hearts, it builds community, and it brings everything together in perfect unity.[9]

Love is the only medicine I know of that, when used according to directions, heals completely yet takes one's life away. It is dangerous; it is uncontrollable; and it can never be taken on any terms but its own. Yet as a healer of the emotions, it has no equal.

Love is the currency of the relational life. In the relational life, we spend love and receive love. That was God's idea from the beginning. It is what He taught us, and it was what He showed us. God wants us to spend love freely, even generously.

Some guard their supply of love, doling it out in portions. But this kind of thinking works with money, not with love.

With money, the more you *hoard* the richer you become. But with love, the more you *spend* the richer you become.

As you can see, love is not like other resources. There is an infinite supply. You can use it and use it, yet there will still be more left over. As a matter of fact, the more it is used, the more its supply increases. We spend love and receive love. When we do, everyone becomes rich. It is God's transcendent economics.

Somehow we just can't wrap our minds around this idea of love. We can't nail it down and say, "There, I've got you." Love is weak yet tough, vulnerable yet strong. It chooses to lose but can never be beaten. It puts itself last yet always leads the way. It is mysterious, yet it came in flesh and stood before us. It is death—yet it is life.

Must we love? That is a nonsensical question. It is like asking, "Must we breathe?" No, we do not have to breathe, and no, we do not have to love. But the consequences of both those decisions will be the same.

*R Invest in love. Yield to love. Be transformed by love. Allow nothing to stand in the way of your commitment to love. Don't use overload as an excuse, and don't spend your last moments on earth apologizing for your life. Set love in order, beginning today.*

---

Where there is love there is no darkness.
BURUNDI PROVERB

# GRATITUDE

*The modern world has had far too little understanding of the art of keeping young. Its notion of progress has been to pile one thing on top of another, without caring if each thing was crushed in turn. People forgot that the human soul can enjoy a thing most when there is time to think about it and be thankful for it.*

G. K. CHESTERTON, BRITISH AUTHOR

---

IN EVERYONE'S LIFE THERE is much to be unhappy about, and there is much to be grateful for. Realistically acknowledging both ends of the spectrum is appropriate.

When we turn to look at our problems, we assess them and make a plan—no matter how small or grand—to work on them. This plan we formulate with our *mind* and motivate with our *will*. Then we look in the other direction at our blessings, finding our obligation for gratitude. Here we may fully engage our *emotions*.

Often we send our emotions to do battle with our problems, and despair results. Then we send our will to express our gratitude, lacking any confirming passion whatsoever.

Of course our emotions ought to be informed about our problems; of course our mind and our will ought to express gratitude. But we should send out that warrior best suited for the duty. And I think there can be little debate concerning the most appropriate assignments here.

If we can adopt such a balanced approach, we will combine a realistic and objective involvement in working on problems with a simultaneous assurance that there is much good in life. We'll recognize that the world is full of beauty, that most people are worthy of our respect and trust, and that the affairs of suffering humans are replete with acts of love, kindness, nobility, and sacrifice. And we'll remember that overseeing it all is a God who knows us well, who loves us anyway, and who is very, very good.

We all have within our grasp much to be thankful for. Gratitude fills. Discontent drains. The choice is ours.

> ℞ Every day write down a specific reason you have to be thankful and post it somewhere visible. Do it as a therapeutic act of discipline. If you wrote a different reason each day, how long would it take before you ran out of reasons to be grateful? Hopefully, fifty years. Or never. Personally, I am grateful that grass is green, that we have vision, that our vision is in color, that four-year-olds laugh once every four minutes, that we are six feet tall instead of six inches, that we have an appreciation of beauty. . . . Furthermore, I am grateful for Handel's Messiah, for oboes, for sunsets, for my woodburning stove, for fishing, for birds, for our capacity to love, for the Scriptures. . . . When you give thanks to God, He then turns it around and gives joy to you.

---

Who doesn't appreciate the small things,
doesn't deserve the big.
HUNGARIAN PROVERB

# WORK ACCESSIBILITY AND RUTHLESS EXPECTATIONS

*The good news is, you're always connected to the office. The bad news is, you're always connected to the office.*

THE WALL STREET JOURNAL, FULL-PAGE AD

THIS 1996 *WALL STREET JOURNAL* ad flaunts a discomforting development: 24/7 work expectations thanks to new accessing technology. The advertisement, hawking a particular computer notebook, continues: "Being out of the office no longer means being out of touch. Connectivity has never been easier. Just think, your people will finally be able to stay connected around the clock. They'll just love that, won't they?"[10]

Lucent Technologies placed their own 1997 version of the same message in the *Journal:* "A Formal Apology. Since inventing cellular and after introducing digital wireless, wireless office systems and cordless phones, it seems that anyone can get ahold of you no matter where you are. Sorry. Sincerely, Lucent Technologies."[11]

It goes without saying that most employers and managers are more invested in the job than the people they supervise. This often makes for a natural asymmetry between their expectations and those of the employees. Meanwhile workers, who might not be interested in 24/7 availability, have fewer places to hide. "Where were you yesterday?" the boss might ask. "I was trying to reach you all day!" Never mind that it was

Saturday and you were camping with the children. Or that it was Christmas Day and you were halfway to Grandma's house. "You know your boss is on vacation," quipped one employee, "when you receive 3 percent fewer e-mails from her."

The penetration of accessing technology goes seemingly unchallenged and is essentially regarded as an unadulterated good. A friend from Vail told of her attempt to take twelve young executives hiking in the Colorado Rockies. At the first break, while overlooking a beautiful vista, seven pulled out cell phones and called their offices. In Alaska, an avid sportsman took three brokers at 3:00 A.M to the Russian River salmon run. Before even setting up, the brokers were on their cell phones working the world markets. "You can be beeped on safari!" observes Peggy Noonan. "Be faxed while riding an elephant and receive e-mail while being menaced by a tiger. And if you can be beeped on safari, you will be beeped on safari."[12]

Communication technology has entered a new era and continuous accessibility is now a real possibility. It is time for a rational discussion of the massive implications this holds for workplace sustainability, morale, productivity, efficiency, innovation, and creativity. It turns out, if you really want to be a good worker, there are times when you must be *disconnected* from the office.

R *Reflect on personal boundaries dealing with the work life/private life interface. Think through the issue according to the context of your own situation and formulate reasonable guidelines. Of course a good work ethic is desirable, and there are legitimate times when long hours are needed. Nevertheless, strive to keep work work and home home.*

---

A good rest is half the work.
YUGOSLAVIAN PROVERB

# POISON VERSUS PEACE

*Discontent doth dislocate and unjoint the soul, it pulls off the wheels. . . . Discontent is a fretting humour, which dries the brains, wastes the spirits, corrodes and eats out the comfort of life.*

THOMAS WATSON, SEVENTEENTH-CENTURY BRITISH PREACHER

THE MANUFACTURING OF needs has been an unqualified success for modern advertising. And in a consumer-driven economy, a seemingly unlimited capacity for need stimulation has been precisely the goal. But what has been good for the economy has been troublesome for the soul. Stimulating need is the same thing as stimulating discontent. While this might lead to short-term economic gain, it will sabotage long-term spiritual health.

In truth, discontent has so many disadvantages one wonders why it is popular. It can suffocate freedom, leaving us in bondage to our desires. It can poison relationships with jealousy and competition. It often rewards blessing with ingratitude as we grumble against God. "Discontent will destroy your peace, rob you of joy, make you miserable, spoil your witness," warns J. I. Packer. "We dishonor God if we proclaim a Savior who satisfies and then go around discontent."[13] And when it has done its work, discontent abandons us, leaving us no comfort in our indebted, marginless, friendless self-pity.

On the other hand, the advantages of contentment are many: freedom, gratitude, rest, peace. They who are content do not have to worry about the latest styles or what to wear tomorrow. They can rejoice in their neighbor's good fortune without having to feel inferior. They do not fret with wrinkles or graying, because they accept what comes. They do not have to worry how they might buy this or that, because they have no desire for this or that. They are not consumed with how to get out of debt, because they have no debt. They have time for gratitude even in small things. They have time for relationships because possessions and the bank do not own them.

"Contentment," wrote Jeremiah Burroughs in 1648, "is that sweet, inward, quiet, gracious frame of spirit, which freely submits to and delights in God's wise and fatherly disposal in every condition."[14] It might not get you a hot tub or a trip to Hawaii, but a life of contentment will enable margin, freedom, and healthy relationships.

> *R Determine to live free. Stop worrying about what you have or don't have. Stop worrying so much about fashion and respectability and what others think. Don't give advertisements power over you. God's acceptance of you is a birthright—don't surrender its freedom.*

---

Better a handful of dry dates and content therewith
than to own the Gate of Peacocks and be
kicked in the eye by a broody camel.

ARABIAN PROVERB

# THE FORGOTTEN GRACE OF WAITING

*Quiet waiting before God would save from many a
mistake and from many a sorrow.*

JAMES HUDSON TAYLOR, NINETEENTH-CENTURY ENGLISH MISSIONARY TO CHINA

---

IT IS NOT surprising so many of us are in such a hurry. The reason for the escalating pace emerges clearly from a straight-forward analysis of escalating progress. What is surprising, however, is how little *awareness* we have that such an acceleration is indeed happening on our generational shift. Even though our age is historically unprecedented, to us each day seems but a carbon copy of the same busyness of yesterday and the same stress coming tomorrow.

God, however, was fond of such words as *wait, rest,* and *be still.* Whatever happened to these words? In the past, people of faith spoke such words and believed in such concepts. Today no one even utters them, at least not in any functionally meaningful way.

To learn the grace of stillness in the midst of busyness is much-needed oxygen for exhausted people everywhere. Instead of being cheered on by the socially acceptable mantra "more and more, faster and faster," perhaps we can rediscover the sacred pace of Jesus. Overload and hurry are not prerequisites for service but enemies of faith. Can we raise new signs, such as "Stop believing that chronic exhaustion is normal, that a listless spirit is inevitable, that burnout is piety"?

The late Bob Benson told of a TV evangelist who developed throat problems and was advised he shouldn't speak for three months. This, he protested, was impossible. So he prayed, and God miraculously healed him. Benson reflected,

> Can you imagine telling God — the God in whom there is no beginning and no ending, the eternal, always was and always will be God, the God who buries tulip bulbs in the darkness of the soil, the God who hides oak trees in acorns, this God — that you don't have three months? It seems bold to me, to say the very least, to say this to God who knew you long before you ever came to be. To suggest to this God — who has promised to gather up all of your life and transform it into the goodness of his purpose — that he should get on with it because you don't have time to dilly-dally around is pretty daring! I can almost hear God saying, "I think I'll just heal him. It will be easier than explaining it to him."[15]

Of course we are to be active on behalf of the kingdom. To put a hammock on a hilltop and admire cloud formations until Jesus comes is not the kind of "waiting" we are advocating. But when our impatience begins to tell God how to run His affairs, we have crossed an important line.

*R When you're not sure what to do, wait. Pray. Seek counsel. Pray again. Expect God to answer your confusion with clearness. He will, in time. Be patient.*

---

Patience is the key to relief.
SYRIAN PROVERB

# VALUE SLEEP

*Have courage for the great sorrows of life and patience for the small ones; and when you have laboriously accomplished your daily task, go to sleep in peace. God is awake.*

VICTOR HUGO, FRENCH AUTHOR

IT IS PERHAPS true that modern Americans get less sleep than at any other time in history. In 1850, for example, the average American got nine and a half hours of sleep per night. By 1950, that had decreased to eight hours. Currently, it is seven hours—and still declining. As a result, fifty million to seventy million Americans (depending on which study you read) have sleep disorders.

Why, under the tutelage of progress, have the hours of sleep declined so dramatically? The answer starts with electricity and the light bulb. We are now a twenty-four-hour-a-day society that seldom shuts down.

Many people in contemporary society have a negative attitude toward sleep. Often these are very productive people who resent the "wasted time." They also tend to be people who need less than the average amount of sleep themselves. Unfortunately, this attitude is often forced on others as well.

Don't get caught in a web of shame thrown by another. A good night's sleep is not an embarrassment. It is not necessary to feel guilty if you are well rested. Sleep is God's idea, not ours. He created the necessity, and "he grants sleep to those he loves."[16]

Let me present you with a decision scenario. Suppose it is thirty minutes before Creation and God has one final detail to decide—whether to include sleep or not. You are imported back so that He might ask your opinion. Five options are presented: To be like fish that do not sleep (or at least do not have eyelids); like giraffes that sleep ten minutes a night; like cows that sleep three hours a night; like dolphins that sleep with half a brain at a time; or to sleep eight hours a night. Which would you pick? For me, the decision is easy: eight hours. Every evening, I am extraordinarily grateful that God allows us to close the book on each day and begin anew the next morning.

The need for sleep is undeniable and should be regarded as an ally, not an enemy. To sleep soundly for a full night is a valuable restorative gift.

> *R Choose to get enough rest. Determine how much sleep you need to feel your best and then determine to get it. Einstein slept ten and a half to eleven hours a night. Personally, I feel best with seven to eight hours of sleep, as do the vast majority of adults. Everything you do, you will do better well rested.*

✺

Sleep is the poor man's treasure.
LATVIAN PROVERB

# TIME AND THE INVENTOR OF TIME

*There is always time enough in a day to do God's will.*
ROY LESSIN, INSPIRATIONAL POET AND AUTHOR

---

DO YOU THINK Jesus would have carried a pocket calendar? Would He have consulted it before making commitments? Would He have bypassed the leper because His calendar said He was late for the Nazareth spring banquet?

Do you think Jesus would have worn a wristwatch? What would have been His reaction if the temple service extended past noon and alarms went off in the crowd? Would He have driven out the clock-watchers along with the moneychangers? What would He have thought of the parishioner I knew who every Sunday timed the pastor with a stopwatch and reported the sermon length on the way out of church?

Do you think Jesus would have carried a beeper? Would Martha and Mary have paged Him to come and raise Lazarus from the dead? Can you imagine Him being paged out of the Last Supper?

The clock and the Christ are not close friends. Imagine what God thinks of us now that we are so locked into schedules that we have locked ourselves out of the Sermon on the Mount: It is hardly possible to walk the second mile today without offending one's pocket calendar. We jump at the alarm of a Seiko but sleep through the call of the Almighty.

The example of Christ, of course, has a cultural context to

consider. Yet beyond this context is a much deeper message: Jesus was not about to permit Himself to be tyrannized by time. What about us?

During a medical trip to the developing world, my wristwatch of twenty years gave out. Upon our return to the United States I decided not to replace it. Living without a watch clearly meant I was handicapped in a certain way. But it also gave an interesting sense of freedom. Finally, after a year, I purchased an inexpensive watch because my patients didn't quite know what to think of a doctor who had to borrow their watches to measure their pulses.

> ℞ *Remembering that time-marking technologies are responsible for a great deal of our time-urgency problem, use them judiciously. Perhaps go on strike occasionally. Try disconnecting from clocks, watches, alarms, and beepers for a day, a weekend, or a week. Consider leaving all clocks—including watches—behind when on vacation. Exiting a vacation workshop where I had just spoken, a dentist took off his watch and flipped it into the swimming pool. You might not wish to be quite this dramatic. But then again . . .*

---

When God created time, He made plenty of it.

IRISH PROVERB

# STRESS SWITCHING

*A man can wear out a particular part of his mind by continually using it and tiring it: but the tired parts of the mind can be rested and strengthened not merely by rest, but by using other parts. . . . Many men have found great advantage in practicing a handicraft for pleasure. Joinery, chemistry, bookbinding, even bricklaying — if one were interested in them and skillful at them — would give relief to the overtired brain.*

WINSTON CHURCHILL

---

UNRESOLVED STRESS HAS a way of usurping our attention and dominating our mood. Not all stress leads to frustration, but when it does, the downside is noticeable. Clear thinking is compromised, efficiency declines, and mistakes increase. Minor annoyance leads to moderate irritation leads to a major explosion. If the cascade is not interrupted, soon unhappy electrons are pinballing around in the brain, blowing out synapses like amplifier tubes.

If the stressful event is not resolving well, oftentimes it's a good idea to step away. When you're stuck and can't move any further, the best thing is to do something completely different. For example, if attempting to balance the checkbook is failing despite thirty minutes of dedicated effort, step away for a while. Many try lying down on the sofa. Occasionally, this works well, but other times it does not work at all—it might even backfire and increase the frustration. The reason: even though your body is on the sofa, your brain is still in the checkbook. The brain operates under its own instructions. Just because you tell it to stop does not mean it will stop. The brain has a mind of its own.

Similarly, just because you tell your mood to improve does not mean your mood will comply. Volitional control over affective functions—while obviously not impossible—is elusive for the majority.

For these reasons it is often better to "stress switch," to do something both different and enjoyable. I cut and stack wood or mow the lawn. I enjoy garden and lawn work and find this therapeutic. Others use sports or jogging. Even a short amount of stress switching seems to work. Any kind of diversion, representing a voluntary change of activity, is often better than inactively ruminating on the stressor.

The body seems to tolerate wear and tear better than the brain does. When stressing the muscles, the nervous system gets a rest. Moderation is the rule however. If the body is pushed to extremes, damage can instead be compounded.

> ℞ *Identify your favorite stress-switching activities. Keep an "open file" on two or three diversions or hobbies. Some examples: cut wood, trim trees, do needlepoint, knit, paint a room, paint a picture, read a novel, watch a movie, keep chickens, work with wood, redecorate a room, refinish a piece of furniture, volunteer at the library, swim, golf, or go rowing.*

---

If the wind will not serve, take to the oars.
LATIN PROVERB

# THE INCOMPREHENSIBLE BRAIN

*The brain is a wonderful organ. It starts working the
moment you get up in the morning and does not
stop until you get into the office.*

ROBERT FROST, POET

EVEN THOUGH WE know that the brain generates both
electrical and chemical activity, we still do not know precisely
what thinking is, or intuition, or consciousness.

For example, how did Einstein's brain do it? In 1905 he
was poor, underemployed, estranged from the world, rejected
by Europe's academic establishment, without a country, and
stung by his parents' disdain for his older Serbian wife. Yet
somehow in that "one miraculous year," at the age of twenty-
six he published five papers that changed our fundamental
understanding of physics forever. Any of these papers — dealing with such topics as time, space, light, energy, speed, relativity, and $E = MC^2$ — would have secured his place in history.
One paper won him the Nobel Prize. How does a brain over-
turn firmly entrenched paradigms with impossibly complex
levels of abstract thought that have nothing to do with measurable day-to-day experience? "The level of genius," wrote one
observer, "is practically incomprehensible."[17]

One Indian memorized the nonrepeating number *pi* to the
30,000th digit, only to be outdone by a Japanese man who
remembered it to the 42,000th digit. One German musician
read an unfamiliar symphony once before conducting it from

memory later that evening. An Edinburgh mathematician was asked to divide 4 by 47. After thirty seconds of giving numbers and having reached 46 decimal places, he said he "had arrived at the repeating point."[18] What do such prodigious feats reveal about the brain's inherent capacity?

Other stunning mental accomplishments come from autistic savants. These are people with severe mental handicaps juxtaposed with prodigious mental abilities. Savants reveal phenomenal abilities of a special type—very narrow but exceedingly deep, sometimes called "islands of intelligence."

Identical twins George and Charles are calendar calculators. They cannot count to thirty but they swap twenty-digit prime numbers for amusement. Give them a date and they can give you the day of the week over a span of eighty thousand years.

Leslie is blind, is severely mentally handicapped, has cerebral palsy, and has never had any formal musical training. Yet upon hearing Tchaikovsky's Piano Concerto No. 1 for the first time, he played it back on the piano flawlessly.[19]

What does this tell us about the human brain—about how it learns, how it calculates, how it performs? What does this tell us about the mind of God, who designed such a brain? We ought rightly to honor not the brain, but the God who created it.

*R̪ Some people are so overloaded processing information that they have no time left for the Scriptures. My advice: absorb data and study facts, but never neglect God's opinion of the matter. How sad to see people who know the uttermost details of science but who ignore Truth.*

∞

One word of truth outweighs the universe.
RUSSIAN PROVERB

# SABBATH REST

*Because people are so busy, because time is the most precious commodity everyone has, most people feel that they cannot possibly waste Sunday doing nothing.*

ATUL DIGHE, ANALYST AND CONSULTANT

WHEN SPEAKING TO a group of stressed-out congressional staffers in Washington, D.C., one attractive young lady in the back raised her hand with an unexpected question: "If we had held to the notion of a Sabbath rest, is it possible we might have bypassed this national state of exhaustion?"

"You might be right," I said. "Perhaps if we unplugged one day in seven from our busy pace, that amount of restedness might prove sufficiently therapeutic to spread over the rest of the week."

God talked about a Sabbath rest long before the Ten Commandments. The post-Creation rest of the Almighty shows up in the second chapter of the Bible: "And God blessed the seventh day and made it holy, because on it he rested from all the work of creating that he had done."[20] He looked upon that which He had made and delighted in it, and then He commanded us to do the same.

This Sabbath rest is not simply for the resting of the body—although it is that. It also is not primarily for emotional resting, although those who are wise will discover such a rest in their Sabbaths. Instead, it is a remembrance: "Remember that you were slaves in Egypt and that the LORD your God brought you out of there with a mighty hand and an outstretched arm. Therefore the LORD your God has commanded you to observe the Sabbath day."[21] This same God who rescued the Israelites from their slavery in Egypt is the One who rescues us from our bondage to sin. *Remember.*

The Sabbath is a time we suspend dominion work and instead worship the dominion-Maker. We cease reaping for our own cupboards and instead bring an offering to Him. The Sabbath rest is not simply the pause: it is the essence. We rest not because we are tired. We cease our labor not because it is finished. We worship not because there are now grapes on the vine and cattle in the stalls. We rest and worship one day in seven simply because He is the Lord.

Yet for the most part, churches today have not developed a practical theology of rest in general, and of Sabbath rest in particular. We read about rest in the Scriptures and say, "Yes, it's true." But underneath it, perhaps even unknown to ourselves, what we mean is "Yes, it's true, but . . . " Perhaps it is time to take a new look, to ask God what exactly He has in mind for us.

*R Recapture the Sabbath rest. Take back the day. Stop your work—and stop thinking about your work. Clear your mind. Calm your spirit. Bless the children. Worship, meditate, pray, nap, walk, enjoy nature.*

———❦———

When God says "today," the devil says "tomorrow."
GERMAN PROVERB

# THE PREDICTION THAT TURNED OUT WRONG

*The course of life is unpredictable . . . no one can write his autobiography in advance.*

ABRAHAM JOSHUA HESCHEL, RABBI AND PHILOSOPHER

SOMETHING INTERESTING IS happening on our generational shift. Interesting, however, is not the only descriptor of contemporary life. It is also a stressful age, a fast age, a dangerous age, an unprecedented age, an exciting age, a busy age, an exhausting age.

But why? Why are we so tired when we have so many labor-saving devices? Why are we so out of breath when we have so many time-saving technologies? Technology promised us more time, not more tiredness. With all this technology and progress, why are we still so overwhelmingly busy?

These developments are surprising. The futurists were not only wrong about their predictions; they were polar opposite wrong. The earlier predictions all indicated that our current problems would be related to boredom, not exhaustion.

Thirty years ago, futurists peering into crystal balls predicted that one of the biggest problems for coming generations would be an overabundance of leisure time. Testimony before a Senate subcommittee in 1967, for example, stated that by the twenty-first century the workweek would be cut in half. Nobody laughed.

The prediction went like this: progress—in the form of labor-saving devices, time-saving technologies, computers, automation, and so on—would greatly increase productivity. As productivity increased, so would wages. As wages increased, the workweek would shrink. People would be working less but earning more. One wage earner per family, working *twenty* hours a week would be sufficient to pay for a house, medical bills, braces, college, weddings, vacations, and retirement.

It was a prediction based on good science and statistics. But it missed—by 350 percent. Currently, we see the median husband-wife unit working *ninety* hours a week rather than the predicted twenty.

Work, however, is only a portion of our overload problem. Because of the rapidly changing conditions of modern living—largely due to progress always giving us more and more of everything faster and faster—we are exceeding human limits in scores of areas simultaneously. We have too many choices and decisions, too many activities and commitments, too many possessions and expectations. We have too much speed and hurry. We have too much change, stress, technology, complexity, traffic, information, debt, advertisements, and media. In short, we are a piled-on, exhausted society.

R̥ *Progress produces strong benefits but also significant negatives. "The first step in problem resolution is correct problem identification." Stop trusting progress implicitly. Discern each new development, accepting only those that serve your priorities and respect your margins.*

———∞———

Wait until it is night before saying that it has been a fine day.
FRENCH PROVERB

# ENVISION A BETTER FUTURE

*The characteristic mood of the times: a baffled sense of drift.*
CHRISTOPHER LASCH, HISTORIAN AND SOCIAL CRITIC

---

IF WE WISH to be emotionally healthy, it is essential to have a vision informing our future—a vision that is long-term, hopeful, and transcendent.

Americans are notorious for our shortsightedness. We live in a state of myopic mania that blurs the future. The horizon is never visible in the middle of a dust storm. But we must have a long-term vision that extends beyond tomorrow. Living only week to week is like a dot-to-dot life.

This vision also needs to be a hopeful vision. One campus contest to define the word *life* had as the winning entry: "Life is the penalty for the crime of being born." Such a vision won't lift the spirit even out of the sub-basement. Repeated medical studies confirm that people who have a more positive outlook have better outcomes; they heal faster, live longer, and are emotionally happier.

We need not only a distant vision and a hopeful vision but also a transcendent vision. We all need a spiritually valid purpose bigger than ourselves that we can live for. We must have something we can believe in, something we can give ourselves to. We must have work, and the work must have meaning. We must have direction, and the direction must have structure. A transcendent vision involves purpose, work, meaning, direction, and structure.

Unfortunately, there has been a wholesale destruction of vision, transcendent or otherwise, in modern-day living, and this destruction is seen worldwide. Aimlessness is like a metaphysical black hole, swallowing up everything in sight. Perhaps the most poignant description of our existential emptiness comes from the French philosopher Jean-Paul Sartre, when he speaks of humankind as a "bubble of consciousness in an ocean of nothingness, bobbing around until the bubble pops."

We have a clear choice. The vision and spirit of the age, which is really a vote for despair followed by the abyss, or the vision of transcendent and revealed Truth.

*R Believe in and work for something larger than yourself — for your family, for the community, for the common good, and for the kingdom. When you do so, every expenditure of emotion will have meaning, and every expenditure of emotion will be reimbursable.*

———

Where the sun is, that's where you
should hang your clothes.
<small>BASQUE PROVERB</small>

# MULTITASKING

*All the really good ideas I ever had came to me
while I was milking a cow.*

GRANT WOOD, ARTIST

---

IT IS CERTAINLY acceptable, when milking a cow, to think about art. It is entirely another matter, however, when operating on a brain aneurysm to also be talking to your real estate agent over the operating room intercom while also watching breaking news on CNN.

The dramatic escalation of busyness in our era has given nearly all of us too much to do in too short a time. The standard strategy for coping with this phenomenon, instead of simply refusing inappropriate activities, is to do two things at once. Or three things. Or four things. . . . It is an extension of the infamous more-and-more-with-less-and-less management philosophy. But someone forgot to do the math.

The idea of multitasking has now become so mainstream that even children talk of it. And of course there is a certain defense for it. In some instances we can become more productive by doing multiple things at once. For example, many people crochet while watching the news. In other instances multitasking is viewed as an absolute necessity. Clerks on the floor of the New York Stock Exchange run around doing five things at the same time. But isn't it a bit bizarre when a forty-eight-year-old broker drops dead on the trading floor and colleagues continue clerking around the lifeless body receiving CPR?

The downside to this rapidly emerging lifestyle has not been well advertised, and now the entire nation increasingly finds itself trapped in a pinball existence. Our society is undergoing a gigantic sociological experiment to see exactly how far we can take a ricochet life without imploding.

With inordinate multitasking, all of life becomes a distraction. Doing two things at the same time, you take 30 percent of your attention off the primary task. This leads to an increased error rate, sacrificing quality for quantity. In the end you finish more tasks but with poorer products and frazzled nerves. I once watched a man in a Mercedes making a left turn through Jerusalem's Zion Gate while talking on his cell phone. He wrecked his passenger door.

Relationally, multitasking is a disaster. We don't really listen anymore; it takes far too much time. Families need focus. Efficient parenting of newborns is a heartbreaking idea. Babies need what they need when they need it, and you either parent them well or you don't.

Jesus never lived like this, nor would He have in a different context. His undivided focus was the person before Him.

*R* *Don't be afraid to judge multitasking. Challenge the idea of efficiency as a guiding philosophy of life. Cut yourself some slack, and the family as well. Stop interrupting. Seek a pace that is humane, sane, sustainable, and godly.*

---

The dog has four feet, but he does not
walk in four roads at the same time.
HAITIAN PROVERB

# LONELINESS, BOREDOM, STRESS, AND THE MEDIA

*In the years ahead, we will live increasingly in fictions: We will turn on our virtual-reality systems and lie back, experiencing heavenly pleasures of sight and sound in a snug electronic nest. The real world will almost be totally blotted out from our experience.*

WORLD FUTURE SOCIETY

---

LIFE IS MEANT to be participatory and relational. In the past, life was "experience-rich" but "stimulus-poor." Today that ratio has reversed, and much of this trend is due to the pervasive presence of media.

In our current environment, it is easy to lapse into a *media-saturated* existence, which eventually leads to a *media-dependent* existence. When lonely, bored, or stressed, the first thing we often do is activate our media surroundings, which usually means turning on the television. In a previous era we would perhaps have visited a friend.

This is not to say that all such media usage for loneliness is inappropriate. But if overused, it will result in more isolation, not less. It is, therefore, wise to guard against media constituting our only barrier to loneliness.

Loneliness and boredom are often traveling partners. While loneliness can motivate us to move toward community, boredom can motivate us to move toward creativity.

We should not fear boredom as we do; it can be useful. People don't tolerate a bored state for long, and it, therefore, becomes a seedbed of imagination. To short-circuit boredom is to short-circuit creativity.

The temptation is to immediately solve boredom with media. When children are bored, we usually rescue them with television, videos, or computer games. Instead, if we allow boredom to build with no possibility of electronics, imagination will begin to surface. This is called *play*. Play is the business of childhood. It is healthy for kids to get bored and have to play their way out of it.

"What could have been long periods of super stagnation (stranded in a hayfield in the heat of August and cow-sitting) forced us to hatch up our own amusements," explains Edna Hong, in describing her growing up years. "What we hatched proves among other things the creative power inherent in boredom, of being placed in a situation so boring that the most fallow imagination begins to improve."[22]

In addition to loneliness and boredom, stress is another factor that drives us to a relaxing media respite. This is acceptable from time to time. But when a media respite becomes media overload, turn off the television. When media saturation becomes physically sedentary and socially isolating, move to restore appropriate levels of physical and social activity, where real healing is found.

*R Allow boredom to nourish the imagination. Create rather than consume. Rediscover and reenergize participatory experience. Don't live a vicarious virtual-reality existence. Instead create a personal-experience reality. In so doing, you will increase physical exercise, connect to others, and build community.*

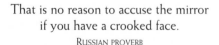

That is no reason to accuse the mirror
if you have a crooked face.
RUSSIAN PROVERB

# BIKE OR WALK

*The human body is the only machine that
breaks down when you don't use it.*

KEITH W. SEHNERT, M.D., PHYSICIAN, AUTHOR, AND SELF-CARE EXPERT

---

SOME THINK THE cause of our national obesity problem is
not that we eat too much, but that we move too little. Our
prosperity has allowed us to be cerebral and sedentary rather
than physically robust. In earlier eras, the sheer harshness of
existence required a physically active, vigorous lifestyle.
During Revolutionary War days, when 90 percent of our population were farmers, physical labor was an indispensable part
of daily activity. Today, however, only 2 percent of Americans
earn their living off the land. Most of the rest of us left our fitness behind on the farm. Now, instead of pitching hay bales,
we push pencils.

When studying in Switzerland for a year, I lived with a
Swiss family. Immediately, I noticed that the Swiss biked and
walked. My "adopted" Swiss father, a physician researcher for
a pharmaceutical company, rode his bicycle to and from work
each day, including a round trip home for lunch. My Swiss
mother walked to town each morning to buy groceries for the
day: bread, vegetables, meat, milk. They were not alone in
these habits. As I daily made my way to the study center, the
streets would be crowded with bicyclists and pedestrians.

As citizens of the most prosperous country in the world,

the Swiss could afford to drive. But they chose a different way. Although the pattern has shifted over the years to more automobile use, I will never forget the example of health set for me that year.

In the United States, however, we go everywhere in our cars. Vehicles have become easy chairs on wheels. We don't even use arm strength to put down the windows. And when we arrive at our destinations, we still don't disembark. Instead we drive up for our banking and drive through for our fast food. Now we even have drive-up churches and, of all things, I once heard of a drive-up baby clinic where you lift your child through the window to a waiting pediatrician.

*R̸ Climb stairs rather than use the elevator. Park a block or two from your destination. Get off the bus or subway one stop early. Any exercise is better than no exercise, even if it is only a walk of ten steps.*

---

We do not walk on our legs, but on our will.
GERMAN PROVERB

# TECHNOLOGY, TIME, AND TWITCHING

*How do we upgrade the competence of human decision making to
match the demands of the hardware? Or could it be that by
information overload and complexity, or by mechanical actions
whose speed outpaces human response time, technologies are
stretching the mind beyond the end of its tether?*

EDWARD WENK JR., ENGINEER AND SCIENCE POLICY ANALYST

I HAVE A fantasy: If a terrorist organization were to simultaneously trigger all the world's alarm clocks, stove timers,
beepers, factory whistles, car horns, doorbells, dinner bells,
digital watch alarms, fuzz busters, car phones, telephones,
intensive care alarms, smoke alarms, fire alarms, burglar
alarms, civil defense alarms, and sirens — namely, every man-
made, adrenaline-shocking device that signals "Hurry!" — do
you think it would be enough to bring Christ back prematurely, out of sheer pity?

Have you ever had a beeper go off in your ear when you
were sleeping? It is one of the most horrifying experiences ever
dreamed up by technology to ambush innocent, already-
exhausted wretches. Although it has happened to me thousands of times, to date I have not even begun to approach
psychic accommodation of the experience. It is fitting that a
society with urgency as its emblem should have tranquilizers
as its addiction. Where are the noises that tell us to slow
down? Which way to Lake Wobegon, that "quiet town, where

much of the day you could stand in the middle of Main Street and not be in anyone's way"?

In defending their quest for speed, Intel chip makers report that human attention begins to wander after one-half of a second. Columnist Bob Greene calls it the "twitching of America." From "fast food" to the "weekend squeeze" to the "Christmas rush," technology and time have us by the throat.

> $R$ Control interruptions and thus develop a more active defense of psychic peace. The average middle manager in America, according to one study, is interrupted over two hundred times a day. Interruptions are a part of modern life, but with effort, they can be modified. Relocate to a quieter room. Go to the library to work. Work late at night or early in the morning. Have other people take messages for you and return them in a batched fashion. Control the telephone. Turn off the beeper. Employ technologies that block interruptions rather than cause them. Reflection, meditation, and contemplation are important, perhaps more than we know. It is not wrong to seek such spiritual respite in the midst of excessively busy lives.

---

To change and to improve are two different things.
GERMAN PROVERB

# WHEN PEOPLE WEIGH AN OUNCE

*Between a living cell and the most highly ordered non-biological system, such as a crystal or a snowflake, there is a chasm as vast and absolute as it is possible to conceive.*

MICHAEL DENTON, AUSTRALIAN MICROBIOLOGIST

LET'S PAY A visit to the terrain of the cell to get a glimpse of perhaps the most spectacular of all human miracles—DNA. The cell, of which we each have one hundred trillion, is the basic structure of living matter. Buried deep in each cell is the nucleus, the epicenter of the cell's functioning. This nucleus contains twenty-three pairs of chromosomes consisting of tightly coiled DNA, and encoded within each cell's DNA are design instructions for the entire human body.

All of these hundred trillion cells began very inauspiciously as one single, microscopic speck—the fertilized egg. Within this tiny first cell is the blueprint for building an entire human body with a complexity that is incomprehensible. Let's do a comparison: I am a grown adult with a sophisticated education including degrees in both medicine and physics, but I can't even figure out how to set the clock on my car radio. On the other hand, here is a single fertilized ovum, smaller than the period at the end of this sentence, that with apparent ease directs the proliferation and differentiation of a hundred trillion cells.

Thirty hours after fertilization, en route down the fallopian tube and headed for the uterus, this single precocious cell undergoes its first division. The resultant twin cells, still bonded tightly together, then continue to divide at a faster rate, roughly twice a day.

Sometime within the first couple of weeks, in addition to *dividing*, the cells also begin *differentiating*. Even though we start out with cells that look identical, after the process of differentiation one cell goes off in the direction of the retina and the other goes off in the direction of the toenail. The secret of this differentiation, which will eventually result in over two hundred different cell types, is mysteriously locked up in the DNA. This is one of God's highest quality tricks, and many world-class biologists would give up tenure just to know exactly how He pulls it off.

This initial single-cell DNA, which determines everything from your handedness, to eye color, to whether you are at risk of premature heart disease, weighs 0.2 millionth of a millionth of an ounce. Stunningly, the combined initial single-cell DNA of every person alive today would weigh a total of one-thousandth of an ounce.

*R Reflect on the level of precision God has displayed in this design. When tempted to feel that your life is out of control, remember that to God, nothing is out of control. God can help you with the details of your busyness, and He can also help you rethink the details of your busyness. Yield both your life and its details to His keeping, and find there your rest.*

≈≈≈

God's help is nearer than the door.
IRISH PROVERB

# ACCEPTABLE LIMITS, UNACCEPTABLE MEDIOCRITY, AND INEXCUSABLE LAZINESS

*It is not how much we do but how much love we put in the doing.*

MOTHER TERESA

SOME WHO FIRST encounter the idea of margin perhaps think it is oriented in the direction of slackness—a wonderful apologetic for the lazy life; a guilt-free excuse for noninvolvement, for camping out in the easy chair while enjoying an NFL-SNL existence. This understandable criticism is fundamentally wrong, but it raises an important issue that must be confronted. If we aim for margin, how can we be sure we won't instead hit mediocrity?

If we slow down and simplify, isn't this the same as quitting? How can we keep the creative tension that leads to appropriate productivity? Is margin anti-work, anti-progress, and anti-efficiency?

Let me be very clear: I believe in excellence, in discipline and self-denial, in lofty visions, and even in suffering. But I also believe in rest, balance, simplicity, contentment, and love. Therefore I believe in margin. Margin is consistent with both sets of values.

Perhaps it can best be clarified by saying that both Scripture and margin condemn a lazy life and extol a loving life.

*The lazy life condemned*—Scripture denounces laziness. The book of Proverbs leaves the sluggard defenseless. Discipline and self-denial are consistently associated with godly living. We are to accept the suffering that comes for righteousness' sake. Therefore work hard.

Margin agrees. Be involved in a life of service. Eschew the gratification of material desires. Live simply—even when simple living is difficult—so that you have time and resources for others. Accept the suffering that honors God, but reject the suffering that comes from the destructive cultural treadmill gone awry.

*The loving life exalted*—Scripture also denounces the recklessness of the driven lifestyle. Hyperactive haste is not the same as seeking God and waiting on His counsel. The Word says: Be humble but not slothful. Be meek but not mediocre. Be broken but not despairing, poor but not lazy, and empty but not indolent. Seek a life of peace, kindness, gentleness, and contentment. And above all, live a life of simple faith and love.

Margin again agrees. Once you have honored God by your work, then honor God again by your rest. Pray. Sleep. Wait. Laugh. Sing. Relate. Communicate. Listen. Care. Love.

Margin then, correctly applied, is the balanced middle ground where both sets of values can be spiritually mated: work *and* rest; community *and* solitude; involvement *and* boundaries; yes *and* no.

> ℞ *Commit to both poles of margin. Decide which direction your weakness lies and concentrate specifically on that deficiency. God commends work—if you refuse, you dishonor both earth and heaven. God also commends rest—if you refuse, you deprecate His counsel.*

---

Work is good provided you do not forget to live.

BANTU PROVERB

# MANUFACTURED NEED

*Advertising may be described as the science of arresting the human intelligence long enough to get money from it.*

STEPHEN LEACOCK, POLITICAL ECONOMIST AND HUMORIST

MARGIN AND THE advertising industry are enemies. Margin requires contentment to thrive, but advertising requires discontent to thrive. As a specific strategy, most advertising consciously stimulates a chronic state of discontent.

Were everyone in America to adopt a scripturally authentic lifestyle of contentment, each of us would need fewer new clothes, toys, furniture, and automobiles. As a consequence, our discontent-dependent, debt-sponsored economy would be put at risk. The only way to avoid such economic risk is to continually convince the public that more and better is desirous. If this *need creation* is successful, a consumption-based economy might be benefited, but at the same time, personal and family stability will be put at risk. Discontent and debt are both destabilizing forces.

Two broad types of advertising deserve mentioning. The first is to remind or inform: "We are having a sale this week," or "When looking for good fried chicken, don't forget us. We serve nightly until 9:00." The second type is to manipulate need: "All the best athletes use Ajax breath mints," or "Use Jake's new and improved fishing lure and you will never have another boring minute of fishing." Nearly every advertisement that interrupts my consciousness is of the latter type.

At first the misrepresentations were subtle and largely overlooked. Then they became progressively more blatant, wrapped in entertainment. Today continuous deceit goes on at absurd levels. Thus we have the intentional stimulation of covetousness through the telling of unashamed lies, both of which Scripture condemns. Yet we sit in rapt attention.

Advertisers use many strategies—visual stimulation and sexual innuendo are two of the more prominent—yet all these are *methods*. What we really need to understand is the *message*. My point is, the message we are given is that we need something. That we actually do *not* need their new products is seen by the advertisers as an obstacle to overcome. They must, therefore, manufacture need.

If we actually needed the thing, advertisers would not have to convince us of it. But, truth be told, we are fairly easy prey.

*℞ Cultivate a continuously skeptical attitude—a therapeutic aloofness—toward advertising. Do not give up your freedom easily in this matter; there is more at stake here than you might suppose. Refuse to be psychologically manipulated. Especially teach this skill to your children. Consider using the remote to switch to another station during television ads. Develop a healthy righteous indignation when the ad attempts to make one group of people (the people without the product) appear inferior.*

❦

Good perfume is known by its own scent<br>
rather than by the perfumer's advertisement.<br>
Afghan proverb

# PLASTIC AND THE PIT

*Money costs too much.*
ROSS MACDONALD, AUTHOR

---

SPENDING MORE THAN we make is one of those modern plastic privileges of dubious advantage. Much of this deficit spending on a personal and family level is because buying has become a national mania. One third of shoppers experience an "irresistible compulsion" to buy. Many buy strictly out of impulse. Others go to the mall with nothing in mind other than recreational shopping.

Today we can obtain specialty cards, not only through our banks, department stores, gas stations, and phone companies, but also from our unions, grocery stores, and online services. The Association of Trial Lawyers has a card, as do fans of Frank Sinatra—all easy to obtain, easy to use, and hard to pay off.

On the front side, this kind of credit is seductive. Out the back door, it is treacherous. The innocent-appearing plastic card draws its life off of our financial margin, becoming more powerful as we sink deeper into debt. Soon we find ourselves looking up from a deep hole, surrounded by possessions we do not really own and left with no room to wiggle.

This love affair with plastic is one of the main reasons we have no financial margin—it is psychologically easier to buy with plastic than with cash. Yet when it comes to fiscal matters, our skills at rationalization are so well developed we scarcely wince when God's Word counters us. We may soon learn that we followed the wrong piper, not to paradise but to the pit.

A huge shift in the financial industry's debt-credit strategy over the past twenty years has come through this widespread use of credit cards. The vast majority of us hold at least one major credit card. Yet even with this level of saturation, several *billion* unsolicited new credit card offers are mailed each year.

One man had twenty credit cards all charged to their limits, and yet was holding on to twenty more "just in case." Even when people go bankrupt, they still receive several credit card solicitations every month. Some even come preapproved.

> *R*  *Either control credit cards or discard them. If you currently have no financial margin and are interested in obtaining some, first, make a budget and, second, cut up your credit cards. The majority of American families would probably be better off if credit cards disappeared from the face of the earth tomorrow. Cards can be convenient, but they also can be extremely dangerous. For many, nothing would rebuild their financial margin faster than the simple act of destroying all their credit cards and instead paying cash for purchases.*

—∞∞∞—

Going to bed without dinner is better
than waking up in debt.
JAMAICAN PROVERB

# BURNOUT

*There is an optimum level of tension which we require in order to perform well. When stress exceeds that level, exhaustion and burnout are the result.*

DONALD ARDELL, PH.D., WELLNESS EXPERT

---

IF YOU WALK into a woods and select a ten-foot sapling, you can bend that sapling over, let it go, and it will return to its normal height and straightness. However, if you bend it again, this time a bit further, then further, then further yet . . . eventually you will hear a snap. Let it go now, and the sapling stays down. It's broken.

This is an effective illustration of what happens from the spectrum of stress to burnout. With stress, first you bend, then you recover. With burnout, first you bend, then you break. And you stay broken.

Burnout is a real phenomenon, not a figment of your imagination or a sensationalized diagnosis by overly dramatic psychologists. It's not only real; it's common. And it is dangerous. The co-morbidity is very high: exhaustion, irritability, anger, paranoia, headaches, ulcers, immune dysfunction, depression, and even suicide.

Burnout is that point where something within you breaks. It is that point where you quit trying, when you finally throw up your hands and say, "I don't care anymore. I don't care who sees me. I don't care who hears me. I don't care about anything. I just want out."

There is indeed life after burnout. It is possible to recover and once again experience passion, enthusiasm, productivity, and excellence. But recovery requires an extended period, and the healing is mostly by scar formation.

Burnout is common among the spiritually minded. They are often very sensitive and tormentingly conscientious. They see the pain, and then they internalize it. They want to help the wounded and rescue the world. But they don't always realize that they were not designed to carry the entire global burden on their individual backs.

> ℞ Find peace in the shelter of the Most High and rest under the shadow of the Almighty. Make the life changes necessary but be careful not to act with clouded judgment. If possible, find someone to walk with and talk to. Find reason for gratitude, stay away from negative people, and surround yourself with prayer. Give yourself plenty of time to heal.

---

The sore is cured but the scar remains.
EKONDA PROVERB

# GETTING AWAY FROM IT ALL

*I am bound to praise the simple life, because I have lived it and found it good. When I depart from it, evil results follow. I love a small house, plain clothes, simple living. . . . To see the fire that warms you, or better yet, to cut the wood that feeds the fire that warms you; to see the spring where the water bubbles up that slakes your thirst, and to dip your pail into it; . . . to be in direct and personal contact with the sources of your material life; to want no extras, no shields; to find the universal elements enough.*

JOHN BURROUGHS, NINETEENTH-CENTURY NATURE WRITER

POWERFUL FUTURE TRENDS are propelling us in the direction of increased complexity, of more and more, faster and faster. The reasons people feel like "getting away from it all" are not dissipating anytime soon. As a consequence, simplicity is a movement whose time has come. Though it has been variously commended and practiced for centuries, simplicity has seldom been more needed than it is today.

If overload is sabotaging our equilibrium, simplicity can help. If we find ourselves being detailed to death, simplicity can restore life. If we find ourselves overextended in our emotional, financial, and time commitments, simplicity is one of the best ways to reestablish margin.

We hear frequent talk about the rat race and the treadmill, about stopping the world to let people off. Given the complicated, rushed nature of daily life in modern America, it is not surprising that many are looking for the exit door. Many fantasize about walking away from their jobs, throwing away the television, and moving to a cabin in the woods. Indeed, in the last few decades many have acted upon the fantasy.

Although moving to a rural location can often add simplicity, it constitutes no guarantee. A columnist writing about life balance for a men's magazine interviewed me recently. As we discussed moving from busy cities, he said, "I tried that. We moved from Manhattan to rural Pennsylvania. There are six people in this town, and five of them are in my family. It didn't help." A fascinating observation. Often we jack up our busyness, put wheels underneath, and then trailer it down the road to our new location. People today can lead a fully "wired" life even with no neighbors in sight.

Simplicity does not guarantee margin, but it is a helpful first step.

> ℞ *The path to simplicity is not so much escaping as it is transcending. Relocation of home address can help, but better is a redirection of heart and mind priorities. Require that all possessions and activities serve your priorities. If they do not, establish control and leave everything that encumbers at the side of the road.*

---

One's own simple bread is much better
than someone else's pilaf.
AZERBAIJANI PROVERB

# WORK PLEASURE, WORK DREAD

*A financial planner told me that the best time for him to catch up was to go to the office on Sunday morning! What kind of planning is that?*

CARRIE WASLEY, COLUMNIST

---

ONE OF THE predicted benefits of progress was shorter workweeks and higher paychecks. Despite the many valid scientific reasons for these predictions, they missed badly. Instead of the projected twenty hours per week, the median husband-wife unit today is putting in ninety hours per week, not including domestic duties awaiting them back at the home front. People now routinely log hours all across the time spectrum whether evenings, nights, or weekends.

Not only did the shorter-hours, higher-pay prediction not materialize, but simultaneously, other work-related problems emerged: fading benefits, unmanageable stress, faster pace, lower morale, and threatened job security. At one high-tech company, an executive who announced long-expected layoffs with severance packages was given a standing ovation. For these frustrated employees, Dilbert was no joke—they couldn't wait to leave.

Work is obviously God-ordained. A life without meaningful work is a tragic life. Each person is healthier—as the entire society is healthier—if we have appropriate, fulfilling work that can be done with pride and integrity. Work overload, however, is a different matter.

Economic necessity, whether real or perceived, is one

reason we work longer hours. Many workers, trapped in low-paying jobs, find it necessary to put in long hours just to stay even as wages struggle to keep up with inflation.

Increasing job insecurity is another contributor to high work hours. Companies who turned thousands of employees out on the street instilled fear in the remaining work force. Threatened workers are hesitant to say no when overtime is required.

Consumptive lifestyles are yet a third reason for work-hour inflation. All the productivity gains since World War II have gone toward producing and consuming more goods and services rather than toward more leisure. People habituated themselves to a lifestyle of high consumption, one they now find difficult to reverse. Trapped in exhausting work schedules by lifestyle excess, they also have high levels of consumer debt that must be serviced.

Work is an important and, ideally, pleasurable aspect of adult life. However, the current drift toward overload is not helping our overall appreciation of this God-ordained responsibility. Keeping work hours and work stress within an acceptable range of tolerance can help keep work both a pleasure and a privilege.

> $R_x$ *Increase work flexibility through simplicity. Many people overwork for one simple reason: they overspend. Overliving your income puts inordinate pressure on work hours. As long as you consume 110 percent of what you make, you will have little choice in cutting back work hours or changing to a less stressful job. Simplicity, on the other hand, brings flexibility to your work options. In this sense, consumption constrains and simplicity frees. Leave a margin.*

———— ∞ ————

He who undertakes too many jobs does none.
BULGARIAN PROVERB

# ANTICIPATION AND MEMORIES

*My Chinese side wonders why Americans are so uneasy with time
on their hands and must busy themselves with activities, the
sweatier the better. Why do they keep changing their minds and
ways, jobs and towns and spouses? . . . Americans are a self-
selected breed programmed by their genes to be forever on the go
and cursed by the Fates never to enjoy luxuriating in the material
comforts and spiritual splendors of home. Is it any wonder then
that they are always asking themselves who they are? They just
don't stay put or reflect long enough to find out.*

BETTE BAO LORD, CHINESE-AMERICAN, WIFE OF FORMER AMBASSADOR TO CHINA

BUSY. PERHAPS THE primary descriptor of modern living.
Booked up weeks in advance, we try to do two or three things
at the same time in an attempt to squeeze still more in. If in
1950 we had ten activities to choose from, today—compliments of progress—we have a hundred. Further complicating
matters, most of these activities are either fun or worthy, and
overload descends upon us in an avalanche.

Activity is a most excellent thing. So is commitment. It is
good to be involved, vital, and energetic. Even activity overload can be appropriate and normal at times. But *chronic* activity overload is a toxic condition.

Activity overload leads to agenda overload. People's
schedules are so full that one does not often see shared agenda.
Friendships that formerly were solidified by shared activities
are now divided asunder by activity overload.

In addition, activity overload and calendar congestion have robbed us of the pleasure of anticipation. Without warning, the activity is upon us. We rush to meet it; then we rush on to the next. In the same way, we lack the luxury of reminiscing. On we fly to the next activity.

For this reason our family intentionally lingers on both of these relatively unremembered sources of delight. Fishing trips are planned at least six months in advance. Because our son Adam spent two summers working in Alaska, our family decided to visit the state. Our planning began eighteen months in advance. We had exceptional pleasure simply envisioning the trip.

When the activity is over, remember. Tell stories. Tell them again. Make a special effort to remember humorous occasions. Spend an evening arranging photos in albums. Frame a picture. Mount a fish. With the gift of remembrance, we don't always have to do a lot—we can do *a little* and remember it *a lot*.

> *R Enjoy anticipation and relish the memories. Have family meetings where you lay out the next year in terms of vacations, trips, birthdays, Christmas celebrations, and so on. Plan pleasurably and well in advance. Create a "memories" budget for such items as quality souvenir purchases, photos, and framing.*

---

The eye never forgets what the heart has seen.
BANTU PROVERB

# PROGRESS VERSUS LOVE

*When institutional conditions create more combat than
community, when the life of the mind alienates more
than it connects, the heart goes out of things and
there is little left to sustain us.*

PARKER PALMER, WRITER AND TEACHER

---

PROGRESS'S BIGGEST FAILURE has been its inability to nurture and protect right relationships. If progress had helped
here, I would have no quarrel with it. But it didn't help. So we
must either teach it to use new tools or put it on the sideline.

Progress builds by using the tools of economics, education, and technology. But what are the tools of the relational
life? Are they not the social—my relationship to others; the
emotional—my relationship to myself; and the spiritual—
my relationship to God? None of the tools of progress have
been of assistance in building the relational foundation our
society requires.

Margin knows how to nurture relationship. In fact, margin
*exists for* relationship. Progress, on the other hand, has little to
say about the relational life. Even our language gives us away.
When we talk of progress, we do not mean social, emotional,
and spiritual advancement. Instead the word is reserved in our
common usage to mean material/physical and cognitive/edu-
cational gains.

In analyzing our age, commentator after commentator will

talk about how much better off we are. Yet invariably, they are referring to money, energy, transportation, housing, communications, technology, and education. However, people have relational needs that go much deeper. And while all the focus was on the material and cognitive, our relational environments have suffered from neglect.

How might we know that the relational environments are where God would have us concentrate? Simply put, these are the same areas Christ spent His time developing and where His teaching is focused. Where do you think God would have us search for answers regarding drugs, crime, divorce, suicide, depression, teenage pregnancies, and litigation — in the material and cognitive realms or in the relational ones? Our society tries in vain to remedy these problems using the popular notions of progress: let's appropriate more money (that is, material/physical answers); let's set up more classes (that is, cognitive/educational answers). But insufficient funds and lack of education are not the problems. The problem is lack of love.

> $R$ Accept selectively from progress those benefits that help faith, family, and friends. But discern carefully, for nothing is pure — especially progress. Our most important human connections must be protected from those contemporary forces arrayed against them: busyness, stress, overload, hurry, complexity, debt, frustration, overwork, multitasking, burnout. The kingdom of God, rightly constituted, is a relational place, and it is our responsibility to keep it that way.

---

No one is so rich that they wouldn't
need their neighbors.

HUNGARIAN PROVERB

# BALANCE OR BURNOUT

*In their Christian graces no one should usurp the sphere of another,
or eat out the vitals of the rest for its own support. Affection must
not smother honesty, courage must not elbow weakness out of the
field, modesty must not jostle energy, and patience must not
slaughter resolution. So also with our duties, one must not interfere
with another; public usefulness must not injure private piety;
church work must not push family worship into a corner. It is ill
to offer God one duty stained with the blood of another.*

C. H. SPURGEON, ENGLISH PREACHER

---

THE HUMAN BODY is a universe, each containing millions of times more atoms than there are stars in space. Ninety percent of these atoms are replaced every year, and virtually 100 percent are replaced every five years. Thus our physical beings are continuously tearing down but also continuously building up.

Veritable factories that never shut down, our bodies exhibit a complexity beyond comprehension. We each are made up of trillions upon trillions of working units, all perpetually moving, metabolizing, combining, interacting, adjusting, purifying, purging, building, and decaying. Yet with all its stunning complexity, the human body *must* function in balance. If this balance is disturbed, disease results.

For physiology to avoid becoming pathology, balance is essential. It is no different in the broader context of life. If life is not in balance, dysfunction results. Yet nearly every force in society today is inherently unbalancing. To maintain balance under such conditions requires a strongly intentioned effort.

Some think balance is unrealistic. One conference speaker on the topic "Balancing Work and Family" surprisingly began his talk with the comment: "Balance is impossible." Some even think balance is sinful. One writer suggested that the concept of balance is an excuse for spiritual laziness.

But in fact there are multiple areas of life where God requires a "decent minimum." This includes, for example, attending to our physical bodies, to our sleep, nutrition, and exercise, to our relationships, to our spiritual life, and of course, to our work. At precisely the same moment that God required such a "decent minimum" in each area, He became the author for the requirement of balance.

Cultivating margin can assist in our quest for balance. Overload leads to burnout; margin leads to balance. Under the conditions of modern living, however, margin has disappeared. We miss margin more than we know. We need balance more than we suspect.

> *R̥ To achieve balance, first regain control over your life. Never completely relinquish your schedule to the unpredictable, commercialized, spiritually inauthentic, and sometimes ruthless whims of the world. Be active in self-examination and intentional in correction. Second, identify each area where God has "decent minimum" requirements. Be sure that adequate resources are given to each. Pain will arise from those neglected areas where imbalance fails God's minimum standard. On the other hand, joy and fulfillment arise from those areas where God's definition of balance is achieved.*

———— ∞∞ ————

Who begins too much accomplishes little.
GERMAN PROVERB

# THE EXPECTATION DEMOLITION SQUAD

*If you can dream it, you can do it.*
*Now there's no limit to your ability.*

EXPECTATION OVERLOAD IS dangerous, functioning as a demolition squad of the simple life. Yet our affluent communications age steadily raises expectations with no restraint discernible. "Your world should know no boundaries," advertises one investment firm. "Life, liberty, and the pursuit of just about anything you please," reads an automobile ad.

As a result, people give almost unbridled permission for their visions to roam well into unattainable territory. Then, when the vision falls short, they become irritated and file suit. Let's examine some specifics.

*Medicine*—Expectations in medicine have risen to unattainable levels. We expect our doctor to know all the answers, our insurance to pay all the bills, and our body to heal all the ills. When these inappropriate expectations are not met we look for someone to blame.

*Plastic surgery*—Upset at nature for not giving them a perfect body, many spend enormous sums attempting to buy one. If we didn't care how we looked on the outside but concentrated instead on the inner qualities of integrity, virtue, and purity, perhaps we would mature beyond this cultural fixation with looks.

*Education*—Society expects us to get an education. And holding a degree, we expect that life will magically unfold. Yet many college students don't know what to study, can't get a job in their fields, and are surprised when an education does not prepare them for such real-life events as relationships, emotional well-being, and spiritual fulfillment.

*Parenting*—Parental expectations for our children often crush the child out of them. We begin hurrying them in education when they are still in the cradle, we want them to be beauty queens or football stars when they are six, and we insist on straight A's when they hit junior high. Whatever happened to unconditional love?

*Marriage*—Our modern expectations of marriage are, at the same time, very low and very high. On the one hand, expectations are low in that we anticipate trouble even on the way to the altar. On the other hand, expectations are high in that we place on our mate extraordinary demands to make us happy and meet our needs. In short, we demand more and put up with less.

*Traditions and rituals*—Weddings and funerals have become painfully expensive, with the expectation bar raised impossibly high and no one having the courage to resist. To be a good fiancé, one must show his love by purchasing the biggest diamond. To be loving parents, we must offer the most expensive wedding. To be good children, we must purchase a "respectable" casket. To be doting grandparents, we must flood the children with Christmas toys.

R*x* *Free yourself from inordinate concern about the opinion of others. If you are successful in shedding that weighty expectation, you will find both margin and freedom awaiting.*

———&———

No matter how full the river is, it wants to swell further.
CONGOLESE PROVERB

# UNDERSTANDING YOUR SYMPTOM COMPLEX

*When our bodies and feelings can't cope any longer with the demands made upon them, when the overload becomes too great, their only course of action is to shut everything down. For many people, physical or nervous breakdown is the only way out of the impasse.*

ROBERT BANKS, AUSTRALIAN THEOLOGIAN, AUTHOR

---

IMPLICIT IN THE idea of margin is the concept of limits. If there are indeed limits, then there is a threshold at which those limits are exceeded. When you cross that threshold, you pass from *margin* into *overload*.

An important practical question therefore presents itself: How does one know when this threshold is passed, when one goes from 95 percent to 105 percent, when one crosses from margin into overload?

The best method for self-diagnosis is to identify your *symptom complex*. Each person will react differently from another person to the stressors of overload. One might experience outbursts of anger; another heartburn; another trouble sleeping.

However, each person will tend to react *similarly* to the way he or she reacted previously, even if it were a different stressor. For example, an individual might encounter different stressors (debt problems, traffic jams, or work deadlines) but in response, always develop the same symptom (upset stomach).

Here is a list of common symptoms that people experience:

• Some people withdraw. They become apathetic and depressed. Work dread is a common form of this reaction.

- Other people become irritable, angry, or hostile.
- Frustration and disorganization are common symptoms. These often lead to mistakes.
- Fatigue, exhaustion, and burnout are also common — particularly interesting in a society that has so many convenience technologies and labor-saving devices.
- Relational problems, moral failures, risk-taking behavior, and excessive self-medication are frequent symptoms.
- Physically, people commonly develop abnormal sleeping or eating patterns, hyperacidity, irritable bowel, headaches, rashes, tics, or palpitations.

Personally, my symptom complex consists of irritability and migraines. I am not normally an irritable person—I don't even *like* irritable people. But when overloaded, it is often the first symptom to arrive. Migraine headaches, my second symptom, are a part of my personality makeup and also a genetic inheritance, and they clearly increase during periods of overload. Understanding my symptom complex helps me to quickly identify overload when it is the cause.

℞ *Identify your symptom complex. While not perfectly reliable, it will indeed be a fairly consistent indicator of overload. When you notice this constellation of symptoms being triggered, then also notice the overloading factors that are responsible.*

---

You can outdistance that which is running after you, but not what is running inside you.
RWANDAN PROVERB

# FASHION, FUNCTION, AND FREEDOM

*One learns first of all in beach living the art of shedding; how little
one can get along with, not how much. Physical shedding to begin
with, which then mysteriously spreads into other fields. Clothes, first.
Of course, one needs less in the sun. But one needs less anyway, one
finds suddenly. One does not need a closet-full, only a small
suitcase-full. And what a relief it is! Less taking up and down of
hems, less mending, and—best of all—less worry about what to
wear. One finds one is shedding not only clothes—but vanity.*

ANNE MORROW LINDBERGH, AUTHOR, *GIFT FROM THE SEA*

---

WHETHER SUBTLY OR explicitly, the fashion demands of
modern culture maintain a stranglehold over the majority of
us. This is not only injurious to our financial margin and
treacherous to our integrity but also chronically destabilizing
to the formation of a virtuous social structure. Those incapable
of meeting minimum fashion demands seem almost doomed to
occupy an inferior social strata.

The nonstop bombardment of advertising does its job
well. We feel there is something inherently wrong with spending money we don't have, to buy fashionable items we don't
really need—yet we all do it. "I do not read advertisements,"
remarked the Archbishop of Canterbury. "I would spend all my
time wanting things." Or, as George Orwell inelegantly but
accurately observed, "Advertising is the rattling of a stick
inside a swill bucket."

Of course the industry understands how to play this game

well. First it cons us into believing we must play by its rules. Then, as soon as we have achieved high fashion in cars, computers, carpets, couches, curtains, and clothes, someone halfway around the world changes the rules—and we must start all over. It is impossible to outpurchase and outperform the fashion industry. As long as we agree to play their game by their rules, they will keep us scrambling in the wrong direction.

We must reverse this flow and grant permission for people to instead follow function over fashion. The opinion levied over and over again by culture says that if you wear plain clothes and drive an old car, you should feel embarrassed. But God never said such a thing at all. We ought to be saying the same things that God says. Does your church give people permission to live simply and not feel embarrassed? If not, then begin making changes. I don't mean in a way that would risk legalism but perhaps in a personal way. Go to the Cross, take the embarrassment yourself, and start allowing others to follow your example of simplicity in fashion.

> *R̶ Follow function over fashion. Until you are able to consistently place function over fashion, it will be difficult to regain margin. This doesn't necessarily forbid you from owning nice things. But it does mean that function and freedom assume their appropriate leadership role in cultural values.*

---

Fashion is more powerful than any tyrant.
<small>LATIN PROVERB</small>

# RUSH HOUR ON THE INFORMATION SUPERHIGHWAY

*Unless we can discover ways of staying afloat amidst the surging torrents of information, we may end up drowning in them.*

DR. DAVID LEWIS, PSYCHOLOGIST

---

DROWNING IN DATA is now an expected part of everyday corporate life, where having too much information is as dangerous as having too little. Information glut is causing off-the-chart stress levels and growing job dissatisfaction, including the Information Fatigue Syndrome: anxiety, self-doubt, paralysis of analytical capacity, a tendency to blame others, time wasting, and in some cases, illness.

There are some who believe the rapidly emerging information superhighway will solve our problems. If our diagnosis were too little information coming too slowly, then the information superhighway would obviously help. But that is not our diagnosis. In fact, we already have too much information coming too fast. How do you put out a fire with gasoline?

As we have seen, there are only so many details in anyone's life that can be handled comfortably. When that limit is exceeded, circuits begin to shut down. We refuse to process any more. Yet progress has given us more information in the past thirty years than in all the previous five thousand years combined. The rate at which information is discovered and disseminated exceeds—by many orders of magnitude—our limited ability to learn.

Everywhere you look, we are surrounded by data. The burgeoning amount of information available has strained all systems attempting to deal with it. One edition of *The New York Times* was 1600 pages long and contained more than 12 million words. The Library of Congress contains more than 100 million documents housed on 650 miles of shelving. If the most conscientious physician were to attempt to keep up with the complete medical literature by reading two articles per day, in one year this individual would be a thousand years behind that goal.

In one year 230 medical journals came across my desk—all of which were dutifully squirreled away for that illusory day when I will have the time to read them. Especially that *New England Journal's* lead article: "Genetic Linkage of the Marfan Syndrome, Ectopia Lentis, and Congenital Contractural Arachnodactyly to the Fibrillin Genes on Chromosomes 15 and 5."

Computerization, using transistors etched onto microchips, has throw the information age into turbo gear. Of course no one can keep up. Our desks are piled high and our brain cells are protesting. We need a surge protector for our synapses.

> *R* *Obviously, you cannot process all the information you encounter. In response, increase your information selectivity. Don't wade indiscriminately through volumes of material. Be ruthlessly selective. Deal decisively with unread periodicals. If the stack is more than six inches high, save the top inch and throw the rest away. If the stack is more than two feet high, throw the whole pile.*

---

Not all the words that were ever uttered are worth
weighing on golden scales.
NORWEGIAN PROVERB

# THE BENEFIT OF A GOOD TRANSMISSION

*Two signposts of faith: Slow Down and Wait Here.*
CHARLES STANLEY, PREACHER AND AUTHOR

———————

THE HEALTHIEST LIFESTYLE comes equipped with four gears. The first is PARK, for the contemplative times. This gear is to be used for rest and renewal. It is our battery-charging gear. This is where we do much of our thinking about values and spirituality, as well as much of our Scripture study and prayer. It is the gear we plan to use as we pick up a novel and head for the hammock or as we sit on a stump and watch the wildlife.

The second gear is LOW. This gear is for relationships, for family and friends. This is the gear we use when talking with someone. Low gear keeps us from being distracted and nervously moving on to the next activity even though we are still in the middle of a conversation. This is the gear we use when the children ask for a story or a back rub. Or when they ask about the death of pets, or sex, or God. No hurry here: just quality.

The third gear is DRIVE. This is our usual gear for work and for much of our play. This gear uses lots of energy, and the faster speed feels good because it is productive. It gets us from place to place quickly and efficiently. This is the gear we mow the lawn in or exercise in.

The fourth gear is OVERDRIVE. This gear is reserved for times that require extra effort and energy. If we have a deadline coming, we kick into this gear. If we are playing a basketball game, we call on overdrive to energize us. This is the gear I use during flu season when my schedule is double-booked. This is the gear most families use getting ready for church.

Unfortunately, many in our society do not come down from overdrive. Our cars are not meant to race at high speeds continuously—the engines would burn up. Neither are our bodies or spirits meant to race continuously. Yet for some, to slow down is unthinkable, and for others, impossible.

> ℞ *Discover where you keep your clutch, and change gears often. Go fast and hard with God's blessing, but only for appropriate activities. If you lack LOW or PARK, expand your transmission. The slow lane in life is just as important as the fast lane—commit to spending more time there.*

---

Alone a youth runs fast, with an elder slow.
But together they go far.
KENYAN PROVERB

# METASTATIC CLUTTER

*If we let culture just happen to us, we'll end up fat, addicted, broke,*
*with a house full of junk and no time.*

MARY PIPHER, PSYCHOLOGIST, AUTHOR

---

AN AXIOM OF modern living: clutter is automatic. Progress gives us more and more of everything faster and faster . . . and this means lots of stuff. The default flow of progress and clutter is downhill, right into the middle of our living rooms. As long as the inflow exceeds the outgo, things pile up.

Progress manifests itself in various ways, but one of the most naturally occurring is consumerism. Consumerism is both a way of life and the primary driving engine of our economy, and it naturally leads to clutter. One has to be unusually intentional and self-disciplined to resist the flow of clutter that assaults our living spaces. Do not underestimate the force of this flow or the level of diligence required to thwart it.

Clutter experts maintain that we *use* about 20 percent of what we own but we *maintain* 100 percent. When examined in this light, it becomes self-evident that we might wish to shift some of our time and attention *away* from maintaining a mountain of things we don't use and redirect that time and attention *toward* living a fuller life.

One way to slow our galloping consumerism is to make deliberate decisions regarding a possession endpoint. How many possessions are enough? Seldom do we address this important issue in objectively measurable terms.

Think specifically about satiety. How much money do we need to earn? Write it down. What kind of car will we be satisfied with? Write it down. How many clothes do we need? How much will we spend on shoes? How often should we update our laptop? What about our chairs and couches? Write it down. Let's not write down legalistic answers for our neighbors; this is about our own personal simplicity campaign. "If everyone swept in front of his own house," advised Goethe, "the whole world would be clean."

Three specific approaches deserve consideration:

*We can buy less.* Of course, for many of us that is like saying we can breathe less. Nevertheless, the less we buy, the less clutter we accumulate.

*We can give away more.* Actively think about things that can bless the lives of others and decompress your clutter at the same time. If you haven't used something in the past six to twelve months, chances are you don't really need it. Think of someone who does.

*We can throw away more.* Go through the house periodically with a front-end loader on a seek-and-destroy mission.

> ℞ *Actively search for things in the house to give away, donate, sell, or throw away. Schedule it: perhaps one drawer a week; one room a month; the entire house in a year. Every year.*

---

A small fountain quenches your thirst
as well as a big one.
<small>BASQUE PROVERB</small>

# THE SOLACE OF SCIENCE

*A little science estranges men from God,*
*but much science leads them back to Him.*

LOUIS PASTEUR

---

THE PEOPLE WHO lived at the time of Christ enjoyed a special privilege: they looked God in the eye. While we do not have that physical proximity to Jesus, we have one advantage earlier people lacked: the new revelations of modern science. While science hardly compares to the physical presence of Jesus, we would be wise not to underestimate it. It provides us an advantage in spiritual perspective previous generations could hardly imagine.

People of faith often tend to fear science. My feeling, however, is quite different. True science is a friend of Truth. It is only the misinterpretation and misapplication of science that ought to be feared. In contrast, truthful science reveals much about the power, precision, design, and sovereignty of God—details we learn nowhere else. And the more we learn about God, the more we rest in the shadow of His vast power.

God has allowed us the privilege of living in a time when great mysteries are being uncovered. No previous era knew about quantum mechanics, relativity, subatomic particles, supernovas, ageless photons, or DNA. These all reveal the stunning genius of a God who spoke a time-space-matter-light universe into existence, balanced it with impossible requirements of precision, and then gave it life.

Does it not stir your heart to realize that in a millionth of a second, a trillion atoms in your body turn over—and yet somehow God makes it work? Does it not deepen your reverence to realize that God is more impressive than a magnetic cloud ten million miles in diameter careening through space at a million miles an hour, or a neutron star that weighs a billion tons per teaspoon?

Does it not give you pause to think that of the ten thousand trillion ($10^{16}$) words spoken by humans since the dawn of time, God heard every one, remembers every one, can recite them all backward from memory, and even knew them before they were spoken? Or that of the $10^{30}$ snow crystals necessary to form an Ice Age, each snowflake—composed of a hundred million trillion water molecules—is unique in all the universe? A British mathematician has determined that the precision seen in the created universe is on the order of $10^{10^{123}}$. How can that fail to impress?

Science is a close friend of the theology of sovereignty. When science discovers, faith rightly grows. The Creator's strength is the answer for the creature's weakness.

> *R Run toward science, not away. Allow science to become a source of spiritual comfort. Once it is realized that God stands behind all creation, then science becomes a display of His genius. And when science is thus seen through eyes of faith, a new vision of God's creative glory brings both solace and strength to anxious hearts.*

---

The rooster said, "I shall cry but whether
the sun rises God knows."

GEORGIAN PROVERB

# TECHNOLOGICAL INCOMPREHENSIBILITY

*"You would need an engineering degree from MIT to work this,"
someone once told me, shaking his head in puzzlement over his
brand-new digital watch. Well, I have an engineering degree
from MIT. Give me a few hours and I can figure out
the watch. But why should it take hours?*

DONALD A. NORMAN, TECHNOLOGY DESIGN SPECIALIST

———————————

IT HAS BEEN estimated that the average person must learn to
operate twenty thousand pieces of equipment, three-fourths of
them "infuriating by design." What could better illustrate contemporary overload than that single statistic? Some elicit our
gratitude, others our exasperation. I have a physics degree, but
honestly, I don't know how to set my watch, set the clock on
my car radio, or program my VCR.

The spontaneous flow of progress is always in the direction of increasing complexity. This is not abnormal but instead
quite expected. It is what development is all about. Yet there is
a Frankensteinian threshold beyond which the complexity
chokes rather than facilitates.

As the shift toward complexity continues, more and more
is removed from our comprehension and influence. We witness it in technology, science, computers, the military, education, economics, medicine, government, law, business, and
more. Once we recognize complexity as a specific problem, its
pervasiveness becomes immediately apparent.

Although technology represents only one aspect of the complexity issue, it is one we can most readily relate to. We all have experienced exasperating moments dealing with machinery beyond our understanding. I was never adept at diagnosing my car's problems, let alone repairing them. Yet thirty years ago when I lifted the hood, at least there were only a dozen moving parts to blame the malfunction on. Now the engine looks as if it came straight from the pages of a science fiction novel.

I once changed our kitchen faucets but had to make five separate trips to the hardware store before the replacement worked. When Linda used the copy machine at a university she encountered the sign "Use at your own risk." From cars to computers to Chernobyl, escalating complexity is the order of the day. And complexity is responsible for more daily stress than we can imagine.

℞ *Seek out only the level of complexity that you need and will use. When possible, encourage simplicity as an antidote to complexity. This requires specific intention and is much more difficult than it might seem but often very rewarding. "Any third-rate engineer or researcher can increase complexity," wrote economist E. F. Schumacher, "but it takes a certain flair of real insight to make things simple again."[23]*

---

Genius can be recognized by its childish simplicity.
CHINESE PROVERB

# SOLITUDE

*It is solitude and solitude alone that opens the possibility of a radical relationship to God that can withstand all external events up to and beyond death.*

DALLAS WILLARD, THEOLOGIAN AND PHILOSOPHER

---

THE TERRAIN OUTSIDE my bus window had been baked by the desert heat. As far as the eye could see, nothing but barrenness. I watched with fascination as the timeless Bedouins sat guarding their sheep under the same relentless sun that had parched the face of Abraham. Suddenly, the Jordanian guide shattered my reverie. "All of the great religions of the world," he said, "were founded in the desert." Then he lapsed again into silence.

The provocation set me back in my seat; I bristled. All you need is a sun-baked desert and a half-baked guru, and presto, a new truth is born.

But God pressed down upon me, taking the oxygen away from my resistance. As I stared at the desert, I went beyond offense to interest. Might it be true that the spiritual quest is intensified in the desert? Surely, if you don't count sun and sand, here is no overload. One has nothing to do . . . but think. Day after day, no change, no distractions. Just focus. Is it possible that one's thoughts might eventually climb to the divine in such a setting? Abraham, Moses, David, Elijah, John the Baptist, Jesus, Paul—all spent time in the desert.

What is it about this desolate environment that facilitates spirituality? Is it barrenness? Heat? Sun? And where today can one find such a desert? In our frenzied, overloaded existence, how is it possible to focus on anything, let alone on God?

After years of reflection, I believe the guide's remark contains a lesson for us. The desert is waiting, poised to teach us. But mostly we do not know about deserts. We do not know what it is like to be alone for weeks on end, clothed only with sandals and burlap, supplied with a small sack of bread and dried fish. Instead, we know cities and highways, noise and lights, activities and entertainment. We know overload.

Most of us would find such a desert experience unbearable. Our skin would shrivel. We would hallucinate from boredom. Despite such dreariness, the experience might yield surprising benefits.

Out of the boredom, the suffering, the barrenness, and the silence would grow a vine called focus. Our thoughts would begin to modulate in the direction of a few central themes. We would stop thinking about where we left the hair spray or what time the Superbowl starts. We would start thinking more about Truth, about life and death, about existence, and about God.

*R* *Use solitude to build a deeper relationship with God and self. Use solitude for rest, for prayer, for strength. Jesus practiced and found strength in periodic solitude. Yet today many are frightened by solitude. Perhaps the more the idea threatens you, the more you ought to consider it.*

---

Solitude is full of God.

SERBIAN PROVERB

# SPREAD GOODWILL

*Two important things are to have a genuine interest in people and to be kind to them. Kindness, I've discovered, is everything in life.*

ISAAC BASHEVIS SINGER, AUTHOR AND NOBEL LAUREATE

---

IT IS PERHAPS strange to think of kindness as a strategy for health. And I would be the first to say that seeking it for inauthentic reasons is a betrayal of transcendent principles. However, when we discover that goodwill and kindness indeed pay strong stress-reducing dividends, it is not wrong to make specific space in our lives for them. If you wish to be emotionally buoyant, be kind to others.

Once overload exceeds a certain threshold for caring, we become self-protective, uninterested in kindness and goodwill. It requires sensitivity to notice possible opportunities for building goodwill, and it takes emotional energy to act on them in the right way. When we are chronically emotionally overwhelmed, sensitivity and emotional energy are lacking just when they could serve us best.

According to Dr. Hans Selye, the father of stress research, one of the greatest buffers against the ravages of future stress is to spread goodwill in the lives of other people. Later, when stress comes to visit you, these people will surround you with their affirmation and support. They will bring you dinner, shovel your drive, stack your woodpile, and speak up for you in the workplace.

"Earn others' goodwill by helping them, and you will help yourself" might sound self-serving. But from another perspective, it is simply God closing His own feedback loop.

Kindness is an action more than a word. Unfulfilled good intentions don't count as much, and they certainly don't reimburse as richly. Yes, to spend time and energy in being kind is margin depleting. Of course it is. That is why it is important to *build up* margin in the first place—so it can be spent on the right priorities.

Plow the fields of kindness and you will reap a harvest of goodwill.

> ℞ *Write simple notes of kindness and encouragement. Be ready with a compliment. Notice opportunities to build others up. Be present at celebrations and crises—whether weddings or funerals, new births or heart attacks. Give simple gifts at tender moments; they need not be expensive. When you see a need, offering to help before being asked is especially kind.*

---

One can pay back the loan of gold, but one lies forever in debt to those who are kind.

MALAY PROVERB

# DISCIPLINE DESIRES

*Gold is like sea water—the more one drinks of it,*
*the thirstier one becomes.*

ARTHUR SCHOPENHAUER, PHILOSOPHER

---

THERE IS GREAT confusion abroad as to how we distinguish needs from desires. The list of what we call "needs" today is certainly much longer than the list was in 1900, which in turn was much longer than the list at the time of Christ. If the list expands each year, what are we to think of this? "The cultivation and expansion of needs is . . . the antithesis of freedom," teaches economist E. F. Schumacher. "Every increase of needs tends to increase one's dependence on outside forces over which one cannot have control."[24]

It is wise to clarify this distinction between needs and desires and to be honest about it before God. Our true needs are few and basic: we need faith, love, relationships with fellow human beings, meaningful work, food, clothing, and shelter. Most of the rest that we call *needs* are instead *desires*, relative to the age and location in which we live.

Let me quickly state that I don't think God limits us only to our needs. He is a generous, gracious God who allows us many of our desires. So if I want carpeting in my house, I should not attempt to deceive God or myself by calling it a need. But at the same time I should realize that God is generous and might well grant the desire.

The important issue is knowing when God says, "Thus far and no more." For me, when there is pride, ostentation, laziness, waste, or excessive comfort involved, then it is a desire I don't even try to bring before God.

In this process we are greatly aided if we tune out advertisements, which are nothing more than artificial *need creation*. If you listen to them and believe them, your financial margin will tend to disappear as you chase a satiation you will never find.

If you want to have financial margin, redefine desires and needs, using God's definition. And in the process, don't listen to advertisements.

*R Consider a broadly defined practice of fasting. It is healthy to periodically separate from the things of the world and do without. In traditional thinking, such fasting pertains to food. But in the context of financial margin, it is good to fast from shopping for periods of time. Use up what you have in the refrigerator and freezer. Wear out whatever clothes you have in the closet. Get along on whatever you have in the house. The world does not stop nor the family fall apart when you unplug from the treadmill of consumerism for a period. About the only momentous thing that will happen is your finances will be resuscitated by a much-needed transfusion of margin.*

———— ✦ ————

The more you have, the more you'll need.
BASQUE PROVERB

# EMOTIONAL REST

*My whole life is a movie. It's just that there are no dissolves. I
have to live every agonizing moment of it. My life needs editing.*

MORT SAHL, COMEDIAN

ASK PHYSICIANS ABOUT the frequency of anxiety or depression in their patients, and you will be stunned to learn how few
people are emotionally healthy and well rested. Despite all the
benefits of modernity, we worry incessantly about our jobs, our
marriages, our children, our looks, our age, our health, and our
future. The high rate of tranquilizer and antidepressant use is a
reliable indicator of our lack of emotional rest.

Physical rest and emotional rest often go hand in hand,
but there is no guarantee the resting of our bodies will produce
rested psyches. The stilling of outward activity does not
always ensure a commensurate quieting of inward activity.
Nevertheless, if we would rest our emotions, a wise first step
would be to seek out quiet. Unfortunately, Walden is nowhere
to be found: lights and noise are to our right; people and
action are to our left.

There are many reasons for the absence of emotional rest
in our midst — so many, in fact, that it would be surprising to
discover true restedness among us. Activity overload deprives
us of rest, yet we are busier than ever. Inappropriate expectations deprive us of rest, yet our culture advertises: "You deserve
the best." Pride deprives us of rest, as we worry about every

new wrinkle and every old shirt. Discontent deprives us of rest, yet ever-present advertising provokes endless dissatisfaction.

Preoccupation with success deprives us of rest—always climb a little higher and get a little more. So does preoccupation with power. Yet success and power are two cogs of the American Dream. Debt deprives us of rest, yet our debt is at unprecedented levels. We worry about our image and our reputation until we have no rest.

Perhaps the greatest root cause of the absence of emotional rest in our society is fractured relationships. When there is fighting in the workplace, contention in the community, bitterness in the church, and combat in the home, rest is not to be found. The saddest of these, of course, is the home. It was intended by God as a haven of peace and security. But when strife enters, rest flees.

Many of the excessively driven regard this type of rest as a luxury, or perhaps even an enemy. Increasingly, in our culture, success is all-important while emotional well-being is secondary. Instead, as your doctor, I must tell you that emotional restedness is an ally, a sustainer, and in the long run, a necessity. It is not wrong to seek a calm spirit.

*R Discipline expectations, tame discontent, and mend relationships. Reconfigure your adrenaline mechanisms to accommodate rest. Learn to subjugate wealth to health. Seek those things that make for peace: a quiet mind and a contented spirit.*

---

Fear and restlessness kill more than do illnesses.
FRENCH PROVERB

# WHAT LANGUAGE SHALL I BORROW?

*In Paris they simply stared when I spoke to them in French;
I never did succeed in making those idiots understand
their own language.*

MARK TWAIN

---

A REMARKABLE FUNCTION of the human brain is language acquisition. The process begins very early. Within a period of months, babies intuitively realize that the strange noises made by people around them are not babble at all but sounds connected to meaning. Once this understanding develops, babies begin a rapid acquisition of the capacity for language.

By a year of age, infants are using one or more words with meaning. By two years, their vocabulary is three hundred words and two-thirds of what they say is intelligible. By three years, the vocabulary has ballooned to one thousand words, 90 percent of which is intelligible. By the time they enter school, the vocabulary has risen to three thousand to four thousand words. The average adult has an *active,* or *use,* vocabulary of ten thousand words and a *passive,* or *recognition,* vocabulary of thirty thousand to forty thousand words.

No other animal has the kind of language capacity God provides humans. Other animals share with us the abilities of walking, running, seeing, hearing, and smelling, but the gift of language is reserved for humans. We were given such a gift, I believe, for a specific reason: relationship, communication, love.

Helen Keller maintained that the gift of hearing was far more important than the gift of sight because hearing allows the gift of speech, and speech allows the nurturing of relationship. Language connects us to the heart of others in a way nothing else can.

As with all of God's gifts, the gift of language can be corrupted. The same language ability that can be endearing and winsome is often instead used to condemn, control, gossip, and curse.

Using language for the building of relationship is primarily helpful on the horizontal earthly plane; we do not necessarily require the gift of language for divine communication. The language of heaven is more than words; it is meaning. Our words are simply vessels to use, vessels that in themselves are empty. If we don't fill the word vessels with true worship and prayer, they will never attain to divine meaning.

Never let us think that we accomplished anything on a Sunday morning because we met and exchanged an hour's worth of words. But rather let us consider whether we filled those words with true devotion. As the hymn says: "What language shall I borrow to thank thee, dearest Friend?"

*R*℞ *Guard your tongue wisely. The brain is capable of thinking at a rate of eight hundred words per minute, far exceeding the speed of caution. Small moments of stress can explode into lingering years of conflict through an unguarded word spoken in irritation. On the other hand, the words of encouragement you speak to another at a point of need will often, down the road, return to comfort during your own need.*

⸺⟳⸺

Words are like bullets; if they escape,
you can't catch them again.
<small>GAMBIAN PROVERB</small>

# NO STRESS, LOW STRESS, AND HYPERSTRESS

*We are hyperliving, skimming along on the surface of life.*
DAVID M. ZACH, FUTURIST

WOULD YOU LIKE a *no-stress* life? A wise person would not accept that option, no matter how tempting it might sound. A stress-free life would be fatal. If we do not have change, challenge, and novelty in our lives, we will literally die.

How about a *low-stress* life? Again, it sounds very alluring. Surprisingly, studies reveal that when placed in a low-stress environment for a period of time and then a high-stress environment for an equal duration, the majority of people prefer the high-stress environment.

There is a word associated with the low-stress life: boring. Teenagers use the word all the time. And I suppose older adults don't like boring any more than teenagers do. It's just been twenty years since we experienced it, so we don't remember how much we dislike it.

How about a *hyperstress* life then? This too, as you might expect, is unsatisfactory. People trapped in a hyperstress life feel out of control, exhausted in body and spirit. Too many demands, too little time.

Let's push the pause button for a second and reflect on the stress balance. Without at least some change and stress, we languish. If, on the other hand, there is too much change and stress, our adaptation mechanism breaks down. God designed the system for a midrange performance. You don't want to drive from Chicago to Los Angeles at two miles per hour, or at two hundred miles per hour, but somewhere in between.

Clearly, our bodies and minds seek a certain level of stress. This is not criticizable. As stress increases, so does our productivity. We have a sense of creative tension that feels good. Deadline pressures focus our attention and keep us on task. At the end of the day we feel quietly pleased with all we have accomplished.

Taken too far, however, the tension backfires. We hit the point of diminishing returns where increased effort leads to decreased results. On top of it all is the sense of frustration, almost a sense of betrayal that all this effort is producing an increasingly unhappy life.

Ignoring the law of limits will land us mired in the swamp of stress overload. When the acceptable tolerances of stress are exceeded, the system breaks down. Because of our contemporary turbocharged change dynamic, most of America is now in a hyperstress environment. When this kind of stress is pushed to the extremes, first fatigue, then exhaustion, then burnout results.

$R$ *Don't begrudge stress, but don't idolize it either. Use it to your benefit, as it was intended. But keep your distance from stress overload—it will happily bite you.*

---

If you see a Hungarian Shepherd dog half-a-kilometer away, keep that half-a-kilometer between you.

# OVERLOAD, THRESHOLDS, AND INDICATOR LIGHTS

*I believe in limits. Climbing teaches you that. You live for the
days when you're on the edge, but you never go over it.
There's an optimum size for every endeavor, and if you
exceed it, you go downhill. With this company, we could
easily become too large and lose everything.*

YVON CHOUINARD, FOUNDER PATAGONIA OUTDOOR CLOTHING

IF WE AGREE that limits are real—a major concession for
some—then the next logical question is, how do we know
when we have reached them? If a car overheats, an indicator
light alerts us to the danger—the engine is about to burn up.
If the electrical system is discharging rather than charging,
another light signals us that the car is about to shut down.

Unfortunately, God didn't equip us with such a warning
system. If we had a flashing red light on the end of our nose to
indicate "95 percent full" followed by a siren when exceeding
100 percent, perhaps we could better gauge our capacities. But
we don't have such an indicator system, and we are not adept
at knowing when we have overextended until we feel the pain.

Without such warning signals, most people are not quite
sure when they pass from margin to overload. Threshold
points are not easily measurable and are also different for different people in different circumstances. We don't want to be
underachievers (heaven forbid!), so we fill our schedules

uncritically. Options are as attractive as they are numerous, and we overbook.

As a result, many people commit to a 120-percent life and wonder why the burden feels so heavy. It is rare to see a life prescheduled to only 80 percent, leaving a margin for responding to the unexpected God sends our way.

When we are on the unsaturated side of our limits threshold we can be open and expansive, saying yes to all kinds of new opportunities and projects and committees and activities. But once we cross the line into the saturated side of our limits, the rules of the game totally change. When we are saturated, we can't factor anything more into our life until we take something away; we can't say yes until we say no to something equally time consuming. As elementary as this principle seems, it remains largely invisible to most.

Thresholds are real, and thresholds are God ordained. He created them. There are times He will take us past them, and at such times we should not hesitate. There are other times when we violate the limits on our own instructions. This can easily be tolerated over the short term. Chronic and extended overload, however, carries a heavy price.

*R̸ Spend some time contemplating your limits threshold—that line between margin and overload. Identify warning signs along the way that can assist in self-awareness. Understanding your symptom complex will help.*

———∞∞———

Once burned by milk you will blow on cold water.
RUSSIAN PROVERB

# FAITH OR PRESUMPTION?

*Your own efforts "did not bring it to pass," only God. . . .*
*Rejoice if you feel that what you did was "necessary,"*
*but remember, even so, that you were simply the instrument*
*by means of which He added one tiny grain to the*
*Universe He has created for His own purposes.*

DAG HAMMARSKJÖLD, SECRETARY-GENERAL OF THE U.N.

---

WE SEE IT all the time — an individual, a group of individuals, or a ministry developing a grand, splashy program that will reach the stars, consume a decade, and cost millions. Who can be against it? It is a taking-the-kingdom-by-force attitude: boldness because God is audacious, fearlessness because "if God is for me who can be against me," and confidence because "nothing is impossible with God."

But how does one know this project is of God? Just because we have a great idea does not mean it is God's great idea. He does His own thinking. And He communicates on His own timetable.

How can we be sure human plans are the result of faith and not presumption? Just because it says so in a fund-raising letter is no guarantee. When we dare to speak for God, there must be integrity at the highest level, as high as heaven is above the earth.

With so much at stake, it is important to understand the full spiritual implications of the stress-limits-overload issue. We must learn where to draw the line between faith and presumption.

What happens if we overextend and find ourselves out on a limb, doing 150 percent of what we ought, and then get into trouble? We cry out to God, "Help!" But God replies, "When you come back where you belong, then I will help you. Remember: *You* are the creature. *I* am God. Use My power, not your own."

Nevertheless, because this is such a difficult lesson for us to learn in our performance-driven, activity-oriented culture, we see people working eighteen-hour days for laudable causes, neglecting their relationships . . . only to have their spouses leave or their children become alienated.

We see others doing wonderful service for God and humankind but neglecting their bodies—sleep, nutrition, exercise. Then comes the heart attack at age forty-eight.

We see delightful, well-meaning servants who overcommit and then wonder why they have no joy.

We see physicians who are so chronically overworked that they resent their patients for being ill.

And on it goes. And on . . . and on . . .

> R̸ *If you are not sure, wait. Pray. Pray some more. Ask for godly counsel. Pray some more. Read the Scriptures. Pray some more. Wait. When God speaks, you will hear Him—if your heart is at Home.*

∽∾∽

God visits us often, but most of the time<br>we are not home.

FRENCH PROVERB

# SETTING BOUNDARIES

*Appropriate boundaries don't control, attack, or hurt anyone. They
simply prevent your treasures from being taken at the wrong time.*

DR. HENRY CLOUD AND DR. JOHN TOWNSEND, *BOUNDARIES* CO-AUTHORS

———————————

CAVING IN TO demands that are emotionally overwhelming,
relationally unhealthy, physically exhausting, and spiritually
inauthentic is not the way to create the space and rest we all
need. This dilemma is best solved by understanding and establishing boundaries.

The concept of boundaries suggests that it is acceptable
and even desirable to erect and defend a perimeter around the
private and personal spaces of our lives. For example, people
have the right to establish the atmosphere in their own homes
regardless of the world's opinion on that issue.

In our family we have erected a sometimes loose boundary
to protect the dinner hour: we do not answer the telephone
while we are eating. Similarly, when the boys were young, we
would not allow the telephone to disturb our evening routines
of reading to them, praying with them, and tucking them in
bed. No matter how important the phone call was, it could
wait. As radical as this might sound, it is actually an elementary form of common sense that has eluded us far too long.

Occasionally, when I am home alone and in a particularly
drained state, I might not even answer the doorbell. After
extensive speaking trips I need to lie fallow, to do nothing, to

recharge my batteries. It is not my desire to be rude or insensitive. But sometimes I simply must rest.

I had a patient call me at 4:00 A.M. to ask if I would renew her Valium prescription. You really shouldn't do this to your physicians—they will not last. Neither can you call your clergy at 4:00 A.M. and say, "I can't sleep. Could you hum 'Amazing Grace'?"

Jesus Himself enforced boundaries every day. He was constantly surrounded by people telling Him what to do. But Jesus *knew* what to do; He was not about to be distracted from the will of the Father.

Boundaries, accurately defined and practiced, are not selfishness but self-care. There is a difference. Don't use the excuse of boundaries to be rude or self-absorbed. Instead use boundaries to establish the kind of margin that will guard your larger priorities for the sustainable future.

$R$ *Control your electronic devices and turn them off when appropriate. Don't answer the phone at the dinner table or during other important personal or relational times. When fundraisers call, inform them you never respond to telephone fund drives and invite them to mail information for you to consider. Consider getting caller ID to screen calls.*

━━━ ∞∞∞ ━━━

Who lives in a quiet house has plenty.
NEW ZEALANDER PROVERB

# NANOSECOND EFFICIENCY

*The goal of much that is written about life management is to enable us to do more in less time. But is this necessarily a desirable goal? Perhaps we need to get less done, but the right things.*

JEAN FLEMING, AUTHOR AND INTERNATIONAL SPEAKER

---

IMPROVING PRODUCTIVITY IN the workplace is the equivalent of bodybuilding in the gym, and efficiency is the steroid. Managers know that time pressure works, that it increases both productivity and efficiency. But who is the one to say when it has been pushed too far? Many video display terminal workers are now monitored electronically. Every key-punch is recorded and if their quotas are not met, their records are tainted and jobs threatened.

Speed: Supercomputers operate at trillionths of a second. Do you know what that means? Neither do I, and I have a degree in physics. A trillionth of a second has no human reference.

Speed: Using electronic linkages, computers can make transactions so fast that the same dollars can finance seven different deals on the same day.

Speed: At international currency exchanges, traders watch their video screens as the constantly changing world currency prices flash before them. If they move fast enough at the right moment, they can make hundreds of thousands of dollars in a couple of minutes. "For us, currencies have a value not for a day or an hour, but for a second," explained one trader.

Speed: In the past, it took weeks to send a letter by Pony Express. Then it took days by mail. Then hours by overnight jet. Now it takes only seconds.

Speed and efficiency are the keys to productivity, and productivity is the key to success. But, of course, we must have quality. So we want more and more speed, more and more efficiency, more and more productivity, with better and better quality. In other words, do more and more with less and less, faster and faster. Continuously. In the end we will have platinum products and dead workers.

"There is more to life," said Gandhi, "than increasing its speed." We've got enough speed. Now let's work on some of the more important aspects of life.

℞ *Avoid short-term flurry. We are notorious for our short-sightedness, living in a myopic mania that blurs the future. The horizon is never visible in the middle of a dust storm. Instead we must have a vision that informs our future and extends beyond tomorrow. Living only week-to-week is like a dot-to-dot life.*

*In particular, don't rush wisdom. Seldom is true wisdom a product of speedy deliberation. In fact, wisdom is almost always slow. The more important the decision, the longer the time you should take to make it. If life's pace pushes you, push back. And take as much time as you need for clearness to develop.*

———✸———

Haste has no blessing.
SWAHILI PROVERB

# THE RELENTLESS POWER OF DISCONTENT

*God has been replaced, as He has all over the West, with
respectability and air-conditioning.*

LEROI JONES, AUTHOR AND PLAYWRIGHT

------

WHY IS CONTENTMENT so hard for us? For one thing, it's
slippery. Contentment is not at all like cutting down a tree,
which, when it is done, is done. It's more like trying to pick up
mercury with tweezers: it keeps squirting away. It's like the car-
rot suspended two feet in front of our face that moves every
time we do. We keep chasing, and it keeps dodging.

Beyond its slippery nature, contentment is difficult to
achieve because of the relentless power of discontent. The battle waged between contentment and discontent is often subtle
but never soft. When we enter the material world for our contentment it pulls us in deeper and deeper, and the pull is
deceptively strong. That for which I long becomes that to
which I belong.

In addition, contentment is difficult because it is a relative
state—at least the world's practice of it is relative. A number
of factors influence this relativism: the age in which we live,
the local culture, the lifestyle of family and friends. If you live
in New York City and all your neighbors drive Mercedes, for
example, you might feel embarrassed to drive a pickup. Living
in rural Wisconsin where many people cut firewood, however,
a pickup reigns supreme.

As a general principle, contentment is relative to the difference between *all we now have* and *all there is to have*. The greater the difference between these two points, the less contented we will be. One of the dubious advantages of progress is how it inexorably increases all there is to have. Progress perceives this as its duty—to give us more and more. This, however, also leads to a commensurate—and paradoxical—increase in discontent.

Before the invention of air-conditioning, for example, no one was discontent to drive in sweltering heat without it. People were *miserable* because of the heat, perhaps, but not *discontent* because they didn't have air-conditioning. You cannot be discontent with regard to something that doesn't exist. Yet when progress invents it for us, the level of expectation rises and with it the level of discontent.

Today, living in Texas without an air-conditioned car, you would likely be discontent. Forty years ago you would not. Some might respond, "Before air-conditioning people were miserable, and now, some are discontent. Isn't it about the same?" No. To be miserable with the heat is not a sin.[25]

> R̸ *Realizing that life today is essentially a comparative experience, divorce yourself from any relativistic standards for contentment. Resist comparing yourself and your material possessions with other people. Decide on an endpoint for enough. Stick with it and discover how freeing it feels.*

---

Everybody else's hens lay more eggs than ours.
BASQUE PROVERB

# SIMPLICITY—WHAT IT IS

*Simplicity in its essence demands neither a vow of poverty nor a life of rural homesteading. As an ethic of self-conscious material moderation, it can be practiced in cities and suburbs, townhouses and condominiums. It requires neither a log cabin nor a hairshirt but a deliberate ordering of priorities so as to distinguish between the necessary and superfluous, useful and wasteful, beautiful and vulgar.*

DAVID SHI, HISTORIAN AND SIMPLICITY SCHOLAR

SIMPLE LIVING OVER the centuries has been variously defined and never fixed. Certain common threads, however, can be identified.

*Voluntary*—If the simple life is forced, it ceases to be simple. Involuntary impoverishment, for example, makes it difficult for people to choose simplicity. The plain life is more profitable when it is chosen as an act of the will.

*Free*—Simplicity is a life of freedom. It is free from anxiety about our reputations, our possessions, our tomorrows.

*Uncluttered*—Because clutter impedes our journey, simplicity seeks to unclutter. We practice deaccumulation. Emotionally, we release our worries and begin anew each day. Like runners of old, we strip down to that which is authentic so we might run the race effectively.

*Natural*—We respect the natural order—the things God has created and the job God has given humankind within that order. We don't just return to nature; we return to the God who created nature.

*Creative*—Life is not boring just because it is simple. Simplicity sets the imagination to work and allows us to rediscover the joys of creativity.

*Authentic*—A simple lifestyle devotes itself to authenticity—those things that have eternal value: people, love, service, worship, prayer, relationships, rest.

*Focused*—We focus on that which is good and true and eternal. This doesn't mean we refuse to wash our car or take out the garbage. But it does mean that we focus intently on seeking the kingdom first. Without such focus, we drift.

*Disciplined*—Comfort is not a legitimate primary goal—authenticity is. Understandably, then, simplicity may at times lead to discomfort. Doing without is often necessary.

*Diligent*—The simple life knows how to rest but also how to work. One of the benefits of simplicity is a return to human labor. It is good to work with our hands. It is good to start and end the work ourselves and to have pride in the process. It is good to plant our own food, to sew our own clothes, to cut our own wood, to walk to work.

A life voluntarily chosen and lived in freedom; a life uncluttered and natural; a life that is focused, diligent, and disciplined; a life characterized by creativity and spiritual authenticity—is this not a healthy life?

℞ *Desire less, give away, share possessions, avoid overindulging, de-emphasize respectability, lie fallow, enjoy solitude, be grateful, don't overwork, fast periodically, bike or walk.*

⸎

If you have a lot, give some of your possessions; if you have little, give some of your heart.
NILOTIC PROVERB

# SIMPLICITY—WHAT IT ISN'T

*Simplicity does not come easily. To withstand the pressures
of society requires constant effort and discipline. On the other
hand, relax. You can't force simplicity. Don't try to
be something you are not. Simplicity is a gift.*

ART GISH, SIMPLICITY ACTIVIST

MISCONCEPTIONS ABOUND ABOUT the simple life. We
can clarify simplicity as much by explaining what it isn't as by
delineating what it is.

*Easy*—Many equate "simple" with "easy" and become dis-
illusioned with simple living when they find out how hard it
can be. To bake your own bread or cut your own wood is not
always the easiest way to accomplish these chores. But doing
them yourself allows for an invaluable independence.

*Legalistic*—Those who choose a simple lifestyle sometimes
set a standard of judgment for the lives of others. Such legalism does not liberate; it kills. It destroys the joy of both the
accused and the accuser.

*Proud*—Simple living can deteriorate into "reverse pride."
It is possible to practice self-exaltation for the patches on your
clothes or the rust on your car. Jesus dealt with the attitude of
self-righteousness and no new teaching is needed.

*Impoverished*—Simplicity doesn't reject money and ownership; it merely subjugates it. We don't seek wealth as a goal in
itself, because it is sinful to do so and because money cannot buy

what we need. Yet money is received and used, for the Father knows how to control it for the purposes of His kingdom.

*Ascetic*—Asceticism rejects all possessions and argues that "things" are spiritually handicapping. While it is true that things can *become* spiritually inauthentic, they are not *a priori* evil. God is a good Creator, and He has created a world full of good things. It is not wrong to use them.

*Neurotic*—Some adherents tilt toward Spartan asceticism because they feel unworthy of any blessing. Such guilt is neurosis, not simplicity. God blames us only for what we are to blame for, and He forgave it all when we asked Him to.

*Ignorant*—We don't achieve such a lifestyle by burning our books. On the contrary, one of the main advantages of simplicity is the opportunity it provides for study and discussion. God created our brains just as He did our hearts, and He expects us to use them both.

*Escapist*—We don't attain simplicity by throwing away our possessions and running off to the woods. Clearly, for some the simple life is facilitated by moving from an overmortgaged house and congested city. But simple living is not a location; it is an attitude. It is not escaping; it is transcending. It is not separation; it is sanctification.

*R̶ Fully understand: This is an adventure, not a luxury cruise. But what a joy to feel the pleasure of the Father while humbly traveling the right road.*

---oooo---

Draw water from the new well,
but do not spit in the old one.
<small>BULGARIAN PROVERB</small>

# GOD'S REPORT CARD

*Take away love and our earth is a tomb.*
ROBERT BROWNING, POET

---

IF GOD'S GREATEST commandments are as inclusive as I believe they are, when life is over and we receive our report card, it will have only one category: relationship. There will be three lines:

- How did we relate to God?
- How did we relate to ourselves?
- How did we relate to others?

We know God's report card contains three categories because Jesus told us. When asked by the Pharisee, Jesus answered that the Shema was the greatest commandment: "'Hear, O Israel, the Lord our God, the Lord is one; and you shall love the Lord your God with all your heart, and with all your soul, and with all your mind, and with all your strength.'" However, He did not stop there: "The second is this, 'Love your neighbor as yourself.' There is no commandment greater than these."[26]

In so answering, Christ laid out for us the greatest imperative of eternity: to love God, ourselves, and our neighbor. This commandment must be the first guideline for all of life's decisions and actions. Nothing is to come before it.

*Love God*—God is our Creator, which means we were related to Him even before birth. He yearns for our broken relationship to be reconciled. He went 99.99 percent of the way and extends a nail-pierced hand for us to grasp. His patience has given us much space to repent. We live in a world that promotes distance, builds fences, buys locks, and doesn't talk on elevators. But God, in Christ, says "Come."

*Love yourself*—God assumes we love and care for self. Some people, however, have no relationship with themselves. To leave them alone in solitude for a day would be punishment. That we are worthy of love is demonstrated by the fact that God loves us. His love validates our worth. The call to spiritually accurate self-love is not a denial of our unworthiness but is instead the result of a journey that goes through personal unworthiness to God's acceptance.

*Love your neighbor*—Created incapable of meeting all our own needs, God gave us others, in relationship, to help. Despite the fact that each individual is of more value than all the careers, education, and money in the universe added together and multiplied times infinity, rightly relating to others seems to be the most difficult item on the contemporary agenda.

Right relationships are a fundamental reason we seek margin, for all healthy relationships require the availability, flexibility, and resilience margin provides. Without margin, our interpersonal connections quickly wilt.

> R̶ *Place the highest possible priority on relationships. If God put it at the top of His list, you should as well. This does not mean that you quit your job or abandon all other commitments. But it does mean you develop an uncompromising conviction that relationship is the primary field God has asked you to plow.*

---

Life without a friend is death without a witness.
<small>SPANISH PROVERB</small>

# MARGIN IN PHYSICAL ENERGY

*Maximum bodily strength and efficiency depend upon three factors: sleep, exercise, and nutrition. Only a body that is well rested, properly exercised, and correctly fed will be able to maintain its energy reserves in the face of serious stress.*

DR. MARTIN SHAFFER, STRESS EXPERT

---

WHEN WE DIP into the tank for some physical energy, we all want the ladle to return with something in it. Unfortunately, for too many of us the tank dried up years ago.

A large percentage of Americans have diminished physical energy reserves because of poor conditioning. Others, such as mothers of newborns and those who work two jobs, are chronically sleep deprived. Still others suffer from chronic caloric overconsumption. These three factors—poor conditioning, sleep deprivation, and obesity—constitute a physical energy desert where no margin can grow. Lacking margin in physical energy, we feel under-rested and overwhelmed. With no strength left, we put our tiredness to bed, hoping tomorrow will be a stronger day.

Those who predicted the human race would evolve into a communal picture of robust heartiness have been shaken by these pathologies of prosperity. In some ways progress is too easy on us. It caters food in overabundance without regard for the requirement of restraint. It provides electricity and artificial lighting without regard for the requirement of sleep. And it supplies transportation and convenience without regard for the requirement of physical activity. As a result we eat too much, sleep too little, and move hardly at all.

Our bodies are, in one sense, sophisticated energy machines. If we properly care for the engine and load the appropriate fuel, the machine will operate reliably. Even when called upon to double or triple its performance, the body is capable of responding by tapping into energy reserves.

These reserves can be enhanced or depleted depending on many factors—some external, some internal, and some eternal. It is wise for us to vigilantly protect these reserves, for if they are drawn too low, ill results follow.

Virtually anyone, no matter how ravaged by insomnia, intemperance, and inactivity, can take steps to reverse deterioration. The body can bounce back; God designed it so. But not without some cooperation from its owner.

Until we accept personal responsibility for our own health, the road to the future will remain paved with aches and adipose. If you are under-rested, overweight, and unexercised, it is your job to change. The good news: *change is possible.*

*R̶ Change your habits. Poor nutrition, poor exercise patterns, and (sometimes) poor sleep patterns are called habit disorders. Breaking old ways and establishing new patterns are necessary. Changing habit disorders often requires changing lifestyles. Sometimes the changes required are small. More often, however, the adjustment entails a new way of looking at and reacting to both yourself and the world around you.*

―※―

The bad habit is first a wanderer,
then a guest and finally the boss.
HUNGARIAN PROVERB

# SAT ON BY AN ELEPHANT

*We are stripped bare by the curse of plenty.*
WINSTON CHURCHILL

---

YEARS AGO IN Siam, if the king had an enemy he wanted to torment, it was easy: give him a white elephant. The receiver of this gift was now obligated into oblivion. Any gift from the king obviously had to be cared for; it could not be given away without causing offense. Additionally, a white elephant was considered sacred and thus required the best nourishment and protection. Soon the extreme costs of caring for the gift drove the king's enemy to destitution.

Today it seems everyone is on the king's hit list. We are increasingly buried under mountains of possessions. Closets are full; attics are groaning; garages are bulging; storage space is saturated. Swollen houses lead to the three-car-garage syndrome: huge homes with spacious garages, yet all the cars parked in the driveway because the garages are already full.

If that little space left in your house is creating an annoying sucking sound, there is no shortage of consumer clutter waiting to occupy the temporary vacuum. For example, if you have $75 million, you could buy a personal submarine over the Internet (www.ussubs.com). Or you could buy a lighted Christmas wreath for the front grill of your car. If you want to light up the life of someone special, you can spend $400,000 for the Heartthrob Brooch: six rubies, seventy-eight diamonds, and chip-controlled, light-emitting diodes that flash with each beat of the wearer's heart. Or you could purchase the world's smallest working model railroad with a nineteen-inch attaché case for only $1,295, battery included. Or you could buy sterling silver thermometer cufflinks, and for only $98 you can take the temperature of your wrists.

Living a consumptive lifestyle is as natural as breathing. To shop till you drop is thoroughly and thoughtlessly mainstream. To step off such a treadmill requires a level of understanding, of intention, of resistance that is hard to come by. But is it possible that the most important answers for our most important problems are not consumption-based answers?

At the beginning of every day we are given assignments with eternal significance: to serve and to love. But when God issued these assignments, He wasn't intending that we serve things and love possessions. He was talking about people. The simpler our possessions, the more time for people.

> *R See owning as a liability rather than an asset. There seems to be a one-to-one relationship between the possession of things and the consumption of time. Everything you own requires a commitment of your work time to pay for it and your leisure time to use and care for it. Don't buy or keep anything if the time spent on it competes unfavorably with family, service, or God. Remember: everything you own owns you. You are free in accordance with the number of things you can do without.*

---

You must leave your possessions behind
when God summons.
YIDDISH PROVERB

# YESTERYEAR'S CHARM

*I wonder sometimes whether we are progressing. In my
childhood days, life was different in many ways. We were
slower. Still we had a good and happy life, I think. People
enjoyed more in their way, at least they seemed to be happier.
They don't take time to be happy nowadays.*

GRANDMA MOSES, FOLK PAINTER

---

MARGIN WAS AN unrecognized possession of the peoples of
the past. Throughout most of the history of the world, margin
existed in the lives of individuals as well as societies. There were
no televisions, no phones, no cars, and no newspapers. The
media could not broadcast the throng of events taking place in
town. With no electricity to extend daylight, few suffered sleep
deprivation. Time urgency had not yet been invented.

Instead, by default rather than choice, people lived more
deliberate lives. They had time to help a neighbor. Their activities more often drew them together rather than pulled them
apart. The past might have been deprived in many respects,
but its people had margin.

Perhaps this is a key to understanding why the past often
holds such charm. Surely we overrate its positives and overlook its hardships. Yet one suspects there must be at least *some*
substance to our nostalgia. It is intriguing to postulate that
margin is the link. Without even knowing exactly what it is
that we miss, we miss margin. Progress devours margin; we
yearn to have it back.

A similar observation holds true in developing countries today. Conditions in the Third World are sad in many respects and sometimes even heart-rending. But after working in several of these cultures I am struck by the recurring impression that the people have margin. They sit and talk, they walk without hurry, and they sleep full nights.

Our family once went to the small island of Carriacou to help Project Hope bring medical care to its seven thousand people. One observer characterized the sleepy life on Carriacou by commenting: "Very little happens on Carriacou, and what does happen, happens slowly. It bustles on Monday, when produce arrives, and on Saturday, mail day. Otherwise, this little island just gazes out to sea."

The clinics were often full, but expectations were low and paperwork minimal. We could perform no lab tests, order no X-rays, do no surgery. Yet sick people got better anyway.

During our brief six weeks, we ate all our meals together, went swimming together, and had crab races on our living room floor together. It was the only time in our parenting when *both* Linda and I tucked in our boys every night. Do you think we miss it?

*R̞ Without romanticizing the past, reflect on the positive features such a life might hold. How can you recapture the more pleasant aspects of that nostalgia without betraying reality? Slow down, rest up, cultivate community, and find contentment in simple things. Progress isn't the only road to joy.*

---

Nothing works, but everything works out.

# MARGIN AND THE HEART

*Once I had a brain and a heart also; having tried them both,
I should much rather have a heart.*

TIN MAN IN *THE WIZARD OF OZ*

POWERING THE CIRCULATORY system is a formidable task, unforgiving of errors. Yet the heart is remarkably effective. Every day this 10 ounce muscle contracts 100,000 times nary missing a beat. Over a lifetime of faithful service, these two self-lubricating, self-regulating, high-capacity pumps beat 2.5 billion times and pump 60 million gallons of blood without pausing to rest.

The body has 60,000 miles of blood vessels, with capillaries so small that red blood cells (RBCs) often must flow through single file and sometimes even distort themselves to fit. The wall of these tiniest capillaries is so delicate it would rupture under a tension 1/3000th required to tear toilet tissue.

Red blood cells are of critical importance to life. "The life is in the blood" is not only good theology but also good biology. The story begins with the critical nature of oxygen. All fires require oxygen, including the energy-releasing fire within our cells. A series of ingenious mechanisms exist to transport oxygen into the tissues. When oxygen is inhaled into the respiratory track, it snuggles against the lining of the lung wall. The favorable diffusion coefficient attracts the oxygen molecule to cross the lining and enter the capillary blood.

Since the oxygen is not very soluble in blood, it can't transfer down to the peripheral tissues on its own. Enter the RBC. The red blood cells contain hemoglobin. The oxygen molecules pile into the RBC by combining with the hemoglobin, each cell carrying a million molecules of oxygen.

Our bodies make over two million RBCs every second. If you took all of the RBCs out of your body and laid them side by side, they would go around the earth at the equator four times.

It is interesting to note that the body believes in leaving a margin. Under normal resting conditions, the RBC releases only about 25 percent of its oxygen to the tissues. This leaves abundant margin for surging to 100 percent—and even beyond—should the need arise during strenuous work and exercise.

℞ *Don't worry. According to researchers, worry is cardiotoxic. It turns out that when God said, "Do not worry about tomorrow,"[27] "Do not fret,"[28] and "Do not be anxious,"[29] He was not only advocating good theology but also good cardiology.*

━━━⊗⊗⊗━━━

The bitter heart eats its owner.
<small>BOTSWANA PROVERB</small>

# WASTED WORRY

*Worry does not empty tomorrow of its sorrow;*
*it only empties today of its strength.*

CORRIE TEN BOOM, DUTCH CHRISTIAN HOLOCAUST SURVIVOR

---

MOST OF US realize that worry is senseless, but that doesn't curb our appetite. Humans have an almost insatiable capacity for fret. No matter what our circumstances, we find some aspect of our experience that tempts worry. Solve a problem in quadrant A, then start worrying about a difficulty in quadrant B. Solve that problem but then find a problem in quadrant C. . . . Worry is its own infinite loop.

A century ago people worried they wouldn't have enough food to last the winter and might die of starvation. Now we worry we have too much food for winter and might die of overeating. A century ago they worried about dying too young, by an accident, or infection, or childbirth. Now we worry we might die too old, with wrinkles and Alzheimer's. A century ago they worried there might not be enough pennies to buy livestock. Now we worry there might not be enough millions to last through retirement.

The parents worry whether Johnny and Susie will grow up emotionally secure, yet also worry when Johnny and Susie don't speak French by age six. The traveler worries it might rain, while the farmer worries it might not rain. The politician worries unemployment is too high while the economist worries unemployment is too low. Progress solves many problems, but it does not solve the worry problem.

Worry often arises from perceptions rather than reality. For example, some drivers worry about an accident every time they approach a stop sign. They might never have an accident, but they will make themselves sick fearing it.

Medical studies reveal that worry is bad for your health, harming the circulatory system, immune system, digestive system, and nervous system. We read such studies and then begin worrying that we are worrying too much. "That's the secret to life," said Charlie Brown. "Replace one worry with another."

David wrote, "Do not fret."[30] Paul wrote, "Do not be anxious about anything."[31] In the most famous sermon in history, Jesus said, "Do not worry about tomorrow, for tomorrow will worry about itself. Each day has enough trouble of its own."[32] *Still* we worry.

There are at least three reasons why worry is foolish:

1. Our emotional energy margin is compromised.
2. Our physical health is damaged.
3. Our spiritual vitality is weakened when we pursue a path other than trust in the sovereignty of God.

*R̴ First, reflect on the power and precision of God. Realize anew that He is aware of your circumstance, He cares, and He has the power sufficient to cover the need. Second, reflect on your own pattern of worry (and ask others if you are a worrier). Calculate how often your worry actually changes circumstances. Then make a serious judgment about which you want more: worry or freedom.*

⸺◦◦◦⸺

Only one sort of worry is permissible—to
worry because one worries.

HASIDIC PROVERB

# TECHNOLOGY AND ACCESSIBILITY OVERLOAD

*I am dying of easy accessibility. Telephones in our homes and offices, cordless phones in our backyards and cars, beepers, fax machines, and e-mail. It's enough to give you a stroke. If Alexander Graham Bell walked into my office, I'd punch him in the nose. If he called, you can be sure I'd put him on hold.*

JAMES M. CERLETTY, M.D., MILWAUKEE PHYSICIAN

---

THE FUTURE ARRIVED yesterday, when the Starship Enterprise landed in our back yard. Slick gadgets are strapped to every belt, plugged into every socket, and stuck in every ear. Overhead, still more gadgets swim in the heavenlies.

As telecommunications rapidly reshape the globe, we sit at the beginning of a universal connectivity unprecedented in human history. Cell phones and pagers, videophones and videoconferencing, telecommuting and fax machines, Internet and e-mail, satellites and the information superhighway. Images of futuristic excitement, to be sure.

But what will be the result of this incredible flurry of seemingly unstoppable activity? Like most modern things, it will be both good and bad—at the same time. The aspect of this development that disturbs me most is accessibility overload.

A major unintended consequence of the flood of accessing technologies is that soon there will be no natural excuse for being unavailable. In the midst of our enthusiasm for the telecommunications revolution, we have not sufficiently discerned the horrifying psychic cost of what columnist William Safire calls *unrestrained reachability*. Don't get me wrong. I like people. Some of my best friends are people. But I also like my privacy from time to time.

"Where were you all day?" your boss or client or bridge partner will say. "I tried to call you five times!" And because virtually everyone will carry tiny cell phones/pagers, you will have no excuse.

"I turned off my pager phone."

"You what?!"

What will this be like for exhausted pastors who are vacationing five states away and one of their parishioners is hospitalized? Do we disturb them? Most of us wouldn't—but some would. What if parishioners die? Do we interrupt pastors' much-needed vacations by requesting they return for the funeral? When speaking in Toronto recently I found two pastors who had encountered this situation in the previous year. One returned home to do the funeral; the other didn't. The first disappointed his family and lost an important vacation. The second disappointed his church family and lost an important ministry opportunity.

Because of progress and technology, universal accessibility is inevitable. Etiquette guidelines will not always be easy to apply. Yet somehow, unrestrained reachability must be controlled for the sake of our margin, our family, our devotion, our sanity, and our rest.

R℞ *Be discerning of all accessing technologies. Use them judiciously. Consider deactivating the answering machine if necessary. If you find it overwhelming to come home to eight messages, turn it off. If the calls are important, the callers will try again.*

⸙

You must keep quiet or say only things that improve silence.
GREEK PROVERB

# INEXTINGUISHABLE DISCONTENT

*The urgency of wants does not diminish appreciably as more of them are satisfied or, to put the matter more precisely, to the extent that this happens it is not demonstrable and not a matter of any interest to economists or for economic policy. When man has satisfied his physical needs, then psychologically grounded desires take over. These can never be satisfied or, in any case, no progress can be proved. The concept of satiation has very little standing in economics.*

JOHN KENNETH GALBRAITH, ECONOMIST

---

HALF A CENTURY ago, my grandfather might reasonably have predicted that advances in affluence, technology, education, and entertainment would bring a commensurate increase in contentment. Such has not been the case. Instead our society is marked by "inextinguishable discontent," observes historian Arthur M. Schlesinger Jr. Satiety largely does not exist. "Give a man everything he wants," said Immanuel Kant, "and at that moment, everything will not be everything."

For most of us, discontent has become a way of life. It has now been fully normalized and mainstreamed. When we are told this is the age of envy, the indictment does not sting. When it is said that our economic system employs greed and envy as its primary engines, our usual response is to yawn and dial our broker.

Contentment is a cause without a constituency, a virtue without a voice. No one talks about it, let alone recommends it. Books dedicated to it are rare. I cannot recall the last sermon

I heard addressing it. It is understandable that secular society would not broadcast an endorsement, but why isn't contentment emphasized within the community of faith?

Discontent as a driving force for a society might make that society rich but will bankrupt it in the end. As the coffer fills, the soul empties. It's like planting a garden with weeds. Come July there will be plenty of green, but in September we'll have nothing to eat.

Contentment facilitates margin; discontentment destroys it. If you wish to be free, consider the incomparable ability of contentment to place you on the right path.

R̸ To help cultivate contentment, develop "counter-habits," as John Charles Cooper calls them.[33] Instead of getting, try giving. Instead of replacing, try preserving. Instead of feeling covetous, try feeling grateful. Instead of feeling inferior before men, try feeling accepted before God. Instead of being ruled by feelings, try enjoying the freedom of contentment.

---

He who has everything is content with nothing.
FRENCH PROVERB

# GREAT EXPECTATIONS

*Poverty wants some thing, luxury many things, avarice all things.*
BEN FRANKLIN

———————————

EXPECTATION OVERLOAD—PEOPLE everywhere are crumbling under its weight. In some ways, it is the most devastating of all overloads, driving the entire train of overload trauma. We are expected to be smart, or at least well educated; to be beautiful, fashionable, and athletic; to drive a nice car (without rust) and to live in a nice house (always picked up); to own nice things (at least as nice as the Joneses'); to be the perfect parent and spouse. And lest we refuse to accept the terms of the first set of expectations, there is a final expectation standing guard over all the others: *we are expected to conform.* Let's examine some specifics.

*Automobiles*—The admission price to the good life expects that we drive a nice automobile—certainly one befitting our career and social status. One day my car was ticketed: "Please move your car. This spot is reserved for the physician." Why did the officer write this note if not for an obvious cultural expectation that an M.D. would not drive a car like mine?

*Homes*—Over the past half-century, Americans have doubled the square footage in their homes even though families are smaller. Partly, this is because of possession overload. But expectation overload is also to blame. Debt is not the determining factor in home size anymore—expectation is.

*Fashion*—Fashion has completely overwhelmed function. Are we sure this is okay with God? If functionality were our only concern, most of us could survive on 10 percent of our clothes budget.

*Income*—We need little income to live a totally God-honoring life. Yes, perhaps we need a huge cash flow to partake of the many benefits of our age. But people now struggling to make it on large incomes could honor God completely with an income far smaller. The rest is consumed in fulfillment of cultural expectation.

*Careers*—We expect our jobs to be stable, our careers to be faithful, our benefit packages to insulate us, and our company morale to meet our emotional needs. But in this era of downsizing, millions have been disappointed, displaced, and depressed by occupational insecurity.

*Retirement*—The expectation of retirement is a distinctly modern notion and, some predict, transient. There is perhaps only a short window of time in a few countries where such a luxury is possible. Yet we see people today with multimillion-dollar retirement plans who are panicked the money will not last. This is directly related to expectations.

> *R Resist inflated housing expectations. Just because you have the ability to buy an expensive home seems to convey a commensurate expectation that you will do exactly that. If you want financial margin for decades to come, resist the expectation to buy larger than you need.*

---

In a small house God has his corner, in a large house
He has to stand in the hall.
SWEDISH PROVERB

# BIG-TICKET ITEMS

*Perhaps in a culture such as ours we should drive around older cars
with a sense of honor, see them as symbols of a higher moral order.*
ERIC MILLER, HISTORIAN AND AMISH AUTHOR

---

DESPITE THE UNPRECEDENTED level of affluence today, a
very high percentage of us struggle with financial margin. The
price tag of the good life tends to rise faster than income. As a
result, people tire of the daily struggle with bills and resolve to
make changes. Simplicity is catching on.

While I am all for simplicity, as long as we are about it, let's
take aim at the highest yield targets. It's laudatory to simplify
across the entire spending spectrum, but obviously we will
decrease financial pressure most effectively when we apply our
attention to the big-ticket items. My wife, Linda, refers to the
25:25 principle. People will work to save 25 cents on groceries
but then spend $25,000 too much on their mortgage.

*Houses*—As a principle, don't assume a mortgage more
than 40 percent of your net spendable income. (The net
spendable income equals the gross income minus the taxes
and tithe.) Included in this percentage are not only the mortgage payments but also the real estate taxes, insurance, utili-
ties, and repairs. Obviously, the smaller the percentage you
spend on mortgage and other associated housing costs, the
larger will be your financial margin. Forty percent is a ceiling. Also, if you have concurrent nonmortgage debts, this

percentage might need to be decreased.

Many people, especially young couples, take on a mortgage that effectively deprives them of any financial margin for decades to come. When the hard reality sets in, they worry, they develop conflicts in their marriages, they begin overworking to try to make ends meet, and they deprive themselves of the joy of giving to the unexpected needs God sends their way.

*Automobiles*—It is time to stop venerating automobiles. If we were to examine the issue honestly, most people pay more for automobiles than is necessary, and the resultant auto loans play a significant role in their overall debt picture. In our family we have never paid more than $4,000 for an automobile. Obviously, if not careful you can get some regrettable vehicles. But mostly, we have had reliable, adequately appearing cars that are satisfactory in every way.

*Traditions, rituals*—Weddings, funerals, graduations, Christmas: every year the price tag rises, and rapidly. Can we agree together that this is not necessary and not a true reflection of love? Personally, when I die, a pine box will be fine. Actually, it is what I *prefer*.

> ℞ *Consider keeping at least one older automobile. Keep it not only for the savings but also for the principle involved, and drive it despite the rust. You save money not only on the purchase but also on insurance payments. Our Swenson family distance record is 205,000 miles.*

---

Great pomp is the coffin of the purse.
HUNGARIAN PROVERB

# NO EXCEPTIONS, NO EXEMPTIONS

*While researchers differ as to the exact figures, they strongly agree on two basic principles; first, that humans have limited capacity, and second, that overloading the system leads to serious breakdown of performance.*

ALVIN TOFFLER, SOCIOLOGIST AND FUTURIST

---

IF I HAD A nickel for every time someone asked me about the role of personality variation on limits and overload, I could make a down payment on the solar system. Personality, genetics, culture, values, expectations, ethnic background, family system, work ethic—all play a tremendous role in determining how the topic of overload applies to each individual. Clearly, every human is different—young/old, male/female, introvert/extrovert, highly productive/highly sensitive. These differences, therefore, must be taken into account when considering human limits.

Just as clearly, however, every human is the same. Every human has limits—without exception—and the universality of that fact ultimately holds sway over all dissenting views. No one is infinite. We all need to sleep, to eat, to exercise, and to rest. The extent we need to do these things varies tremendously. Nevertheless, the law of limits is real for each individual and just as binding as the law of gravity.

Combining these two generalizations—we are all different, we are all the same—we see that for each person we can draw a line that represents the threshold of his or her personal limits, but for each person that line will be drawn at a different place compared to others.

What about those extraordinary people who seem to accomplish so very much and never get weary? People who only sleep two hours a night, or who create a hundred-million-dollar business in just five years, or who have ten children and a sixty-hour job as a corporate executive yet get voted "parent of the year"?

Indeed such stories are breathtaking. But this does not mean that I should feel guilt if God has not given me those same abilities. We should not be in the business of telling God how He should arrange the personalities in His kingdom. It is, after all, His kingdom, and He has the right to do with it as He wants.

These exceptional people are interesting and their accomplishments laudable. But remember, even exceptional people have limits. Unfortunately, if we follow many of them into the future, we often would find the same painful consequences of chronic limit violation the rest of us experience: physical illness, emotional burnout, relational strain.

*R Accept the fact that God made you as He did. Understand how your limits might be different from those around you. Rather than kick against it, celebrate it. God knows what He is doing, and He must have had His reasons.*

---

It is just as useless to tell an old person to hurry
as it is to tell a child to go slow.
BASQUE PROVERB

# MARGIN AND THE HEALTHY FAMILY

*If you don't have enough time for your family, you can be one
hundred percent certain you are not following God's will for your life.*
PATRICK M. MORLEY, AUTHOR AND MEN'S MOVEMENT SPEAKER

THROUGHOUT HISTORY, THE family has functioned as
the great shock absorber of any society. A family belonged
together, not by choice, but by birth. Thus, when a person was
wounded, it was the family's responsibility to welcome those
wounds back home, into its midst, for healing. When a person
was bruised, bereaved, or bankrupt, it was the family's responsibility to provide comfort. Of course, the family has never
functioned perfectly, and cruelty rather than comfort was
sometimes the result. Nevertheless, as an institution for healing and housing, the family was irreplaceable.

That same institution is now itself being severely wounded
by the conditions of modernity. Stress and overload strain the
bonds of family. Escalating complexity, speed, and intensity
constitute a horrible context for our interpersonal relationships. All human connections require time and energy. Yet in a
marginless landscape, time and energy are in short supply.

When asked what factor has done more damage to families than any other, Dr. James Dobson answered:

> It would be the almost universal condition of fatigue and
> time pressure, which leaves every member of the family
> exhausted and harried. Many of them have nothing left

to invest in their marriages or in the nurturing of children. . . . If a scale-back from this lifestyle, which I call "routine panic," ever grows into a movement, it will portend wonderfully for the family. It should result in fewer divorces and more domestic harmony. Children will regain the status they deserve and their welfare will be enhanced on a thousand fronts. We haven't begun to approach these goals yet, but I pray that a significant segment of the population will awaken someday from the nightmare of overcommitment and say, "The way we live is crazy. There has to be a better way than this to raise our kids. We will make the financial sacrifices necessary to slow the pace of living."[34]

*R̰ Make spending time together a priority. Consider having family meetings—perhaps once a week or at least once a month. Keep an agenda and update it each time. Plan family vacations well in advance and enjoy the anticipation. Appoint a treasurer and save together in a glass jar for enjoyable family goals. Run errands together. Enjoy family field trips. Watch a movie together—unplug the phones, push the couches together, light a fire or a candle, make popcorn. Have family days when you don't allow visitors or other interruptions. Guard the family mealtime. If you are calendar driven, schedule your family on your calendar.*

---

May the roof above you never fall in, and those gathered beneath it never fall out.

IRISH PROVERB

# STRESS REDUCTION, STRESS MANAGEMENT

*You can regain your sense of balance and control by changing your environment and by changing your expectations.*

ROBERT S. ELIOT, M.D., CARDIOLOGIST

---

THERE ARE TWO broad strategies for dealing with stress:

- *Stress reduction* — decrease your stress load
- *Stress management* — control your stress response

Any balanced approach for dealing with stress problems should incorporate a program of stress management combined with wise stress reduction tailored to the individual need. Although most books dwell on stress management, I strongly feel both approaches are important. Margin can assist with either approach but is much more closely related to stress reduction.

*Stress reduction* — If you live in a heavily overloaded environment, it makes simple common sense to lessen the offending agent. When the stress load is severe and chronic, stress reduction is more important than stress management.

Significant stress reduction often requires courage. It may mean rearranging life: getting a different job, living with less income, establishing boundaries (saying no), creating some margin — in short, making different choices. Once you have identified the stress dynamics in your life, it is important to remedy the destruction even though at times the remedy might require radical change.

*Stress management*—Most stress books and seminars, however, emphasize stress management. This is an important concept to teach, as we can blunt the ill effects of stress by changing our reactions. Our *perception* of the event matters a great deal, and our *response* to that perception matters even more. As was written even in ancient times: "Men are distressed not by things, but by the views which they take of them."

Stress management is accomplished by realizing we do have some control in our response to stressors. We can learn how to relax in the midst of strife, to slow our heart rate, to talk to ourselves positively, to behave rationally. This approach is essentially teaching ourselves how to take the wires off our hot buttons. It is not always easy, but it is possible.

Both strategies are important. Stress reduction takes back control of your circumstances; stress management takes back control of your reactions.

℞ *Put more control in your life. The first thing to tell yourself in any stressful situation is that you have more control than you think. Before external stressors can make us miserable, they must first have our permission. If we can learn to walk above stressful circumstances, we will have discovered a key not only to stress, but also to spiritual maturity.*

———⟨∞⟩———

The brain is capable of holding a conversation
with the body that ends in death.
RUSSIAN PROVERB

# LIKE WEEDS IN A GARDEN

*Reality is the leading cause of stress amongst those in touch with it.*
LILY TOMLIN, HUMORIST

ONE WOULD HAVE hoped that the process of progress would have been kind to our emotional life, making it ever easier to replenish our reserves. It might have seemed reasonable to speculate that as our society improved in the areas of education, affluence, and entertainment, we would see a commensurate improvement in overall emotional well-being. Such has not been the case. These advancements have not resulted in unburdened emotions and liberated psyches. But why not? Our babies seldom die anymore, and famine is virtually unknown in the industrialized West. We have telephones when we get lonely, air conditioners when we get hot, aspirin when we have a toothache, and television when we get bored. Why then do so many remain so emotionally drained?

I am not suggesting that emotional turmoil and emptiness is an invention of modernity, for this type of pain has been with us since the beginning of humankind. Yet as our survival needs were secured by civilizational improvements, might we not have expected that emotional disorders would increasingly disappear? Anxiety, depression, suicide and suicide gesturing, personality disorders, obsessive behaviors, eating disorders, panic attacks, substance abuse, rage disorders, phobias, psychoses—these are not diagnoses on the verge of extinction.

Instead these maladies seem to thrive in our society like weeds in a garden. And they drain us emotionally dry.

Is it possible we are living in a "deteriorating psychic environment"? Over the last several decades, the number of therapists has risen dramatically. Spending for mental health is close to one hundred billion dollars annually. Alarmingly, the psychopathology has now drifted down past adolescence, entering even the elementary school age.

Where is this coming from? Where will it lead? And what can we do about it? Perhaps it is time to look in a different quadrant for our healing.

It is neither ungrateful nor disrespectful to ask progress some hard questions at this point. Progress has indeed given us much. But it is becoming increasingly apparent that having bigger houses, fatter wallets, and more education does not deliver commensurate emotional wholeness. It is also becoming obvious that the very single-minded dedication with which we pursue progress has itself become a part of our problem.

Just because civilization dresses up with the golden gown of progress does not mean it has become the kingdom.

*R* *Accept progress for what it is —good at some things, horrible at others. Do not trust progress to supply your emotional buoyancy. Instead of blindly being led down the broad road of progress, follow the narrow uncrowded path of Truth. Seek a life of love, joy, peace, patience, kindness, goodness, faithfulness, gentleness, and self-control.*[35]* *There you will also find all the happiness you seek.*

---

By sitting in a golden cage, no crow becomes a swan.
INDIAN PROVERB

# EXPECTING THE UNEXPECTED

*Living is entirely too time-consuming.*
IRENE PETER, WRITER AND HUMORIST

IT DOES NOT take much in the way of observational powers to realize that the world is a defective place. Things routinely go wrong. It happens every day to every human in every quadrant of life.

In theological terms, it is called fallenness. But even those not spiritually minded can detect a distortion in the cosmos that consistently thwarts perfection. The practical implication of this reality is that life seldom flows perfectly. Cars break down and people break down. Snowstorms slow interstates. Babies cry all night with ear infections, and mothers break their ankles getting out of bed. Fathers strain their backs shoveling snow and then contract influenza while waiting to be seen at the clinic.

The expense report is past due but the receipts have gone missing. The two o'clock appointment called and will be fifteen minutes late but the three o'clock appointment arrived an hour early. The elevator doesn't work for the third time this month. A close relative was diagnosed with cancer. The car needs new brakes but the service station has no openings until Thursday. The stalled car on I-90 creates a traffic jam resulting in another missed flight.

Expect the unexpected. Nearly everything takes longer

than anticipated. If you want some breathing room, increase your margin of error. If you are chronically late, for example, try adding extra margin to your scheduled activities.

What implications might this have for travel plans? Moderns don't like arriving early and barely agree to arrive on time. We often plan our schedules so that we can arrive "somewhere in the vicinity"—meaning give or take ten minutes. But when traffic is snarled, or unexpected snow falls, or we get a late start, or the car is out of gas, we begin to hurry. And worry. The entire experience quickly erodes into yet another urgency-induced panic attack.

To short-circuit such routine distresses, plan to arrive early. With an earlier estimated time of arrival, you can slow down the driving, enjoy the day, and actually begin to anticipate with pleasure the event in front of you. The best way to meet your planned ETA (estimated time of arrival), of course, is to have an earlier ETD (estimated time of departure).

> ℞ *Create buffer zones. If you have a busy schedule with nonstop appointments, consider creating small buffer zones between some of the obligations. A coffee break for the spirit. Even an occasional ten or fifteen minutes can allow you to catch up, make phone calls, close your eyes, pray, call your spouse, reorient your priorities, and defuse your tension.*

---

Everything takes longer than it does.
ECUADORAN PROVERB

# ESTABLISHING MEDIA LIMITS

*Television has the culture by its throat.*

NEIL POSTMAN, COMMUNICATIONS PROFESSOR AND AUTHOR

---

MODERN MEDIA IN its various forms have penetrated all aspects of contemporary life. It is hard to imagine a life—or even a *single day*—that is not saturated start-to-finish with media. The average American consumes 3,500 hours of media per year, nearly twice the hours per year spent working.

Much of this is acceptable, and at times perhaps even laudable. Movies and television can inform, stimulate, and entertain. Newspapers and magazines keep us up-to-date. Music can lift our spirits, massage our souls, and stimulate our senses. The Internet can do all of the above, at least potentially. But everything in a fallen world has a downside, and in that regard, media is as bad as it gets.

Anchoring the top spot in the media winner's circle is, of course, the omnipresent television. It has reshaped every aspect of our society, from entertainment to news to political life to religion. Nationally, we spend over two hundred billion hours per year in front of the television, with the average viewer watching between fifteen and thirty-five hours per week. It is hard to overemphasize the impact of something so temporally dominating.

The younger the adult age, the more likely we are to be frequent movie attenders or to rent movie videos. The easy accessibility of videos has both reshaped and inflated movie viewing habits. Movies continue their slide in the direction of objectionable elements, but this tendency has been mainstreamed and seems hardly to elicit a yawn.

Children at ever younger ages are drawn into the movie/video habit, especially with the common use of videos for babysitting. For overloaded parents, it is simply too tempting to put in a video and place the kids before the set, where they are well behaved and entranced. And for busy, stressed-out, exhausted parents, there is nothing so attractive as quiet children.

Radio can be a wonderful companion on the road, in the lonely hours of the night or, for that matter, at *any* hour. Music, the mainstay of radio programming, is a special gift from the creative genius of God. Unfortunately, the gift has been counterclaimed by the dark side, and the battle rages for the heart and soul of a nation.

Records ruled the music world until 1982, when sales were eclipsed by audiocassettes. In 1992, CDs passed cassettes. The unique captivating power of music is nearly inexplicable in terms of its psychology and omnipresence.

*R If you are overloaded, consider establishing some media limits for yourself and the family. Turn off the television earlier and get some needed sleep. Turn off the stereo and talk at the dinner table. Decide viewing and listening limits — in both content and time — as an act of intention rather than randomness. Have standard rules that make sense. Don't force yourselves into re-deciding every week. More is not necessarily better.*

⊶⊷

The best armor is to keep out of range.
ITALIAN PROVERB

# FROM SUPERSTRINGS TO CELLS

*I seem to be a verb.*

BUCKMINSTER FULLER, ARCHITECT AND ENGINEER

WHEN FIRST DISCOVERED, the subatomic particles proton, neutron, and electron were thought to be the fundamental building blocks of all of nature. Surely nothing could be smaller. Since, however, over two hundred tinier and more fleeting particles have been found. One such particle, for example, is called the *xi* and has a life span of one ten-billionth of a second.

Whenever scientists devise new technology to penetrate deeper atomic levels, they find yet another little critter winking at the camera. Some physicists now speculate that perhaps humans are infinite, not only in the eternal direction, but also in the subatomic direction.

The proton, neutron, and electron are made up of even smaller fundamental subatomic particles called quarks. But perhaps underlying all of existence are the newly postulated superstrings, each a hundred million billion times smaller than the nucleus of an atom. Might this be the bottom of our subatomic existence or are we "infinite in all directions"?

Mix together these subatomic particles, add a bit of mysticism, and out pop some *atoms*. Take about twenty of the most common elemental atoms—especially carbon, oxygen, hydrogen, nitrogen, phosphorus, and sulfur, which account for 99 percent of the dry weight of every living thing—add a bit of mysticism, and out pop some pretty sophisticated *molecules*. Organize molecules in just the right way, add a bit of mysticism, and—this is the really tricky part—out pop some living *cells*.

Not only are the subatomic particles flashing in and out of existence faster than a New York cabby changes lanes; not only are the atoms turning over at a rate exceeding a billion trillion per second; and not only are the molecules continuously rearranging themselves in a dance we might call the nanosecond shuffle . . . but the cells are doing the same. It is almost as if God, working at the speed of light, is continuously tinkering with His invention.

The body contains about one hundred trillion cells, each with approximately a trillion atoms. These cells, like just about everything else in the body, are continually being torn down, remodeled, and replaced.

If God put this all together, He must be very clever. And powerful. And precise. Does He know the position of each of these subatomic particles, all the time—even when they come in and out of existence in less than a trillionth of a second? Certainly.

The point is, such a God can be trusted with the details of your life. After rearranging subatomic particles all morning, the specifics of your life probably seem a bit unchallenging to Him.

> ℞ *Learn to trust God's precision in the management of your affairs. Nothing is so small that it escapes His attention, concern, or expertise. Margin is easier to pursue when you remember the Designer and Sustainer of the universe stands with you.*

---

There are no miracles for those that have no faith in them.
FRENCH PROVERB

# PERCHANCE TO SLEEP

*Sleep is the golden chain that ties health and our bodies together.*
THOMAS DEKKER, SEVENTEENTH-CENTURY ENGLISH PLAYWRIGHT

WE ARE TRAPPED in a sleep gap. As many as fifty to seventy million Americans have some type of sleep disorder. Many round-the-clock cities never go to sleep—factories, grocery stores, service stations, and restaurants are often open through the night. After pushing the limits to the breaking point, we push some more. Students pull all-nighters studying for exams, nurses check on sleeping patients and watch the monitors, while taxi drivers listen to the all-night station on their radios and drive denizens of the dark around town. Mothers of young children work all day in the office and then work all night in the nursery.

Shift workers, a growing percentage of the labor force, miss an extra five days of work per year solely for the reason of fatigue. In addition they use more caffeine, suffer more drug abuse, and take four times more sleep medication. The total annual cost of insomnia to U.S. businesses, including absenteeism, medical costs, and decreased productivity, is an estimated one hundred billion dollars. Even though sleep is not optional, evidence is mounting that sleep deprivation has become a massive public health problem.

Many people don't sleep well simply because they have poor sleep habits. Develop a healthy pattern of sleep. Retire at a similar time each evening; arise at a similar time each morning.

Have a quiet room and a good mattress—you will spend a third of your life there. If you suffer from cold feet, warm the sheets with an electric blanket. Don't engage in disturbing conversations immediately before bedtime. Instead begin relaxing about an hour or so before retiring. Give yourself time to unwind from the day. Don't have a big meal within two hours of bedtime. Limit the intake of caffeine in the evening, and if necessary, in the afternoon as well. If you are a clock-watcher, turn the clock toward the wall. If sleep is delayed by racing thoughts or creativity, keep a notebook or even small tape recorder next to the bed. As soon as a thought threatens your somnolence, write it down—then forget it.

Margin and resilience are greatly enhanced by a good night's sleep. Sleep was God's idea, and good sleep is restorative. To be well-rested is a blessing, not a waste of time.

> R In addition to the suggestions above, consider an exercise program for sounder sleep. Healthy physical tiredness probably has no equal as a sleep-inducing sedative. Don't exercise vigorously just before going to bed, however. While a routine of stretching exercises or a leisurely walk can be an excellent prelude to a good night's sleep, a six-mile run is not a good idea.

———— ⧂ ————

The loss of one night's sleep is followed by
ten days of inconvenience.
CHINESE PROVERB

# RUN OVER BY GOOD INTENTIONS

*Monday is Spanish, Tuesday is Scouts, Wednesday is tutoring and, if it's Thursday, it must be tennis. Parents wind up feeling like maniacs and the kids don't have a moment to breathe.*

LINDA LEWIS GRIFFITH, COLUMNIST AND FAMILY COUNSELOR

---

RUSH THROUGH BREAKFAST . . . hurry out the door . . . speed to work . . . punch the clock.

Deadlines and demands; busyness and bustle. More productivity needed; higher efficiency demanded. Ratchet up another notch; ricochet off the walls.

Finally, saved by the bell. Run to the car. Tear through traffic. Dash in the door. Lunge for the sofa. Collapse in exhaustion.

Speed. Too much speed. We are wheezing and worn out. Our relationships have been starved to death by velocity. Our children lie wounded on the ground, run over by our high-speed good intentions. How did it ever come to this?

Our nanosecond culture is toxic to relationships, as nearly every family knows. Surveys and studies reveal time pressures to be at the top of our relational complaints. No one has the time to listen, let alone love.

Fast-lane families are headed for head-on collisions. They don't have the opportunity to eat together. Shared, unstructured leisure time disappears. Communication suffers, problems multiply, tempers flare. But it takes time to make up.

Stress flows downstream. When parents are hurried, children are hurried. We *must* have some room to breathe.

In a slower era, every day and any place, people had time for each other. At the store, the gas station, or the church there was time to visit. At the breakfast table and the dinner table there was time to visit. Marginlessness, however, finds everyone overcommitted, self-protective, late, and in a hurry. It is time for a change. For the sake of our families, it is time, perhaps, for a slowdown crusade, or a campaign of mellowness. It is time to rediscover the fine art of relational dawdling.

> R̸ *Schedule a regular family night (once a week, once a month) where hurry is banished. Slow the pace of talking. Listen! Don't interrupt. Perhaps play a board game, read stories out loud. Go on a slow family walk, and see who can spot the smallest detail in nature. Explain your intentions at each meeting to reinforce the slow-is-good-when-loving-each-other message. The curricular objectives for this activity are rest and recreation, and joy in each other's presence. It is also an instructional module in appropriate slowing to counteract the routine cultural destruction of family sanity.*

---

None but a mule denies his family.
SAUDI ARABIAN PROVERB

# BOREDOM AND SUFFERING

*All of man's troubles stem from his inability to
sit quietly in a room alone.*

BLAISE PASCAL, FRENCH PHILOSOPHER

---

CONTENTMENT IS HELPFUL in enduring boredom and suffering. Children today use the word *boring* frequently. It is intended as the ultimate verbal scourge, and basically it means "I'm discontent. Entertain me." The prevalence of this word is an unsettling indicator of where our children are in relation to contentment.

As I was growing up, we used our imagination and creativity to make our own fun. Today electronic entertainment rides a nonstop conveyer belt that passes directly into the dormant souls of the young. It is not a favorable development. I cannot be optimistic that this trend will miraculously result in a mature sense of contentment in later years. Over time a decaying log will not turn into a house. All you get is a bigger pile of decay.

> A man said to the universe:
> "Sir, I exist!"
> "However," replied the universe,
> "The fact has not created in me
> A sense of obligation."[36]

Stephen Crane's words remind us of a truth: God is not indebted to us. If life is boring, then it is boring. We work to make it better, but our duty throughout the working is contentment. If life is tough, so it is tough. Our duty is contentment. If there is suffering, why would we expect anything different? Our duty is contentment.

Life can be painful. Most people do not choose this pain; it comes with living. Contentment, however, is different. Contentment or discontent is a matter of the will, a choice. After a disappointing harvest, one Appalachian farmer remarked, "Well, I had my teeth set for lots of corn this season but the Lord saw fit to give us cucumbers instead. So I'm enjoying the cucumbers."[37] There is a freedom that accompanies such lighthearted contentedness, and the presence of the freedom weighs more than the absence of the corn.

The entire journey of life should be an ever-deepening exploration into this freedom of contentment. It is a discipline, to be sure, often rigorous and unpleasant. Yet as life wears out and winds down, as strength wanes and abilities shrivel, what better reward could we ask than the ability "to sit quietly in a room alone" with a smile on our face and true joy in our heart. "Rejoice," said the apostle Paul from prison. "I will say it again: rejoice."[38]

When we choose obedience, God, in His wonderful way with surprises, can redeem the pain and suffering in our lives and can turn the destruction into benefit.

*R Labor hard for the reward of contentment. It is a far greater prize than piled-up riches and will bring a freedom that transcends circumstances. Accept from God's hand that which He gives — not resignation, not complacency, but contentment. Even pain and suffering that seemingly cannot be corrected, He can redeem.*

---

The contented person can never be ruined.
CHINESE PROVERB

# FAMILY MATTERS

*Making family your top priority means standing against a culture where materialism and workaholism are rampant. It means realizing that you may not advance as fast in your career as some of your colleagues—at least for a few years. It means being willing to accept a lower standard of living . . . knowing you're doing the right thing for your children, giving them the emotional security they'll draw on for the rest of their lives.*

CHUCK COLSON, FOUNDER, PRISON FELLOWSHIP

---

ON ONE OCCASION I was giving a parenting talk at a medical conference. In a stunning display of self-disclosure, the physician preceding me revealed how forty years earlier her five-year-old son said, "Mommy, who do you think I would rather die—you or Sparky?" This child, for no precipitating reason and with no apparent malice, said that if he had to choose, he would rather his mommy die than his dog.

It was difficult for me to follow this story with a talk on the deficiencies of modern parenting, particularly because the physician who shared her heart is a genuinely compassionate person. Yet, at the same time, the brutal poignancy of her painful testimony underscored the importance of my call to invest in the priority of our families.

"This is a selfish world," says the world's oldest (103 years) practicing pediatrician, Leila Denmark.

Parents are working their brains out to buy nice homes and cars. If we're ever going to make America better, we've got to tell [parents]—no matter how educated, how poor or how rich—to take care of [their children]. When I worked in the slums in 1918, that's where all the bad kids were because their parents didn't take care of them. Today, you find them in the suburban homes of the finest doctors and lawyers; their kids have gone bad because they have no time for them.[39]

I am a pro-work person. But, simply stated, work must assume its rightful place, leaving also sufficient time for the family. Today, however, there is a mathematically shocking "hemorrhage of time" away from the critically important institution of family and toward the institution of work.

The way our society and our work environments are currently structured, we give the least time to those we value most. If we are wise, we will understand that success as defined by the world isn't success. Success in God's eyes is measured by love. One day He will push the delete button, wiping out all the time clocks, bank statements, productivity sheets, and 401k plans. All that will be left is love. And when love judges the universe, it will be transparently clear: family matters.

*R Some "at least" suggestions to protect the priority of family: Have a family dinner once a week; a family meeting once a month; a family reading evening once a quarter; a family hotel overnight once a year.*

---

To love is to choose.
FRENCH PROVERB

# RETREAT TO THE PAST?

*No one in his senses would choose to have been born in a previous
age unless he could be certain that he would have been born into a
prosperous family, that he would have enjoyed extremely good
health, and that he could have accepted stoically
the death of the majority of his children.*

J. H. PLUMB, HISTORIAN

MANY AMONG US might wish to turn back the clock, to
retreat to a simpler, easier time. We long for the quiet of nature
rather than the blast of rock music and car horns. We want to
be more directly involved in the elements, whether planting
the seed that feeds our family or digging the worms that catch
our fish. Perhaps we even long to raise our own animals or
build our own log home.

Much debate continues over such nostalgia. Is it healthy,
or is it escapist? Is sentimentality an ally or a deceiver? Often
the past seems more idyllic than it was. We forget the horrid
problems of yesteryear and in the process also overlook the
blessings of today. Our historical memories are selective. To
pine for a misrepresented dreamland is not a spiritually authentic thing to do.

When simplicity author Art Gish was confronted with the
question of turning back the clock, his answer was enlighten-
ing: "The analogy of a clock is not helpful. It is not the question of a clock, but a compass. The issue is not chronology, but

direction. And that we can decide. . . . We are not retreating, but looking ahead to perceive what is important. Simplification implies leaving things behind and moving to a new future."[40]

Perhaps the best solution is a combination approach. Is it possible to accept the best that the past had to offer and combine it with the best of the future? In both cases, the principles of *direction* and *selectivity* will be our guide. We travel in the direction of our priorities, and we select only that which is consistent with those priorities.

From the past we might select a slower pace, fewer alarms, more physical activity, less time urgency, less complexity-intensity-overload, and a more stable sense of community. From the future, we might select the miracles of health care, travel, and communication, plus some of the conveniences of modernity—like running water and hot showers.

Instead of escaping, we are transcending . . . holding on to that which is good and rejecting that which is destructive.

*R* *Live one day in 1850. You might be surprised at how interesting and slow-paced this adventure turns out to be. Use only the technology that existed during that era. This, of course, never precludes walking, reading, conversing, or sleeping. By suspending our hurrying technologies, it will quickly become apparent just how large a role these modern devices play in the unreasonable pace of modern life.*

———∞———

Don't throw away the old bucket until you know
whether the new one holds water.
<small>Swedish proverb</small>

# STRESS AND GOD

*I love going back to the States but was really struck by the fast
pace that was everywhere. The lifestyle is slow and relaxing
here in Africa. America is years ahead on progress and
also years ahead on stress.*

BETTY ARNOLD, MISSIONARY

---

IN THE MODERN era, stress is an everyday household word, which should perhaps strike us as a bit bizarre if observed from a long-distance perspective—we have more affluence, education, and technology . . . and stress? . . . than any people in history? Somehow, it seems, the good life comes packaged with the requirement for sedation.

Although we use the word *stress* in a negative connotation, it actually is a value-neutral concept. In the medical sense, stress is the body's response to any change required of it or any demand imposed upon it. Such a definition is contrary to the popular thinking that defines stress as an unpleasant circumstance, such as tax time or a screaming baby. Stress is *not* the circumstance; it is our *response* to the circumstance. It is not "out there" but rather "in here."

It makes little difference if the situation we react to is a positive one, such as buying a new home, or a negative one, such as bankruptcy. Although the ultimate consequences of *frustrating stress* can be very different from the consequences of *rewarding stress*, nevertheless, the initial adaptive response mechanism is similar in both cases. Merely encountering the word *stress* should not connote a positive or a negative feeling. The word only describes an entirely normal psychophysiological process without which we would die.

It will surprise many people to realize that God is responsible for the stress response. As described in my book *More Than Meets the Eye: Fascinating Glimpses of God's Power and Design*, the human body is designed with staggering complexity and precision. Part of this design involves the stress mechanism. We often curse it, but actually it is beautiful, intricate, and completely essential. We depend on it day in and day out, for the routine and for the extreme. It keeps both our body and our brain operating at vigilant and productive levels. But, of course, if abused, it knows how to abuse back. Stress definitely knows how to get even.

> $R$ *Thank God for His design. If He created the stress response and if it is essential for life and well-being, perhaps we should consider for a moment that God knew what He was doing. Maybe He was establishing a governor for our efforts, thus preventing us from inflating our role in the drama of life. Instead of blaming God for the design of our stress mechanism, perhaps we should instead blame progress, culture, and ourselves for the unauthorized stimulation of stress exceeding the original design specifications.*

---

Do not blame God for having created the tiger,
but thank Him for not giving it wings.
ETHIOPIAN PROVERB

# OVERLOAD DEFINED

*Even if our lives are full of only good and useful things, there can
be too many of them and they can cause us to end up harried and
worried and overworked. We've gotten into that predicament by
choice and we can choose to get out of it.*

BRUCE LARSON, PASTOR AND AUTHOR

---

DEFINITIONS ARE IMPORTANT, and the definition of overload is more important than most. It has been said that "a problem well-defined is a problem half-solved." Overload is
definitely a problem, so let's see if defining it well will put us
on the road to a solution.

> Overload: A state of *chronic* overage that leads to *dys-
> function* in at least *one* important area where *God* requires
> a *decent minimum*.

*A state of chronic overage* . . . It is important to realize that
short-term, acute overloading is a universal occurrence and not
the topic of this book. Short-term overload is unavoidable:
Christmastime, tax time, deadline time, daughter-getting-
married time. Such extreme but transitory busyness is indeed
exhausting. But if you budget wisely, you can plan for healing
post-activity. Not *acute* overload but *chronic* overload is the cul-
prit—activity that presumptively exceeds God-ordained limits for extended periods of time.

*That leads to dysfunction* . . . We are not suggesting that
there is one single sentinel symptom of overload that in and of

itself cements the diagnosis, but instead myriad possible morbidities. Overload in one person might be manifested by depression, in another by insomnia, in another by credit card debt, and in still another by family conflict. The presence of any of these various dysfunctions can certify that unhealthy overloading has occurred.

*In at least one important area* . . . The overloaded person need not exhibit multisystem failure: single-system failure is sufficient to secure the diagnosis. Your bank account might be great, and your body trim and well conditioned. But if your family relationships have been devastated by overload, then that one important area is enough to qualify.

*Where God requires* . . . God Himself makes the diagnosis. If you have questions about whether your lifestyle and commitments constitute an offense, lean an ear to what the Scriptures say.

*A decent minimum* . . . In multiple categories of life (work, nutrition, emotions, service, devotion, rest, exercise, church, community, love) God has expressed strong opinions about our performance and requires that we at least meet His "decent minimum."

> ℞ *Using these criteria, make a diagnostic effort to screen your life for unacceptable and unsustainable levels of overload. Be careful not to overdiagnose—ebbs and flows of stress are inevitable. But don't underdiagnose either. Also remember that if you are doing this evaluation together with another, overload is both perceived and measured differently by different people.*

---

Bandage up your finger and take a walk in the village to
see how many medical people you will meet.
BULGARIAN PROVERB

# GOD THE CREATOR ... OF LIMITS

*Don't think God has ordained you to carry the entire space-time universe on your own back. God created it, God sustains it, and God intends that "the government will be upon his shoulder."*

CARL F. H. HENRY, THEOLOGIAN

---

LET'S REFLECT FOR a moment on God's opinion of human limits. If God is the infinite Creator and we are the finite creatures, He obviously had some decision control in our design.

My best guess: Limits were God's intention from the beginning. He decided early on that limits were not only good but also necessary. It was His way of preempting any ambiguity about who is God and who is not. He is the Creator—the One without limits. We are the created—the ones with limits.

Because God is the author and creator of my limits, then it is probably okay with Him that I have them. He probably does not expect me to be infinite and is a little surprised when I try. It is okay with Him if I am not all things to all people all the time all by myself. As a matter of fact, it is probably *not okay* with Him if I assume otherwise.

We often get into all kinds of trouble by inflating our role in the drama of life. Perhaps this is one of the main reasons God created limits. He knew that without limits, we would overreach, swell with pride, and become independent. We would get priorities all messed up, and life balance would be neglected. He would have been right. So to address that problem preemptively, He created limits.

We are not infinite. None of us has more than twenty-four hours in a day. We do not have an inexhaustible source of human energy. We cannot keep running on empty. Limits are real, and despite what some stoics might think, limits are not even an enemy. Overload is the enemy.

As the author of limits, God put them within us for our protection. We violate them at our peril. God is under no moral obligation to bail us out of our pain if we attempt to do more than He asks.

It is okay for me to have limits—God doesn't. It is okay to get a good night's sleep—God doesn't sleep. It is okay for me to rest—God doesn't need to.

We don't know a lot about what heaven looks like, but this much we know: God is not pacing the throne room anxious and depressed because of the condition of the world. He knows, He is not surprised, and He is sovereign. It is okay if we have limits. He is able.

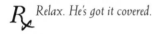 *Relax. He's got it covered.*

---

The earth does not shake when the flea coughs.
AUSTRIAN PROVERB

# HEALTH THROUGH SERVICE

*Doing nothing for others is the undoing of one's self. We must be
purposely kind and generous, or we miss the best part of existence.
The heart that goes out of itself gets large and full of joy. This
is the great secret of the inner life. We do ourselves the
most good doing something for others.*

HORACE MANN, NINETEENTH-CENTURY EDUCATOR

A UNIVERSITY OF Michigan study followed several thousand people for a decade to see how social relationships
affected their health. Those performing regular volunteer
work showed dramatically increased life expectancy.
Additionally, men not involved in such altruistic activity had
two and a half times more illness during the study than those
who volunteered at least once a week.

It turns out that when you are helping others you are also
helping yourself. Whatever the service—whether noble and
sacrificial or small and simple—when you meet other people
at their point of need, God meets you at your point of need.

Overloaded people, however, are painfully uninterested in
service. Instead they are trapped in survival. A recent front-
page newspaper article, touting the benefits of volunteerism,
ran under the headline: "Overworked, overstressed, who has
time to volunteer?" Yet another reason margin is so important.

Ten years ago, a 110-mile-per-hour windstorm blasted
across our county, leveling trees, power lines, and buildings,

and causing $60 million in damage. Within days, people from several eastern states began quietly arriving in town, volunteers from the Mennonite Disaster Service. Some stayed as long as a month, living in university dormitories vacated for the summer. Most of them were involved in the rebuilding of barns. I don't remember what I did those weeks after the storm, but I will never forget what they did. They served. Every time I think of the disaster, I think also of their gift.

I recently heard of a man who, while traveling on the interstate system, pays not only his own toll but also the toll for the car to follow. In so doing, he is making deposits in at least three emotional bank accounts: his own, the teller's, and the driver's following.

My wife, Linda, is always alert for ways to serve others. Stopping at a convenience store recently for some ice cream, she happened to mention at the counter that it was for cherry pie. "Sounds great!" responded the youthful clerk. Fifteen minutes later, Linda brought him a huge piece of fresh cherry pie a la mode. That evening, alone in the store, he was nourished by service. A simple thing; a magnificent obsession. And the gift goes on . . .

> *R You can serve friends or strangers. You can serve visibly or anonymously. You can serve in small projects or grand proposals. You can serve in your home or on the other side of the world. But if you want to be healthy, serve.*

---

God is a busy worker but He loves to be helped.
BASQUE PROVERB

# OUR BODY IN PARTICLES

*We speak of the body as a machine, but it is hardly necessary to
say that none of the most ingenious machines set up by modern
science can for a moment compare with it. The body is a self-
building machine; a self-stoking, self-regulating, self-repairing
machine—the most marvelous and unique
automatic mechanism in the universe.*

SIR J. ARTHUR THOMSON, SCOTTISH BIOLOGIST

WHEN GOD SET out to create humanity He put his genius
on display. If we wish to learn more about His ingenuity and
precision we don't have to go any further than the mirror. The
pinnacle of creation, we are crowned by God "with glory and
honor."[41] As a scientist with training in both medicine and
physics, it is easily apparent to me that the majesty of God is
revealed in the human body.

The human body contains $10^{28}$ atoms (1 followed by 28
zeros). With the universe itself containing perhaps only $10^{20}$
stars (estimates range as high as $10^{24}$), it could be stated that the
human body is about a million times more complex than the
universe. No physician has ever understood it, nor ever could.

According to isotope studies, 90 percent of our atoms are
replaced annually. Every five years, 100 percent of our atoms
turn over. In the last hour, one *trillion trillion* of your atoms have
been replaced. If all the people on the earth were to count this
rate of atomic turnover in the body, each person would have to

count ten billion atoms per second to keep up. Only God can monitor something of this magnitude — causing such dramatic exchange and disruption, yet holding all things together.[42]

The fundamental particles that comprise us — carbon, hydrogen, oxygen, iron, and so on — have been floating around since the beginning. They roost within us for a while, and then move on down the road to inhabit our neighbor. Some of the atoms that resided within our childhood frames are now probably doing their similar work within a child's body in Mongolia.

Yes, our bodies are indeed discreet units. But we also leak, both physically and metaphysically. As a consequence, we share our physical existence with our neighbors, however remote. Through myriad mixing devices, God brings us together constantly.

If after glimpsing the activity, intricacy, balance, and precision of life at this level, you do not suspect a God standing behind it all, then my best diagnostic guess is that you are in a metaphysical coma.

> *R* *When you witness the body self-correcting — healing an infection or repairing a broken bone — think of God "standing in the shadows keeping watch over His own." Faith consists of things beyond our seeing but is also buoyed by visible evidences of a Creator who cares. Remember, if He can keep the complexities of your physiology straight, He can surely also help balance the stressors of your day-to-day life.*

———≈≈≈———

God heals, but the doctor gets paid.
BELGIAN PROVERB

# THE PERIODIC DISCONNECT

*Paradoxical as it may seem, modern industrial society, in spite of an incredible proliferation of labor-saving devices, has not given people more time to devote to their all-important spiritual tasks; it has made it exceedingly difficult for anyone, except the most determined, to find any time whatever for these tasks. In fact, I think I should not go far wrong if I asserted that the amount of genuine leisure available in a society is generally in inverse proportion to the amount of labor-saving machinery it employs.*

E. F. SCHUMACHER, BRITISH ECONOMIST

WHILE SPEAKING RECENTLY at a physician's meeting, a doctor from the Mayo Clinic came up to me and said, "We all need margin. We are too stressed and trying to do too much. But it is impossible."

I looked him in the eye and responded, "You can have it beginning tonight. When you get home, go downstairs and find your circuit breaker. Find the switch labeled 'Main Switch' and flip it to 'off.' Do it every evening at 7:30. You'll have all the margin you need."

He is not going to do this, of course, and neither would I and neither would you. But is it possible? Of course. We all use the language of victimology, even though we indeed have choices. "The loss of felt choice is an everyday experience," explains psychologist Larry Crabb. "But we must state clearly that loss of felt choice does not mean loss of actual choice."[43]

A few years ago there was a power outage in the Twin

Cities area, where two hundred thousand people were without electricity for forty-eight hours. Soon thereafter an editorial appeared describing the experience. "Something interesting happened," said the observer. "Kids played outside until dark. Neighbors visited over back yard fences. Husbands and wives took long leisurely walks hand-in-hand that I had never seen on the street before. As soon as the power was restored, everyone disappeared inside."

Why does it take an electrical storm or a twenty-inch snowstorm to slow us down and join us together? Why can't we make it happen ourselves?

Increasingly, overloaded people are checking into local motels just to escape. If you can afford it, this is a periodic option that the entire family might enjoy. Use an indoor pool during winter. Order a pizza, cuddle on the bed, and watch a family movie. Thirty years from now, it might remain as one of your most vivid memories.

> $R$ Consider selecting a personal or family "disconnect time" — a set time each day or a set evening each week. During disconnect time, shut out the external world. For example, tell your friends, your relatives, your neighbors, your church, and your work: "Every evening from 5:30 to 7:00, we are disconnecting. Don't try to reach us then; we'll be unavailable."

---

If the family is together, the soul is in the right place.
RUSSIAN PROVERB

# THE HEART OF OUR NEIGHBOR

*Strive to love your neighbor actively and indefatigably. In as far as you advance in love you will grow surer of the reality of God and of the immortality of your soul. If you attain to perfect self-forgetfulness in the love of your neighbor, then you will believe without doubt, and no doubt can possibly enter your soul.*

FYODOR DOSTOYEVSKI, RUSSIAN AUTHOR

WE KNOW RELATIONSHIP is critically important to God because He does all His work there. That is why progress missed Him. Progress keeps telling us to search for buried treasure inside bank vaults, while all the time God has it buried in the heart of our neighbor.

Even if we have little time for healthy relationships, we all instinctively understand their importance. Due to the antagonistic influences of marginless living, however, relationships are an increasingly rare commodity. Overloaded contemporary life attempts to "derelationalize" us, which is perhaps the English equivalent of the German word *Zerrissenheit*—"torn-to-pieces-hood."

Today it is possible to live in a city surrounded by one million people and be alone for a lifetime. We become a number, and no one ever loved a number. The systems of modernity swallow us alive. Bureaucracies, corporations, institutions—all conjure up images of structures that inhale people and exhale cement.

God, however, is a personal God, and relationship is very

important to Him. He created us as relational beings—not because He had to but because it suited Him. We are relational and dependent whether we acknowledge it or not, whether we want to be or not. We ought not kick against this, however, for it was meant as a gift. God gave us to each other for reasons of benefit, not torment.

I am convinced that God could have created us one person per planet and scattered us across the universe. But He did not. He gave us to each other, and He did it for purposes of benefit. He created us connected, and it is not right for us to undo His finest work.

Admittedly, sometimes it seems like the requirement of relationship is part of the penalty for the Fall. We know in medicine, for example, that the greatest stressor on the face of the earth is the presence of other people. But we also know that the greatest blessing on the face of the earth is the presence of other people. God meant it for blessing, and it is time we recovered His original intention.

Margin begets healthy relationships. And healthy relationships beget margin. This is the kind of feedback loop that makes the world a better place.

*R̄ Don't trust the vitality of your relationships to the normal flow of culture, because right now culture isn't helping much. Be intentional about building community. Invite people over for dinner. Join a small group. Stick with the same doctor, auto mechanic, and church. Move less often.*

---

Though he eats alone, he calls the whole village
to help launch his boat.
Vietnamese proverb

# EXERCISE FOR THE MIND AND SPIRIT

*You can't sit around all day and
expect rest for the soul at night.*

ERIC MILLER, HISTORIAN ON AMISH LIFE

ONE HUNDRED PERCENT of people who exercise to the point of cardio-respiratory fitness will experience an increased sense of well-being. *One hundred percent.* People report that they feel better, they sleep better, and they have more stamina, confidence, focus, and productivity.

Exercise has a tranquilizing effect on the body. It helps to decompress stress and is good medicine for anxiety or depression. Along with increased energy, it grants increased alertness, increased independence, increased dignity, and increased self-esteem. Because of these benefits, an exercise program is often recommended, not just for physical conditions but for a wide range of mental and emotional problems as well. Unfortunately, and understandably so, these are also the same people who often lack the strength to begin such an exercise program, or to sustain it once begun.

Those who have difficulty maintaining an exercise program might try scheduling it in the morning. Morning exercisers seem to maintain a conditioning program better than those who choose the evening hours. One study revealed that three times as many morning exercisers were able to sustain their regimen compared to evening exercisers.

Another hint for sustainability is to discover the kind of exercise most practical and enjoyable for you. Don't start playing racquetball if you hate the sport; you will sabotage your own success. Find an activity that you have a natural affinity for, and something that doesn't cost much in terms of accessories — such as special jogging shoes, green fees, lift tickets — unless you have the resources. Some enjoy tennis, some jogging, some swimming, some simple walking. Even gardening is a wonderful exercise and qualifies for the physical and mental benefits we are seeking, as well as producing inexpensive and healthy food.

The brain is connected to the body. Signals flow continuously back and forth. Not surprisingly, the brain likes to see the body well cared for. When the mind and the body are both speaking kindly to each other, the spirit finds rest.

R Exercise away your problems. Many people "sweat to forget" and find it highly effective. While mental strain is often destructive, physical strain is almost always healthy. Of course, our overloaded lives often don't allow time to exercise, and our emotional exhaustion makes it seem unappealing. But at least one study revealed a jogging program equal to antidepressants in treating that mood disorder. Consider exercising with another person. Faithfulness to a workout schedule is much easier when the responsibility is shared.

⊸∞∞⊷

From walking — something; from sitting — nothing.
BULGARIAN PROVERB

# A PERSONAL STORY

*I feel like that hamster on the exercise wheel. Only the hamster is dead and the wheel is still spinning around.*

BOSTON BUSINESSMAN

I KNOW ALL about overload. In 1982 it sat on my chest and blew smoke in my face.

As a result, I decided to make a change in careers and, at the same time, to embark on a journey of investigation and a pilgrimage for renewal. Having always loved teaching, I changed from the private practice of medicine to the world of academic medicine, also cutting my work hours.

My nonmedical time I dedicated to balancing my life, nourishing my relationships, and better understanding the forces that were so chaotically propelling our culture. If we were all riding a cork in the middle of the Atlantic during hurricane season, I wanted to better understand the wind and waves.

Where was all the stress coming from? Why were so many people so unhappy even though they had so much? Why were so many relationships so fragile?

During the subsequent decade of research, one contemporary phenomenon impressed me as being responsible for more pain than I would ever have imagined. I noticed it in the lives of my patients, in the lives of my colleagues, in the lives of my friends and neighbors. I even noticed it grimacing back at me in the mirror. It was the pathological absence of margin.

The more I studied the phenomenon of margin, the more I understood its importance. And the more I understood its importance, the more I yearned for its freedom in my own life. Carefully and even forcefully, Linda and I carved out margin from our social and professional landscape. As we did, 90 percent of our pain disappeared.

Despite our chosen voluntary restraints, still we find life very full. At the end of a tiring week, we fall into bed and sigh: "How do people manage who have no margin?"

I lived sixteen years without margin: college, medical school, residency, and practice. And since that decision in 1982 to slow down and simplify, I have lived more than twenty years with it. I can say with certainty that if margin were taken away from me now, I would beg shamelessly to get it back.

*R⁘ Sometimes the quest for margin involves significant trade-offs in finances. Count the cost before making the change, and decide in advance if the increase in financial pressure is adequately counterbalanced by the decrease in overload. In your calculations, remember, of course, to factor in an understanding that the greater the degree of simplicity of lifestyle, the less the income needed to support that lifestyle.*

---

It's no time to go for the doctor when the patient is
dead.
IRISH PROVERB

# DECREASE SPENDING

*Their property held them in chains . . . which shackled their courage and choked their faith and hampered their judgment and throttled their souls. . . . Enslaved as they are to their own property, they are not the masters of their money, but its slaves.*

St. Cyprian, third-century Bishop of Carthage

---

THERE ARE THREE ways to increase our financial margin: decrease spending, increase income, or increase savings. Among these choices, the best is to simply reduce our spending. It sounds easy, but as we all know, in practice it is hard to sustain. The context of our culture screams against restraint, and every message we receive—from the ads on television to the specials in the newspaper to our coworker's new sweater to our neighbor's new van—all urge us to cave in.

A friend who once owned a catalog store explained customer spending patterns: "When people run out of money, they stop shopping," he explained. "But this only lasts about six weeks. Then, whether their financial situation has improved or not, they start buying again."

Doesn't that match what you know to be true about human nature—whether in dieting or exercise or no-shopping resolves? Understanding this simple fact of human psychology leaves us in a stronger position than we were in before. We now recognize that even our best resolves usually only last a short time and require conscious renewal on a regular basis.

There are two facets of decreased spending: short term and long term. Even a short-term spending freeze—a day, a week, a month—is helpful in reestablishing financial margin. In contrast, the long-term approach requires a vastly different level of commitment and is better thought of as a lifestyle change. Short-term resolves are considerable in number but limited in effect; long-term resolves are limited in number but considerable in effect. For example, a moratorium on eating out for a month is probably sustainable and would improve the average family's financial margin by one hundred to two hundred dollars. But a decade-long moratorium on eating out would be very difficult for most families, even though it would improve their financial margin by ten thousand to twenty thousand dollars.

*R Resisting impulse buying is a very effective way to decrease spending. A large percentage of purchases are sheer impulse. Retailers stack these items near the cash register. These are the things you didn't go to the store to buy but bought anyway. If you want financial margin, don't buy on impulse. Buy only those things you know you need and can use. If you have difficulty in this area, make a list of needed items before going to the store and don't deviate from it. It goes without saying that big-ticket items, such as a car, boat, or house, should never be bought on impulse.*

If you make a habit of buying things you do not need,
you will soon be selling things you do.

FILIPINO PROVERB

# THE DARK UNDERTOW OF DEPRESSION

*It is almost impossible to convey to a person who has not had a depression what one is like. It's not obvious like a broken arm, or a fever, or a cough; it's beneath the surface. A depressed person suffers a type of anguish which in its own way can be as painful as anything that can happen to a human being. He has varying degrees of fear throughout the day, and a brain that permits him no rest and races with agitated and frightening thoughts. His mood is low, he has little energy, and he can hardly remember what pleasure means.*

JACK DREYFUS, FOUNDER OF THE DREYFUS FUND

---

THE SUFFERING OF depression is often unbearable. If you look, you can see it in the eyes: privately tortured eyes reflecting a sea of pain, always misty, ready to overflow at the slightest provocation. When I sit next to such a patient in the examination room, I ask a gently probing question and pass them the tissue box at the same time. As the pain surfaces, the tears spill over.

In medical practice, depression is a daily finding. It is not limited to a certain socioeconomic group or a certain educational level. No one is immune. Like a flu virus, it strikes any age, any race, any occupation, at any time. Unemployment does heighten the risk, but even successful business executives, such as Jack Dreyfus, suffer from it. High school dropouts might have it, but so do many Harvard graduates. Nihilistic unbelievers feel its pain but so have some of the greatest preachers in the history of the church. An increasing number of children and adolescents are being diagnosed with it, and on the other end of the spectrum, many elderly spend their last days caught in its grip.

Researchers at the National Institute of Mental Health are attempting to identify "Agent Blue," the unknown factors that cause such a high rate of depression in our society. The Institute is concerned because the increasing rates of depression and suicide in Western countries cannot be explained by genetics or by better reporting mechanisms.

But where is this "dark undertow" coming from? Where is emotional resilience hiding these days? One of the major contributing factors to Agent Blue is the AWOL—the American Way of Life. In our desire for more and more, faster and faster, we have sacrificed much. We outrun our emotional supply lines and then are surprised when we are weary. We overload our margins and then are shocked when we break.

*℞ Understand the cultural forces that contribute to depression, and then move to defeat them. Slow down. Lower expectations. Learn to laugh. Communicate often. Love more. And don't be afraid to seek professional help; treating depression is one of the success stories of modern medicine. And together, let's stop blaming the victim.*

---

The death of the heart is the saddest thing
that can happen to you.
CHINESE PROVERB

# MARGIN AND THE SOVEREIGNTY OF GOD

*We are living in a world that is absolutely transparent, and God is shining through it all the time. That is not just a fable or a nice story. It is true. If we abandon ourselves to God and forget ourselves, we see it sometimes, and we see it maybe frequently. God shows Himself everywhere, in everything — in people, and in things and in nature and in events. It becomes very obvious that God is everywhere and in everything and we cannot be without Him. It's impossible. The only thing is that we don't see it.*

THOMAS MERTON, MONK AND POET

GOD'S POWER IS undeniable; His precision is impressive; His sovereignty is on display. How can such power fail to dominate our every thought and action? Why do we not trust Him more?

It is not that God has failed to clearly demonstrate His nature or that He has been lax in instructing us. It is just that we are slow to understand. This world is too much with us.

What we need is a new vision of God. The real God. Not some vague image we fold up and stuff in the back drawer of life, but the kind of God who parts the Red Sea and shakes Mount Sinai. The kind of God who stuns the physicists with symmetry, the mathematicians with precision, the engineers with design, the politicians with power, and the poets with beauty.

The Scriptures build our understanding of God's sovereignty on a practical level — by that I mean the kind of knowledge that affects our everyday behavior. But science is also a fascinating source of revelation, and increasingly so.

The spiritual implications of modern science are impossible to dismiss. They are a stick of dynamite under the front porch of our spiritual complacency. When we lift any stone of the universe, God's fingerprints stare back at us. Everything is there, waiting to be discovered. All the evidence we need, and more.

When we understand the sovereignty, power, design, majesty, precision, genius, intimacy, and caring of an almighty God, it takes away our fear. It removes our frustration. It allows us to sleep at night and trust Him with the running of His own universe. It allows us to have margin. It allows us to resume our proper role in the order of things rather than taking over His role. It allows us to seek His will rather than follow our own mind.

The more we understand about God's power, the less we worry about our weakness. The more we trust in God's sovereignty, the less we fret about our future.

> *R̄* *Don't accept that science is an enemy of faith. In fact, God Himself is the creator of science. Put away your scientific inferiority complex and accept from God all that He has to show you. From the far-away galaxies to your own genome, there is much to celebrate.*

⸺ ∞ ⸺

God sits on high and sees far.
UKRAINIAN PROVERB

# LIFE AS A VAPOR

*One life—a little gleam of Time between two Eternities.*
THOMAS CARLYLE, SCOTTISH HISTORIAN

---

THE SCRIPTURES OFTEN refer to the brevity of life. James, for example, says that life is a vapor or a mist: "You are a mist that appears for a little while and then vanishes."[44] In essence, what God is saying is that life is like a puff of steam. Throw a drop of water on a hot skillet, stand back, and *poof*. That, says God, is your life. I sometimes argue with God on this point. "I am a doctor. I know about life and death. Life is not a vapor; it is seventy or eighty years." God replies: "Let's talk about it again in a billion years."

David then joins the discussion, saying that life is merely a breath: "The span of my years is as nothing before you. Each man's life is but a breath."[45] Paul contributes as well, calling our afflictions momentary: "For our light and momentary troubles are achieving for us an eternal glory that far outweighs them all."[46] "Momentary?" I ask God. "Why did Paul choose that word? His troubles were interminable, not momentary."

God replies, "I am trying to tell you something about the temporary nature of suffering. I am doing this to encourage you through stressful times. It might *seem* to you like a long struggle. But here is a secret: your perceptions about suffering are incorrect. Troubles are momentary, fleeting, vaporous. You need only hang on for a vapor's length of time, and then you'll be Home.

A vapor's length of time is not too long to do what's right."

In the following poem I am especially struck by the line: "Pain in itself not hard to bear, But hard to bear so long." Whatever the circumstances of this poem, the pain of the poet, Frederick William Faber (1814–1863), is now over. And from his new perspective, he understands why God used the phrase "momentary troubles."

> O Lord! I live always in pain, My life's sad undersong,
> Pain in itself not hard to bear, But hard to bear so long.
> Little sometimes weighs more than much, When it has
>      no relief;
> A joyless life is worse to bear, Than one of active
>      grief.[47]

As a result of modern physics, we now understand that the duration of time is indeed variable and elastic. At the speed of light, eighty years and a vapor's length are precisely the same duration—and the Scriptures teach "God is light." This is not only scientifically interesting but also functionally useful. For if our life is indeed only a vapor, it reframes our entire perception of suffering.

> *R Replace your current perception of the duration of both life and suffering with God's instruction that suffering redefined is actually momentary. Life, in fact, is vaporous. And a vapor's length of time is not too long to do the right thing.*

---

A day is long, but a life is short.
RUSSIAN PROVERB

# EXERCISE FOR THE HEART

*Most of the medical symptoms caused by inactivity are well known and they are alarming. A body that isn't used deteriorates.*

KENNETH COOPER, M.D., EXERCISE GURU

---

BY SOME STANDARDS, there are five aspects to a fitness evaluation: cardiorespiratory endurance, muscle strength, muscle endurance, flexibility, and body composition. Fitness in each of these five is recommended, but by far the most important and beneficial is cardiorespiratory endurance. Those who wish margin in physical energy would do well to begin with their heart.

Think of your heart as the horse that plows your fields. You abuse it and abuse it and abuse it — but it never complains. And then one day in the middle of a furrow, it drops dead.

Don't abuse your heart. It is your workhorse. Every day it beats 100,000 times and pumps 1600 gallons of blood over 60,000 miles of vessels. Say thank you to your heart. Buy it roses. Encourage it every chance you get.

One way you can encourage your heart is by conditioning it. Through exercise you can cut your heart rate from eighty beats a minute down to sixty. In so doing, you would save your heart 30,000 beats a day and eleven million beats a year. As a token of its appreciation, it would send you back a gift. Try it for a few months and see what the gift is.

A common misconception people have is that they already live an active life so why all the fuss? They are on their feet all day, up and down stairs, lifting, bending, stooping, and generally on the go continuously. They always come home tired. Therefore they get plenty of exercise. It is important to recognize, however, that although this might be a busy lifestyle in one sense, it is not conditioning exercise.

A specific fitness program aimed at conditioning the cardiorespiratory system focuses on the body's ability to deliver and use oxygen. Aerobic conditioning trains your heart, your lungs, your blood, and your blood vessels in such a way that they can deliver more oxygen faster and more efficiently to the body. Once oxygen use is optimized, fitness results. You will feel much better—guaranteed.

> ℞ *Perform thirty to forty-five minutes of exercise—walking, jogging, swimming, bicycling, and so on—three or four times a week. Walking is perhaps the most sustainable activity. When walking, you should be able to talk as you go—if not, you are walking too fast. On the other hand, if you can sing a song, you are walking too slowly. For accountability and sustainability, consider walking with someone else. This accomplishes three goals in one: cardiac conditioning, friendship nurturing, and stress relief.*

---

If you have to drag a dog to the hunt,
neither he nor his hunting is any good.
EGYPTIAN PROVERB

# HOW MUCH WORK IS ENOUGH?

*Success has made failures of many men.*
CINDY ADAMS, SYNDICATED COLUMNIST

THE WORK ETHIC is an important Puritan remnant and part of what developed our national greatness. It is an essential component of maturity. It contributes to integrity on the job. It often results in the fundamentally important ability to pay our bills along life's way. As parents we are pleased to see it evolve in our children. But emphasizing the importance of a work ethic should not be taken as a defense of workaholism. A work ethic is laudatory; workaholism is intemperate.

Let's rethink work for a minute. What are we exalting? Is it work as God defines it, or work as we define it? Is it *work*, or is it *success*? Be cautious of your definitions and motives.

A biblically authentic work ethic does not mean that work is all-important, that our ability to earn money defines our worth, that other important relationships and spiritual obligations take second place, or that people should be layered according to their professional levels.

Work is so dominant in our value structure that many will not—or cannot—even bring themselves to ask the question: *How much work is enough?* It seems heretical. But it is essential that we ask such questions about every aspect of our lives. Idolatry is often marked by unchallengeable presuppositions.

I commonly see two extremes regarding work: work

avoidance and workaholism. Both are unbalanced and a deviation from God's intention. While not working at all can be devastating, working too hard can likewise be devastating, only in a more socially acceptable way.

A nearly universal psychological truth in modern society is to obtain our identity and esteem from our work. While granting that work is a significant *part* of our lives, it is not the *essence* of our lives. This distinction is important because if we achieve our esteem through our work, when we want more esteem we work more hours. But if we are already putting in fifty hours a week and feeling empty, increasing to sixty hours a week is a hollow answer. You cannot correct a wrong by doubling it.

Ultimately, our identity comes from God and is not contingent on our job description or how many hours we work. At the deepest level of our spirit, life flows more smoothly if we agree with God's definitions.

> *R Develop interests outside work. When the sole meaning of your existence is found in work, the tendency is to escalate hours on the job. But then if you are laid off, disabled, or retired, your whole life is crushed. Instead, when the workday, workweek, or work career is ended, there should be another level of meaning waiting to absorb your efforts. Strive to make work interesting and enjoyable, but more than that, strive to make life interesting and enjoyable.*

---

If work were a good thing, the rich would have
grabbed it a long time ago.

HAITIAN PROVERB

# FAMILY STRESS

*I love my children more than life itself. But just because you love people doesn't mean that taking care of them day in and day out isn't often hard, and sometimes even horrible. If God made mothers because he couldn't be everywhere, maybe he could have met us halfway and eradicated vomiting, and colic too.*

ANNA QUINDLEN, PULITZER PRIZE-WINNING JOURNALIST

REMEMBER ANDREA YATES, the Texas housewife who drowned her five children in the bathtub one morning in 2001? Inhuman, grotesque, unthinkable. Except . . . stress sometimes does brutal things to people.

What is it like when you are stressed out, mentally ill, and have five bouncing-off-the-walls children under the age of seven? Best-selling author Anna Quindlen, a mother herself, remembers "the end of a day in which the milk spilled phone rang one cried another hit a fever rose the medicine gone the car sputtered another cried the cable out *Sesame Street* gone all cried stomach upset full diaper no more diapers Mommy I want water Mommy my throat hurts Mommy I don't feel good."[48] I am not excusing anyone of anything. But I am saying that the damaging effects of stress need to be taken seriously.

Stress is not an esoteric pathogen that we might encounter some time in the distant and theoretical future. It is a problem that handicaps the best of us on a daily basis, and causes others of us to snap in the worst way imaginable. This is a burden from which families must be protected.

The modern stress epidemic has pummeled all aspects of society, but families have sustained perhaps the most painful level of damage. Every study on family functioning reveals stress to be at or near the top of the list of problems. Human relationships in general do not fare well under this kind of pressure.

Well-meaning parents who feel trapped between a rock and a hard place—wanting to have solid careers but good families as well—have attempted a difficult balancing act. There is the promising career but also the dirty clothes. And then there is the soccer practice on Saturday morning. And the new version of Sony PlayStation that "all of the other kids have." And the compounded debt, and the telemarketers calling during dinner, and the TV blaring in the background, and the baby crying . . . all while you're trying to decide what to wear for the important meeting tomorrow. Soon there are harsh words, and sleepless nights, and no time to reconcile. . . .

Margin well applied can safeguard the family from the pervasive harmful effects of stress.

> ℞ *Budget enough time and energy to act as a firewall against the malignant effects of stress on your family. Make time for togetherness, shared experience, gentle conversation, and unstructured leisure time. Make space for healing and for love. Get enough sleep; your family will thank you.*

---

The one who first shuts up in an argument
is from a good family.
SLOVAK PROVERB

# CONSUMER ORGY

*Don't forget it: he has much who needs least. Don't create necessities for yourself.*

JOSÉ ESCRIVA, CATHOLIC SAINT

---

THE *GOOD LIFE* has now become the *goods life*. We now have more shopping malls than high schools, and in many communities the mall has become the center of community life. Mall mania leads to recreational shopping, compulsive shopping, and therapeutic shopping. As many as one-third of shoppers express an irresistible compulsion to buy, often in reaction to stress, anxiety, or depression. Forty percent of these compulsive shoppers admit their closets are filled with unopened items.

Not only do we want more, we want bigger. Houses are three rooms larger than they were twenty years ago, even though families are smaller. Our cars are bigger, shoes are larger, furniture is overstuffed, tubs are huge, and now they have a mattress one size up from king. "We're having a harmonic convergence for bigness," observes Jon Berry, editor of *Public Pulse*.

Florida attorney Stacey Giulianti is a case in point. "I've got a 61-inch TV, which, diagonally, is one inch bigger than my own mother," the twenty-nine-year-old lawyer said. "I've got an 11-speaker surround-sound system. I've got oversize plush couches and a monster-size kitchen with a huge bread maker and a commercial-size mixer. And I've got a large master bedroom with a walk-in closet that was the size of my bedroom in my old house." He has a soaking tub, twelve-foot cathedral ceilings, and an enormous Infiniti four-by-four truck that they never drive off-road. "Life is messy," he points out, "and it's nice when you're done with your day to be able to come home and soak in the big tub, grill in your big backyard, and watch your 61-inch TV. It allows you to escape the daily stress."[49]

Where is one to store this cultural largess? In ever larger houses, of course. Today many garages are as large as entire houses were in the 1950s. One California mansion we saw from a distance has twenty bedrooms, twenty-five bathrooms, plus both indoor and outdoor Olympic-size pools for a thirty-two-year-old man, his wife, and daughter. Ironically, he made a fortune in the mini-storage business.

"We tend to measure success with a thingometer," observes author and financial counselor Russ Crosson. But things consume time, and out-of-control consumerism leads to possession overload. Perhaps it's time for a new measure of success.

> $R$ *Stay off the treadmill. Harvard economist Juliet Schor explains how, instead of an earn-and-save cycle, most Americans have adopted a work-and-spend cycle. This involves a nonstop and accelerating treadmill of working more, wanting more, buying more, owing more, and then working more again. If you buy an expensive house and automobiles, obviously these purchases need to be paid for. Things are paid for in dollars; dollars are earned by working; working consumes time; and time is what you are trying to gain. Therefore fewer things = less work = more time.*

---

He who buys what he doesn't need steals from himself.

SWEDISH PROVERB

# WHAT KIND OF POWER?

*Week after week we witness the same miracle: that God is so
mighty he can stifle his own laughter. . . . Does anyone have the
foggiest idea what sort of power we so blithely invoke?*

ANNIE DILLARD, PULITZER PRIZE-WINNING AUTHOR

IN AN IMPRESSIVE show of power, God created science. On
an even deeper level, He *designed* the science that He created.
How exhilarating to be not only fascinated by the science, but
also captivated by the Designer who stands behind it all.

But know this: this same God is uncontrollable. When you
come to know Him, it will only be on His terms. To know
Him is to trust Him; to trust Him is to rest in Him. He will
give you the rest you seek, but only after He has shaken the
foundations of your life.

What kind of power do we so blithely invoke? He spoke
the universe into existence. Nothingness obeys His voice. He
controls time, space, matter, and light. He monitors the position of every elementary particle. He is sufficient unto
Himself. He does not need anybody or anything to accomplish His purposes. He answers to no one. He obeys only His
own counsel. He works on thousands of levels all at the same
time. His scientific sophistication is unfathomable. He created
the laws of physics and appears to be a "pure mathematician."
His intelligence is so superior, according to Einstein, that in
comparison "all the systematic thinking and acting of human

beings is an utterly insignificant reflection."

Look up the word *omnipotent*. Either He is or He isn't. And if He is, we had better prepare ourselves to accept the consequences. "It is madness to wear ladies' straw hats and velvet hats to church," concludes Dillard. "We should all be wearing crash helmets. Ushers should issue life preservers and signal flares; they should lash us to our pews."[50]

Let the record show: God's power is impressive. It should not be underestimated. The deficiency comes not from a lack of God's power but rather a lack of our own faith. Busyness is sometimes what happens when we forget who God is.

> *R̶ Reflect on the word* omnipotent. *If God has infinite power, what implications does that have for your life? Do you suppose He would share some of His power with you if it were in your best interest? But perhaps, you think, He doesn't know that I need it. Reflect on the word* omniscient. *Either He is or He isn't. He knows what you need even before you do. But perhaps, you think, He doesn't care. Reflect on the word* compassionate. *Either He is or He isn't. If God is all-powerful, all-knowing, and all-caring, you don't need to run your life by yourself any longer. What is keeping you from trusting Him with your family, your finances, and your future? And, for that matter, with your margin?*

---

Everything has an end with the exception of God.

DUTCH PROVERB

# THE SECRET OF CONTENTMENT

*If your godliness has freed you from the desire to be rich
and has helped you be content with what you have,
then your godliness is tremendously profitable.*

JOHN PIPER, PASTOR AND AUTHOR

---

CONTENTMENT IS NOT only a good idea; it is our duty. If God recommends something, we *ought* to do it. If God requires something, we *must* do it. As J. I. Packer has emphasized, contentment is both commended ("Godliness with contentment is great gain"[51]) and commanded ("Be content with what you have"[52]).

Such a forceful endorsement by the Almighty should make contentment a prominent concern for each of us. Instead we make it a secret concealed by our indifference to it. When the apostle Paul wrote, "I have learned the secret of being content," his use of the word *secret* was intentional.[53] Those things we expect to bring contentment surprisingly do not. We cannot depend on it to fall into place through the progressive evolving of civilization, for contentment arises from a different source.

Most of us do not know how to uncover this secret and, to be honest, have never seriously tried. Our quest is not for *contentment* but for *more*. This quest brings us into an immense maze, where before us lie dozens of avenues. Some are wide, luxurious, downhill, and tempting, and we see a rush of our friends entering them. They lead to beautiful houses, comfortable cars, exotic vacations, and affluence. Other avenues, equally popular, lead to prestigious colleges, distinguished jobs, important friends, and power. Still others direct us to beautiful spouses, beautiful children, deep tans, and popularity.

All the while, off to one side, courses a narrow uphill road, unadorned and unpopular. It is dusty from its sparse use and lonely from lack of travelers. The sole treasure at its end is an elusive commodity called "godliness with contentment."

Godliness is an attitude whereby what we want is to please God. Contentment, explains J. I. Packer, "is essentially a matter of accepting from God's hand what He sends because we know that He is good and therefore it is good."[54]

Contentment is the freedom that comes when prosperity or poverty do not matter. To accept what we have and "to want but little," as Thoreau advised. The more we choose contentment, the more God sets us free. The more He sets us free, the more we choose contentment.

> *R Instead of desiring security and savings, desire to know the secret. Be entranced by this secret. Pursue it. Fall in love with it. Understand there is a doorway here that leads to something much deeper than prosperity. Only those willing to search in the right places will be rewarded with this gift of contentment. When sought, it is never found by us but instead is revealed to us.*

---

A harvest of peace grows from seeds of contentment.

INDIAN PROVERB

# BUSY, BUSIER, TOO BUSY

*We live in the age of the half-read page, the quick hash and the
mad dash, the bright night with the nerves tight, the plane hop
with the brief stop, the lamp tan in a short span, the brain strain
and the heart pain, the catnaps until the spring snaps . . .
the land where the fun's gone.*

CHUCK SWINDOLL, SEMINARY PRESIDENT AND AUTHOR

----

WE LIKE FAST food, fast cars, and fast answers. We want to simultaneously boot up, download, and cell phone. We struggle to squeeze more work into fewer hours only to find out that the more we do, the more there is to do. When such speed and busyness have matured, they give birth to fatigue. And Americans are, if anything, exhausted. We are a nation of the "hard-wired and dog-tired." People careen through their days like impetuous electrons that have jumped their orbits.

Busyness is not a synonym for kingdom work: it is only busyness. And busyness is sometimes what happens to us when we forget who God is. Busyness displaces the power of the present moment. The present moment is infinitely small, yet God resides there. When we hurry, we look beyond the present, and in so doing, miss it entirely. We are aiming for something in the future, but not in the moment.

Christ, however, lived and ministered in the moment. He accepted daily ministry opportunity as it came in the person standing before Him. He didn't follow a daily agenda, didn't consult a to-do list, and never seemed to hurry. All of these notions seem peculiar to us today, smacking of a sluggard rather than a savior.

Perhaps instead of reflexive busyness we should assess all activities according to their spiritual authenticity. If we have twenty things to do and can do only ten, how do we select? We must have Christlike criteria with which to judge our choices and then be willing to actually use these criteria as a guide for daily living.

If we are already too busy, why look for more things to do? For example, why do we even glance through the section of the paper that describes what is happening in town this week? Our problem is not lack of activity; our problem is lack of time. So throttle back, contemplate your course, consult God, and carefully choose your way.

> R Remember Who it is that gets things done. God is the multi-plying coefficient for our labors. We might only do 50 percent of all that we had planned tomorrow and yet accomplish 500 percent more in terms of eternal significance—if our efforts are sensitive to the promptings and empowerment of the Holy Spirit. God can do in ten seconds what it takes us ten years to do. Let's trust more and do less. Is it busyness that moves mountains . . . or faith?

---

Have faith—God calls forth life even from eggs.
INDIAN PROVERB

# SAYING NO

*Some people can't say no. They take on too many relationships and too many responsibilities. They enroll in too many courses, hold down too many jobs, volunteer for too many tasks, make too many appointments, serve on too many committees, have too many friends. They are trying to be all things to all men all at once all by themselves. They equate dedication with exhaustion.*

DR. J. GRANT HOWARD, THEOLOGIAN AND AUTHOR

WITH TODAY'S VAST menu of tempting activities, learning to say no is increasingly a mathematical necessity. Because of the inexorable proliferation of progress, we always have more options, opportunities, and obligations . . . but no more time. If we have thirty hours of things to do in a twenty-four-hour day, we must learn to say no to six hours worth of possibility. This is not bad news; it is only good math. The straightforward implication is that we need priorities that teach us what to accept and what to decline.

Regaining margin in our lives will never happen unless we develop such an ability to say no, *even to good things.* On the one hand, it is easy to say no to bad things: root canals, flexible sigmoidoscopies, IRS audits. But it is difficult to say no to things that are interesting and enjoyable. Yet twenty-four hours is only twenty-four hours, and it will not expand to accommodate our mathematically unreasonable commitments. Every person living under the remarkable conditions of modernity must learn this same lesson: the clock, without bothering to consult us, forces fixed external limits universally.

Our leaders are the subgroup with the greatest difficulty accepting such limits. These high-performing individuals rose through the ranks by challenging limits and by doing more, not less. When confronted with the twenty-four-hour day they try to find ways around the threat, only to discover that this is one limit that will not budge.

Thankfully, many leaders have begun to adopt a healthier approach. They are viewing the word *no* as an ally rather than an enemy. It keeps them focused. *No* helps them to differentiate the things that are most important from all the other options clamoring for attention.

"Some leaders have difficulty saying no because their sense of self-worth demands that they make themselves indispensable to their organization," observe Richard and Henry Blackaby. "These leaders take pride in the fact that they are in great demand and that their calendars are brimming with places to be and things to do. . . . Healthy leaders, on the other hand, graciously, yet regularly, say no to many opportunities presented to them. They say no far more often than they say yes."[55]

R Begin to regard the word *no* as a friend, a concept that guards both sanity and effectiveness. It is only a two-letter word, yet one of the most difficult to speak. If you do not learn to say no, however, overload will overwhelm.

—◦◦◦—

Say no from the start; you will have rest.
AFRICAN PROVERB

# RECONCILE RELATIONSHIPS

*When we allow ourselves to feel like victims or sit around dreaming up how to retaliate against people who have hurt us, these thought patterns take a toll on our minds and bodies.*

MICHAEL MCCULLOUGH, DIRECTOR OF RESEARCH,
NATIONAL INSTITUTE FOR HEALTHCARE RESEARCH

BROKEN RELATIONSHIPS ARE a razor across the artery of the spirit. Stemming the hemorrhage and binding the wound should be done as quickly as possible. Yet all too often it takes months or years. And sometimes the bleeding never stops.

Medical studies give abundant evidence of what we already intuitively know: conflict in relationships is harmful to our health. For example, we now have liberal evidence that hostility is cardiotoxic; a person with unresolved anger has a significantly higher chance of dying prematurely from a heart attack. Research has additionally shown that reconciling conflicts improves the immune system, lowers blood pressure, and optimizes mental health.

Notice that it is not revenge that heals. It is not litigation, or time, or distance that heals. It is forgiveness and reconciliation that bring wholeness.

True reconciliation is one of the most powerful of all human interactions. Warring individuals who have done battle for years can erase all antagonism in a matter of minutes. This is not a matter of human psychology but rather a divine gift. One of the great privileges of our adoption into God's family is the access we have to this mysterious healing power of the Spirit. If you have not seen it happen, or if you have only seen it happen rarely, then yearn for it. Pray for it. Beg for it. And know that it is one of the gifts God most enjoys giving.

Although there is no formula, there are principles. It helps to bring God close — through our brokenness.[56] And it helps to accept God's grace — through our humility.[57] This gift, you see, is mostly a matter of emptiness and yielding. In our brokenness we confess, yielding our *wrongs*. In our humility we forgive, yielding our *rights*. And when confession and forgiveness are completed, our frozen winter of pain will also yield under the warmth of the Son.

> ℞ *Write a letter, make a phone call, or ask forgiveness for some rift of the past. Even if you feel the fault lies with the other person, if you wish to be healthy, forgive. Declare unilateral peace. Then forget about it. Don't revisit the injury. Don't nurse the grievance any longer, for love keeps no record of wrongs.*[58] *Forgive, and then forget. As you give them freedom, you give yourself rest.*

---

He who forgives ends the quarrel.
AFRICAN PROVERB

# THE SEMIVISIBILITY OF MARGIN

*There are times I almost think I am not sure
of what I absolutely know.*

KING OF SIAM, *THE KING AND I*

IF THIRSTY, WE needn't be told that water is what we lack. If
sleep deprived, we needn't be told that sleep is what we yearn
for. If exhausted from a thirty-mile walk, we needn't be told
that rest is what our body craves. If bankrupt, we needn't be
told that money is what we require.

Why, then, when we so desperately need margin in our
lives, is it necessary to explain our need for it? Why don't we
understand it by instinct?

Some burdens and pains in life are visible while others are
not. To say that some are "visible" means they can be perceived
with one of the five senses or they can be quantified or measured. If you smash your finger with a hammer, you don't have
to guess about why it hurts. Physical pains are obvious and visible. In much the same way, financial pains are usually visible.
If a financial statement reveals imminent bankruptcy, the
source of your distress is not obscure.

Other pains, however, cannot be perceived by the senses
in quite the same way; neither can they be quantified or measured. They are invisible or, perhaps more accurately, semivisible. Emotional, psychological, social, relational, and spiritual
pains often fit this description. The pain is real, but the details

of cause and effect are hard to sort out. It often requires months of introspection to clarify wounds in these areas.

In this same way, margin is semivisible. Living without it does not cause a sensory pain but instead a deep-seated subjective ache. Because the ache and heaviness are only semivisible, it is hard for us to talk about. We feel weak if we complain. We feel vulnerable to the slings and arrows of the contemptuously stoical. It is hard to justify our inner pains when we don't even know who the enemy is. How do we talk about our anguish when we don't have a vocabulary to use?

Living without margin has, to date, been unseen and unexplained—but not unfelt. Yet it is not buried so deeply that we must send the philosophers out to find it. Even a simple country doctor can explain the concept. And once explained, the fog lifts.

Very seldom do people attempt to refute the diagnosis. Instead most say, "So *that's* the problem." It is as if a switch is tripped in their understanding. Instantly, they have hope that their burden is finally being understood.

> ℞ *Be as concerned with accuracy of analysis as you are with effectiveness of therapeutics. The only effective remedies are those that flow from correct diagnoses. The subjective and semivisible environments of life are actually more important than the quantifiable environments. Do not underestimate them, and stop devaluing them.*

---

The reverse side also has a reverse side.
JAPANESE PROVERB

# HUMAN LIMITS AND THE POWER OF GOD

*There is a sense of relief in remembering that I'm not God.*
STEVE BROWN, RADIO BROADCASTER AND PROFESSOR

THAT HUMANS HAVE limits is scientifically undeniable. It is, as a matter of fact, patently obvious at the most elementary level. The brain is not capable of memorizing the entire contents of the *Encyclopedia Britannica* in five minutes. The body is not capable of running from Dallas to Minneapolis in five minutes. The spirit cannot send a note of encouragement to every hurting soul in the world in five minutes. We are limited. We all possess a certain level of strength, stamina, and resilience, but always within the context of limits.

Why, then, do we resist acknowledging what is so obvious? Some find the idea of limits threatening on a personal level. Others feel it inhibits their vision — their reaching for the stars and achieving feats previously thought unattainable. Others feel that their best work lies yet on the other side of impossible. Others feel the very real pressure from bosses or the onerous expectations of never-satisfied parents.

Still others believe that God is disappointed when we acknowledge limits — that in this discussion God also is implicated as being weak. But saying that *we* have limits in no way suggests that *God* has limits. And to say that all the spiritual work in the kingdom must be done with human effort misses the point of God's power altogether. It is very freeing to realize that God has the resources to get the job done, and that rest is still a part of His will for us. Conversely, it is lack of faith, coupled with an inadequate view of God, to think that we have to work continuous twenty-hour days at 120-percent capacity. To acknowledge human limits does not dishonor God. It is only telling Him what He already knows. Instead it dishonors Him to *deny* limits. It insults His creation wisdom.

Margin is not an abdication of faith. On the contrary, spiritually authentic margin is the very essence of faith. It is the acknowledgment that God has sufficient strength and wisdom and that He does not need my contribution to make up His deficiency in any area.

All of life is a gift. It is God—not myself—that supplies my need. God is not only sufficient, but He is lavish with His bounty and power.

Striving is not only foolish, it is also sin. Rest is spiritually normative. Waiting is spiritually wise. Frenzy, on the other hand, is a type of spiritual treachery.

*R Work diligently to develop both a psychology and a theology of human limits. Limits are real, and limits are not even the enemy. Overload is the enemy. When we come to the end of ourselves, God stands ready to be God. Let Him.*

---

He who leaves God out of his reckoning
does not know how to count.
ITALIAN PROVERB

# THE DIFFICULTY OF SIMPLICITY

*It is still not easy for me to choose to live in less style than others;
I would like a bigger, more elaborate house, more fashionable
clothes, and all those other things that go along with the marks
of success in this society. I've not chosen the "controlled" life
style because I like it, but because I believe God does!*

LORRY LUTZ, FORMER MISSIONARY

WHAT FACTORS MAKE the simple life hard to obtain? If we embark on this journey, let's first decide how much of the currency of fortitude we need to bring with us. There will be tollbooths along the route, with the costs sometimes unreasonably high.

No sooner have we started out the gate but we encounter our first problem: society's disrespect. If we choose to de-emphasize fashion and status, we will not gain the admiration of our peers. From the outset we need to decide who it is we are trying to please.

Continuing down the narrow road of the simple life, we repeatedly encounter another problem: our expectations. After decades of convenience and affluence, we not only desire but also expect ease and satiation. Gratification of our appetites has become a widespread goal not seriously challenged. If we do not reprogram such expectations, we will experience recurrent frustration in our search for simplicity.

Our lack of discipline presents us with yet another obstacle.

We have not needed much discipline during this era of abundance, and we have thus lost interest in it as a component of lifestyle. Most of us have grown soft. But the simple life is not easy, and discipline is necessary.

Finally, our own mistaken opinions of how things ought to be also trip us repeatedly. Theological confusion has permitted us first to look at what we want and then to build a theology that justifies it. For example, somehow we have incorporated a high money demand into our theological construct. Yet little money is needed to live a fully *God-honoring* life. True enough, we do need a lot of income to live a fully *society-honoring* life. But God doesn't require a badge of wealth as a prerequisite for kingdom participation. Somewhere along the line I think we missed a step.

> *R⃰ Prepare yourself in advance for the possible social costs of the simple lifestyle. Making the changes can be freeing but sometimes painful as well. Worn carpeting can be embarrassing, and old cars can be exasperating. On the other hand, authenticity is its own eternal reward. Note: It helps immeasurably if you are surrounded by a community of like-minded friends who support your value structure rather than a society where envy has been normalized.*

---

To know how to do it is simple, the difficulty is in doing it.

CHINESE PROVERB

# PHYSICAL REST

*People in the Western world have leisure. We do not need to slave*
*every minute in order to eat. But only a few appear to have rest.*
*Profit-making work began to swallow Sundays and holidays.*
*No wonder everyone has been getting so tired. Obviously much*
*of this fatigue takes place in the name of making more money,*
*even though the pantry is already stocked.*

DORIS LONGACRE, MENNONITE SIMPLICITY AUTHOR

---

CONSTANT ACTIVITY IS a characteristic of our age. If we are not active we feel slothful. If we are not productive we feel guilty. A healthy twenty-eight-year-old man sitting on a lawn swing for an entire Sunday afternoon would more than likely feel the need to apologize to his neighbors.

Such busyness comes from a societal value system that idolizes productivity. I am not saying that productivity is wrong. I am only saying it must not be idolized. Productivity has no more spiritual value than does rest. Industriousness might be good for an economy, particularly one like ours. But that does not mean it is healthy in all respects.

As a physician I clearly affirm that *activity* is not only good, it also is necessary. But so is *rest*. Our bodies were designed in such a way to require rest. Sleep is the clearest example and one that cannot be violated. Many Americans, however, get the activity-rest cycle out of balance. Millions get too little activity, and millions more get too little rest.

Work in our culture often dominates other areas of life. To be sure, work is very important. But there are other activities that are also important. The people who work the hardest and rest the least naturally rise to the top, from where they drive the entire system. They set the rules, which maximize productivity. Too often love and relationship come far down the list. It is little wonder rest cannot find a resting place.

Leisure might be the name we give our time away from work, but it is not a synonym for rest. Many return exhausted from vacation because our vacations and weekends have ceased to be restful.

Americans do not tolerate an activity vacuum well. The slow, contemplative life is largely foreign to our experience. Therefore when "leisure time" appears on our schedule, we select from the many activity options society offers. This is not inherently wrong. Neither is quiet reflection always right. But when we work hard and then play harder, it is no wonder we feel fatigued so often.

Although progress may not approve, it is important to rest physically.

> *R̶ God first designed our bodies to need rest, then He instructed us in the Scriptures to get rest. Do it. Don't be shamed into thinking it is wrong. You dishonor God when you fail to work, but you equally dishonor Him when you fail to rest.*

───◆◆◆───

A good rest is half the work.
YUGOSLAVIAN PROVERB

# TAKING EVERY THOUGHT CAPTIVE

*If the brain were so simple we could understand it,*
*we would be so simple we couldn't.*

LYALL WATSON, BIOLOGIST

---

THE BRAIN—PRIDE and joy of the nervous system—is staggering in its abilities and complexity. "In man is a three-pound brain, which, as far as we know, is the most complex and orderly arrangement of matter in the universe." Thus wrote scientist and author Isaac Asimov.[59] In so stating, he was giving God a compliment, even though he remained an avowed atheist up to the end.

The basic cell of the brain is called the neuron, of which there are ten billion to one hundred billion. In addition to long extensions called axons, each neuron has ten thousand tiny branching fibers and filamentous projections called dendrites. Each neuron is thus in contact with ten thousand other neurons, for a total of one hundred trillion neurological interconnections.

If you were to stretch out all the neurons and dendritic connections in the brain and lay them end to end, they would extend one hundred thousand miles and circle the earth at the equator four times.

One way to visualize these dendritic connections is as light switches, either in the off or on position. The brain holds $10^{14}$ bits of information and thus has a storage capacity one thousand times that of a Cray-2 supercomputer. Unlike the parts of a computer, however, nerve cells are highly individual. No two cells are exactly the same, nor do they respond to the same incoming information in the same way. Each neuron is unique in all the universe.

The brain is capable of firing at ten thousand trillion computations per second. The capacity of the brain is such that it can hold the information equivalent to twenty-five million books, capable of filling a bookshelf five hundred miles long. In contrast, the Library of Congress has eighteen million volumes.

The brain can be a conduit of distress or a channel of blessing. Overloading our synapses with excessive multitasking will leave us besieged by anxiety. If we live in an emotional gutter and perseverate on problems and pain, then we will be battered by our thoughts. If, on the other hand, we yield our spirit to the Spirit of God, our surrendered thoughts can lead us to green pastures and still waters where He restores our soul.

℞ *"Take captive every thought."*[60] *Prioritize the functioning of your remarkable brain for the right purposes. Carefully use your cognitive abilities and memory for purposes of truth and peace. "Whatever is true, whatever is noble, whatever is right, whatever is pure, whatever is lovely, whatever is admirable — if anything is excellent or praiseworthy — think about such things."*[61]

⸺≋⸺

If you are a fast talker, at least think slowly.
<small>CRETIAN PROVERB</small>

# MUSCLES AND FLEXIBILITY

*What one needs is not great knots and boulders of muscle on the*
*arms and the back, but rather a collection of good usable muscles*
*all over the body —enough to make one active, and*
*cheerful, and equal to all the demands of life.*

MARJORIE BARSTOW GREENBIE, HISTORIAN AND WRITER

---

ONCE PROGRESS DELIVERED us from the need to use our muscles in earning a living, we lost both strength and stamina. It is a loss, however, which can be recovered.

Muscle conditioning, while perhaps not as important as cardiorespiratory conditioning, is nevertheless a vital and often neglected aspect of overall physical fitness. As such, it is a helpful ally in securing physical energy margin. If you wish vitality and energy for the day, strengthen your muscles. While weight lifting and calisthenics do not constitute overall aerobic conditioning, they can give enhanced strength, speed, agility, and self-esteem.

There are two aspects to muscle fitness: strength and endurance. In a weight training program, for example, lifting heavier weights with fewer repetitions is for strength, while lifting lighter weights with more repetitions is for endurance. As we age, muscle strength declines more quickly than does muscle endurance.

I do not support weight training for the vanity of it. But neither should it be forsaken simply because it is misused by bronzed bodies who flaunt it. The simple fact is, progress wrongly released us from the need to use our muscles, and if we do not use them we lose them.

Flexibility exercising is another dimension of fitness. It is the least demanding in terms of wear and tear. You can do it at the bedside before retiring, and you seldom huff, puff, or sweat. Yet despite its ease, it can help increase mobility and decrease aches and pains, particularly in the back.

As we age, our flexibility becomes constricted. We have twenty-eight joints in the neck alone. Unless resisted, every year we naturally lose some mobility. Similarly, the lower back stiffens, often resulting in discomfort. Another example: If you were to keep your arm at your side for one month, it would result in a "frozen shoulder."

Watch the limber contortions of young children as they pretzel up on the floor to read a book. Compare that to your own creaky hinges. Undergoing a program of flexibility can help you regain some of this lost range of motion with laudatory results.

Muscles and joints: they were created to be used. Oblige them.

> ℞ *Develop a systematic program to help your muscles and joints resist the normal effects of aging. Lift weights, even small ones. Move your joints, especially those that bother you the most. Doing this consistently will enhance both your quality of life and your quantity of strength.*

---

The willing dancer is easily played to.
<small>HUNGARIAN PROVERB</small>

# CULTIVATING SOCIAL SUPPORTS

*There is perhaps no more effective way to relieve psychic pain than to be in contact with another human being who understands what you are going through and can communicate such understanding to you.*

DR. FREDERIC FLACH, PSYCHIATRIST

NOT ONLY IN common sense but now also in good science, the importance of healthy social supports is irrefutable. We do not simply think they work: we *know* they work. Studies consistently reveal a link between nurturing friendships and personal well-being.

Whether family and friends or community and church, the existence of intact, functioning, healthy, nurturing systems of social support are as good a resource for replenishing depleted energy reserves as can be found. Love, affection, nurturing, intimacy, connectedness, bonding, attachment, empathy, community—these are "feel good" words for a reason: because they *are* good.

If you find yourself emotionally empty, go to a caring friend. If you are bruised and bleeding, the empathetic response of another will stem the hemorrhage of emotion and begin the process of healing and filling. According to research, empathy is in itself therapeutic.

Researchers have also studied what is called "the disclosure effect." If we have a frustration inside and are able to reveal our heart to a safe friend, simply disclosing the problem will improve our well-being in measurable ways. It is not necessary for our friend to *fix* the problem—all he has to do is listen.

Many of us have unsatisfactory relationships and are afraid to risk intimate emotional contact. So we withdraw and "hide from love," only to find that isolation is unhealthy as well. The obvious answer is not to abandon people contact but to learn how to make our relationships mutually nourishing. As we become more active and effective in nourishing families, nourishing friendships, nourishing churches, and nourishing community, we will also discover that our own emotional health is nourished.

As an added note, we can say that not only verbal expressions of caring are important, but the physical are as well. We all need human contact. We all need to be hugged from time to time. Have you ever noticed how, when a child climbs onto a parent's lap and snuggles in, the entire room feels caressed by the warmth of it?

> ℞ *Develop a network of caring friends. Keep updated. Send notes of encouragement. Remember birthdays and anniversaries. Run errands together. Have coffee. Develop traditions. Go for walks. Persist despite lulls or disagreements.*

———⊗⊗⊗———

There's no physician like a true friend.
ROMANIAN PROVERB

# WORKING FASTER FOR LESS

*On every level of life from housework to heights of prayer, in all
judgment and all efforts to get things done, hurry and
impatience are sure marks of the amateur.*

EVELYN UNDERHILL, BRITISH DEVOTIONAL AUTHOR

---

IN ANY WORK environment, increasing the speed of work is
a common strategy for increasing productivity. It works. But
only up to a point. Once you exceed a certain speed threshold,
completion of a task becomes harder rather than easier.
Concentration becomes distracted. Results are flawed. Hurry
leads to mistakes. A second attempt at completing the task is
now compounded by the frustration of a failed initial effort.
The worker becomes stressed and irritable, further complicating the completion effort.

Once after I finished speaking in central California, my
host was late taking me to the departure location. Because of
unfamiliarity with the area, he was quickly scanning signs for
the San Jose Airport exit. Finally, at top speed, he suddenly
pointed to a blurred sign disappearing behind us. "I think that
was the way to the airport!"

"Yes," I said, "I think it was."

We drove around the loop a second time, only to have
him say, "I think we missed it again."

It took four attempts to finally hit the exit ramp. I made
my flight, with ten seconds to spare. This relatively straight-

forward task was sabotaged by one factor: hurry.

In construction work, the motto is "Measure twice, cut once." If you cut the board quickly and it is too short, you can't put the board back together again for a second chance.

How about medicine? Is it possible we hurry too much and miss important diagnoses? All the time. If we have one patient per day, that is not sufficient. But if we have one patient per minute, that is far too many. Somewhere in the middle is a balance that is professionally sustainable and diagnostically optimal.

Excessive haste does more than harm the product. It also increases injury, disability, and absenteeism, and ultimately poisons workplace morale. At some threshold point, doing more and more, faster and faster becomes a flawed strategy. It is best to stay on the right side of that line.

> ℞ *Discover the pace that works best for your desired effort, then stay within acceptable tolerances. If you work too slowly or too rapidly, both production and efficiency will suffer.*

---

Work is twice done by the person in a hurry.
IRANIAN PROVERB

# A LAND DEVOID OF SPACE AND TIME

*I feel like a minnow in a flash flood.*
CHICAGO HOMEMAKER

---

OFTENTIMES A CONCEPT is better illustrated than described, perhaps because real-life examples bear a better resemblance to our daily affairs.

In Washington State, thirty-two dairy cows ate themselves to death after one of them shook loose a pipe on an automatic feeding machine and spilled tons of grain. The cows feasted to their desires, but soon found themselves in the graveyard. Does this mean that eating grain is bad for farm animals? No. Eating grain is fine: eating overload is not.

A single mother and her four children had a combined one hundred rehearsals or concerts in the month of December. God bless 'em. Perhaps this was exactly the right choice for such a talented family. Most of us, however, find the entire month already overloaded even before such additions. Be careful not to spoil the celebration with too much celebrating.

Buy a satellite dish, and you can choose from 1,100 movies a month—a wonderful cure if your diagnosis is chronic movie deficiency.

There are 450 English language editions of the Bible and 63,000 new books every year. A college student can choose from over 500 possible baccalaureate degrees. There are more than 60 kinds of Musak and more than 50 medical specialties.

The average grocery store has 30,000 product choices. There are 177 kinds of salad dressing, 184 kinds of cereal, 250 kinds of toothpaste, and 551 kinds of coffee. It is also reported that the average store has 22 doors of frozen desserts. Oreos now come in Original, Mini, Chocolate Creme, Chocolate Creme Mini, Reduced Fat, Doubled Stuf, Fudge Covered, Fudge Mint Covered, Double Delight Peanut Butter & Chocolate, Double Delight Mint'nCreme, and Double Delight Coffee'nCreme. Choice overload is also decision overload.

The plane carrying American pop singer Aaliyah and eight members of her entourage was substantially overloaded by several hundred pounds. It crashed on attempted takeoff in the Bahamas. This does not mean that we should avoid small planes. Nor does it mean we should avoid flying to the Bahamas. It only means we should not overload airplanes and then ask them to fly.

At a physician conference, one doctor came to me and said, "Do you know the difference between God and a physician? God doesn't think He's a doctor."

*℞ Work hard. Dream large. Serve sacrificially. But always with a knowledge of God-ordained limits. Don't cross the line unless God first grants permission.*

———∞∞———

You can't load a small boat with heavy cargo.
<small>CHINESE PROVERB</small>

# TIME, ETERNITY, AND DIMENSIONS

*Time is eternity wrapped up; eternity is time unwrapped.*
FRIEDRICH CHRISTOPH OETINGER, SCIENTIST AND RELIGIOUS MYSTIC

---

TIME IS THE one constant in a rapidly changing world. Seconds are like the steady dripping of a leaky faucet. Time moves only in one direction—forward. Aside from God Himself, nothing has ever been able to change the direction of that flow. And it moves at the same pace for all people. Whether naked tribesmen in their Irian jungles or bespectacled professors in their Oxford classrooms, it makes no difference. Time is a resource we all share equally. In any twenty-four-hour day, nobody gets a minute more or a minute less. Time just *is*.

And then Einstein came along and threw the rulebook into the fire. He proved that time only works in the usual way when we are comfortably in our routine frame of reference. Once we step out of that frame of reference, however, time changes. When in the larger universe—a universe of many frames of reference and great speeds—time warps dramatically.

By allowing us to glimpse this fact, I believe that God is hinting at something. Through Einstein's relativity, He is allowing us a "sneak peak" revelation into the nature of heaven. When God hints in such a way, it is usually worthwhile to follow His lead and try to discern His message.

There are many theological opinions about God's exact relationship to time. The orthodox position—and my own belief—is that God stands outside of time. Time was a specific invention of His; in other words, time had a beginning. God created time when He created space and matter. When our age is over, God will un-invent time, and then eternity will take over.

Time seems rigid to us because we exist in only one time dimension: a straight line. If we were able to perceive time as having two or more dimensions, many of our questions about God's miraculous powers would be easily answered. Because God operates in more than one time dimension He can move around within our single time dimension and see everything happening simultaneously.

This is hard for us to perceive but not at all hard for God to do. We should never fall into the trap of thinking that if something is hard for us to imagine, it is therefore hard for God to do. Fortunately, the spiritual universe is neither obligated nor constrained by the meagerness of our comprehension.

> ℞ *Fill your time with authenticity. Soon we shall all be on the other side, wishing we had filled our moments exclusively with truth and love rather than with the tyrannizing trivia of an overloaded age. "It is precisely because of the eternity outside time that everything in time becomes valuable and important and meaningful," wrote Dorothy Sayers. "Therefore Christianity . . . makes it of urgent importance that everything we do here should be rightly related to what we eternally are."*[62]

---

Age and time do not wait for people.
CHINESE PROVERB

# THE EAR AND A DISTANT CRICKET

*NOISE: A stench in the ear. Undomesticated music. The chief
product and authenticating sign of civilization.*

AMBROSE BIERCE, ICONOCLASTIC WRITER

---

JUST AS THE eye converts photons into electrical signals that
can be "seen" by the brain, so the ear converts sound waves
into electrical signals that can be "heard" by the brain—no
less a miracle. In some ways the ear actually outperforms the
eye. It can hear over an even wider range of sound intensity
(one trillion times) than the range of light intensity over which
the eye can see (ten billion times).

The eardrum has the same thickness as a piece of paper
and is exquisitely sensitive to any vibration. It can vibrate as
slowly as twenty times per second and as fast as twenty thousand times per second. Even sound waves that move the
eardrum less than the diameter of a hydrogen molecule can be
perceived by the brain as sound. It is this sensitivity that makes
it possible to hear a cricket chirping one-half mile away on a
still night.

The sensitivity of the hearing mechanism is very impressive. The reason "sound" happens at all has everything to do
with the sensitivity of the equipment God designed for us and
almost nothing to do with the energy of the sound wave itself.
A noise loud enough to pain the ear, for example, measures a
mere 0.01 watt of energy.

The sound energy generated by our speaking is likewise negligible. A person could "talk continuously for one hundred years and still not produce the sound energy equivalent to the heat energy needed to bring a cup of water to the boil."[63] Thus it is the extraordinary sensitivity of the ear itself that permits hearing.

The ear has a million moving parts and is yet another evidence of the microprecision of God. Yet as with so much of life, the creature abuses the gift. The ear is increasingly assaulted by an epidemic of noise and commotion. Noise is to the ear what excessively bright lights are to the eyes.

Noise is toxic to the sensitive cells of the ear, the cardiovascular and nervous systems, and our mental and spiritual health. "Noises usually drown out the voice of God," maintains Gordon MacDonald. "Few of us can fully appreciate the terrible conspiracy of noise there is about us, noise that denies us the silence and solitude we need for this cultivation of the inner garden."[64]

> R Realizing that excessive noise leads to stress, seek to diminish the ambient level of noise in your life. "Regular times of quiet are absolutely necessary," wrote Dietrich Bonhoeffer. "After a time of quiet we meet others in a different and a fresh way."[65] Adds theologian John Stott: "I've learned the necessity of stepping back, looking where I was going, and having a monthly quiet day to be drawn up into the mind of God."[66]

⸺✥⸺

We have two ears and one mouth,
learn to use them in proportion.
GHANIAN PROVERB

# LEARN TO LAUGH

*Always laugh when you can; it is a cheap medicine. Merriment is a philosophy not well understood. It is the sunny side of existence.*

GEORGE GORDON BYRON, ENGLISH POET

---

THE THERAPEUTIC BENEFITS of laughter are well established in modern medicine as state-of-the-art, stress-reducing therapeutics. We don't yet fully understand *why* laughter works, but we do know that people who laugh readily heal faster.

Only a few months after birth the hilarity begins. By the time babies are four months old, they are already laughing once every hour. The peak age of laughter is four. I don't know if God is behind this symmetry, but *four*-year-olds laugh once every *four* minutes, or *four* hundred times a day. Children are remarkably buoyant and resilient—laughter deserves much of the credit.

Adults, on the other hand, laugh on average fifteen times a day. If we were to follow four-year-olds around and laugh every time they do, positive things would happen to both our bodies and spirits. Laughter lowers the pulse and blood pressure and seems to improve immune function. One psychiatrist recommends thirty minutes of therapeutic laughter every day. Some call this "inner jogging."

The most valuable kind of laughter is when you laugh at yourself; you'll never run out of material. "Blessed are those who laugh at themselves for they will never cease to be amused." In addition, laughing at our own problems has a way of putting them into perspective. After a hurricane in southern Florida devastated his house, one person put a sign up in the front yard: "Open House." It didn't help him rebuild, but it surely helped him weather the storm.

Pious traditions have held differing views on laughter. Some have regarded life, faith, sin, and redemption so ponderous that mirth was inappropriate. One man in Jonathan Edwards' parish was fined for smiling in church. On the other hand, Martin Luther once remarked: "If you're not allowed to laugh in heaven I don't want to go there."

Humor is a medicine. It works better than most pills and costs much less. I am not implying that life is essentially humorous—it decidedly is not. But God, perhaps because He knew we would need it, has given us the free gift of laughter. I, for one, am grateful.

R̥ *Laugh often, freely, and loudly. It is an inexpensive shortcut to well-being. If you are not wired for it or if your heritage precludes it, at least make friends with people who laugh readily. Memorize a few jokes, and post your favorite cartoons around the house.*

❦

Many families are built on laughter.
INDIAN PROVERB

# THAT WHICH MATTERS MOST

*When you gonna wake up and strengthen the things that remain?*
BOB DYLAN, MUSICIAN

LIFE HAS A way of getting away from us, of cascading out of control. Soon we are scrambling to keep our balance, desperately trying to keep our head above water. At such moments, we are seldom guided by transcendent principles but instead by survival pure and simple. When the phone is ringing and the doorbell is ringing and the kids are fighting and the baby is crying and we are trying to get ready for a meeting that started ten minutes ago, it is hard to sustain lofty thoughts. Priorities are lost in the din. And modernity, to be sure, has lots of din.

Inherent in the understanding about overload is the need to prioritize. If our lives are besieged with excessive clutter, crowded schedules, and continuous interruptions, then we have some choices to make. If we have more to do than we can possibly do, then we have some decisions to make. And such choices and decisions, if pursued wisely, will be guided by eternal priorities and God-honoring criteria.

Many people often do not consciously realize what their priorities are. A French anthropologist, Claude Lévi-Strauss, once remarked, "History is something that happens to people; what happens is always different from what people would rather have done." Upon first reading that statement I realized it was both true and tragic. And I determined that it would never happen to me. Priorities matter.

The following are principles to use in establishing and guarding priorities:

- Obtain priorities from the Scriptures.
- Look through God's eyes, and then act on what is seen.
- Seek *first* the kingdom of God, and everything else later.
- People are more important than things.

"Things that matter most," advised Goethe, "must never be at the mercy of things that matter least."

> R℣ *Listen to God's advice. Take control of each area in your life where He has given explicit instructions. When you bring your balancing problems to God, you will discover that He never assigns twice as much as you can possibly do. Instead the Father reveals the appropriate priorities to use and then always provides whatever time and resources are needed to accomplish His will.*

---

Better to spend a day thinking it over than a week working for no purpose at all.

BALTO-FINNIC PROVERB

# THE PHENOMENON OF INCREASING COMPLEXITY

*Civilization is a limitless multiplication of unnecessary necessaries.*
MARK TWAIN

EACH DAY THE world becomes more complicated. The automatic, default direction of progress is toward escalating complexity. Much of this trend is to our liking, for we delight in sophisticated, impressive hardware, whether space shuttles, supercomputers, artificial hearts, or global positioning satellites.

But there is another aspect to this story. Complexity can bless, but it also can irritate. And most of us do not need a larger irritation burden complicating our already overloaded lives. At such times we might consider strong, determined, selective moves to keep our lives, our schedules, and our technology within a range of acceptable complexity.

Medicine, for example, has become enormously complex. When the *Physician's Desk Reference* first appeared in 1947, it contained 300 pages. Now it has 3,000 pages, and no doctor on the face of the earth knows all those medicines. When our University of Wisconsin clinic received new charts, I counted 2,605 blanks for patient information. My heart sank. When were we actually going to take care of the patient? A single sentence in an insurance contract contained 136 words. When President Clinton proposed health care reform in 1993, the report was 1,342 pages long, a document no human had ever read, or understood. "It was enormously complex," stated one senator. "It was almost frighteningly complex."

When United began flying the sophisticated 777s, they sent a mechanic on every flight to teach the first-class passengers how to use their seats. In San Francisco an absentee ballot for a primary election was 173 pages long. Discover Card and Sprint combined to advertise their services for placing long-distance calls: "Calling with your card is easy," the ad stated. All you had to do was punch in forty-two digits.

All new technologies will have both positive and negative consequences regarding complexity. Our responsibility is to clearly understand this dynamic and then make day-to-day decisions regarding which consequence dominates. It is not enough to look only at how much the technological trend is helping. We must, more importantly, also understand how much it is hurting. No amount of trendiness or glitz should tempt us to accept complexity if it harms the all-important emotional, relational, and spiritual dimensions of life.

> ℞ *Even as your ambient life becomes ever more complicated, take pains to be sure your spiritual life does not. "Every age has its own characteristics," wrote A. W. Tozer. "Right now we are in an age of religious complexity. The simplicity which is in Christ is rarely found among us."*[67] *In truth, the gospel message is radically simple: God says, "I love you. I don't hold your sins against you. Won't you let me rescue you?"*

❦

Simplicity is the seal of truth.

LATIN PROVERB

# THE LAST SHALL BE FIRST

*Content makes poor men rich; Discontent makes rich men poor.*
BEN FRANKLIN

---

MRS. NGUYEN THI AN has lost everything . . . except her contentment. Her husband, a pastor in Vietnam, was thrown into prison when their church was closed. Without official papers, she and her children were forced to live on a balcony. Yet her faith has forged a sanctuary out of her surroundings, from which she greets us:

> My Dear Friends,
> You know around here we are experiencing hardships, but we thank the Lord He is comforting us and caring for us in every way. When we experience misfortune, adversity, distress, and hardship, only then do we see the real blessing of the Lord poured down on us in such a way that we cannot contain it.
>
> We have been obliged recently to leave our modest apartment and for over two months have been living on a balcony. The rain has been beating down and soaking us. Sometimes in the middle of the night we are forced to gather our blankets and run to seek refuge in a stairwell.
>
> Do you know what I do then? I laugh and I praise the Lord, because we can still take shelter in the stairwell. I think of how many people are experiencing

much worse hardships than I am. Then I remember the words of the Lord, "To the poor, O Lord, You are a refuge from the storm, a shadow from the heat"[68] and I am greatly comforted.

Our Father . . . is the One who according to the Scriptures does not break the bruised reed nor put out the flickering lamp. He is the One who looks after the orphan and the widow. He is the One who brings blessings and peace to numberless people. I do not know what words to use in order to describe the love that the Lord has shown our family. I only can bow my knee and my heart and offer to the Lord words of deepest thanks and praise. Although we have lost our house and our possessions, we have not lost the Lord, and He is enough. With the Lord I have everything. The only thing I would fear losing is His blessing!

Could I ask you and our friends in the churches abroad to continue to pray for me that I will faithfully follow the Lord and serve Him regardless of what the circumstances may be?

As far as my husband is concerned, I was able to visit him this past summer. We had a twenty-minute conversation that brought us great joy.

I greet you with my love. Mrs. Nguyen Thi An[69]

*R Only a few have mastered the freedom of contentment at the highest levels. Seek out someone of that caliber, such as this gentle woman, and use that person's life as a model of godliness.*

———∞∞∞———

God is the comfort of the poor.
GEORGIAN PROVERB

# NOT A MODERN INVENTION

*Blessed be the true, simple, and humble people,*
*for they shall have a great plenitude of peace.*

THOMAS À KEMPIS, FIFTEENTH-CENTURY ASCETIC WRITER

IN OUR COMPLICATED age, many contemporary thinkers are discussing and writing about the concept of a simple lifestyle. We encounter with regularity such phrases as "the plain life," "intermediate technology," "intentional communities," and "contrast culture." We are enamored with the Amish, wanting to tour their villages, eat their food, and bring home their quilts. Even the popular country look in home decorating has become, at least in part, a manifestation of the nostalgia many share about things simple and past. Glitz and gaudiness are out; fireplaces and rocking chairs are in.

Simplicity as a contemporary application is both attractive and timely. But it is certainly not a new concept. The spiritually minded have long sought it as a way of facilitating the contemplative life. The monastic orders and the Desert Fathers practiced simplicity, often including vows of poverty, extreme asceticism, and complete separation from the world.

Through the seventeenth and eighteenth centuries, many of those who traveled to the New World in search of religious freedom—from the Puritans to the Quakers—sought a simple, godly lifestyle. America of the nineteenth century also saw its simplicity movements. Perhaps the most lasting impressions were made by the Transcendentalists, a group who were in many ways spiritually motivated but not within the context of orthodox Christian doctrine. Two of their number, Ralph Waldo Emerson and Henry David Thoreau, were articulate prophets for this "plain living and high thinking," and their legacy continues to influence many today.

The modern era has witnessed such simplicity causes as the hippie communes and cultural dropouts. In addition, there has been significant activity within the church, although not always mainstream. From the International Consultation of Simple Life-Style to the Mennonite Central Committee, some in the church seek to find the posture of proper theological balance in an age of complexity and affluence.

In the rich and varied history of the simplicity movement, adherents have desired less stress and more joy, fewer distractions and more focus. For myself, I feel a spiritual affinity with simplicity for two reasons. First, it was the chosen lifestyle of Jesus, and second, Scripture commends it.

> *R Hebrews 12:1 admonishes us to "throw off everything that hinders." What hinders you from the pursuit of fundamental priorities? In what specific ways might you rid yourself of distractions that obscure your focus? Consider making one significant step in this direction—perhaps something that has kept you in debt, or cluttered your mind, or consumed too much time, or usurped energy and resources away from more essential priorities. Get rid of it, and then assess the results three months later. Remember: simplicity is about freedom, not about guilt. If you don't feel the freedom, then don't do it.*

---

He who wants what God wants of him will
lead a free and happy life.
JAPANESE PROVERB

# DIFFERENT PEOPLE, DIFFERENT STRESSORS

*Whoever wishes to live a quiet life should not have been born in the twentieth century.*

LEON TROTSKY, RUSSIAN REVOLUTIONARY

THERE IS A significant difference from person to person regarding how much stress is desirable or what type of events are stressful. A stressor that for one might be pleasure, for another might be pain. For one, the spice of life; for another, the kiss of death. Different stressors, different personalities, different results.

*Type A*—The type-A personality is commonly characterized as "driven." Type As have a drive to control others and a competitiveness characterized by a need to win. They think multiple thoughts and do multiple actions at the same time. They are very productive and usually the leaders of companies, programs, or institutions. They live on a high level of adrenaline, however, and often have significant health problems because of it.

*Introvert or extrovert*—The introvert is a personality type vulnerable to the stresses of the crowd. Introverts like to be alone. They appreciate quiet and time to think and feel in their own internal world. They generally do not like having a large number of social interactions, going to parties, or meeting new people. The majority of Americans (three to one), however, are extroverts, and extroverts are energized by such social exchange. Extroverts usually don't understand introverts and try to push them into situations where they simply don't wish to be.

*Depressed and anxious*—People with generalized depression or anxiety feel pressure from stressors that are inflated or sometimes not even there at all. They will be burdened much of their lives simply because they perceive stressors as more of a threat than they really are. And it is often our perception of the stressor that damages us more than the stressor itself.

*The elderly*—Some evidence indicates that mental stressors induce more tension in the elderly than in the young. Performing serial seven subtraction is only mildly stressful for those in their twenties. Many elderly, however, are hyper-responsive to such stimuli and become agitated in performing the task.

*Children*—Pediatricians, child psychologists, and developmental experts all believe that our current age is more stressful for children. Most adults agree. Social change is too rapid, competition is too stiff, and expectations are too high. Added to the host of already oppressive burdens are children's insecurities about family stability. Children today are "hurried"—exposed to more stressors at younger ages without the maturity necessary to process these stressors in a healthy manner.

> $R$ *Know yourself—then accept yourself. God made each of us differently, for a purpose. It is not only good that we are different from each other; it is very good. We each have our own unique personalities and our own various tolerances for stress and overload. Learn yours; then proceed accordingly.*

---

Eggs and metal should not be put in the same sack.
GHANIAN PROVERB

# EYES THAT SEE

*To simulate ten milliseconds of the complete processing of even a single nerve cell from the retina would require the solution of about 500 simultaneous nonlinear differential equations 100 times and would take at least several minutes of processing time on a Cray supercomputer. Keeping in mind that there are ten million or more such cells interacting with each other in complex ways, it would take a minimum of 100 years of Cray time to simulate what takes place in your eye many times every second.*

JOHN K. STEVENS, BIOMEDICAL ENGINEER

---

THE EYE, CLAIMS one influential neo-Darwinian theorist, "is stupidly designed." My first reaction upon reading his comment was frank laughter. If the *eye* doesn't impress a biologist, what will it take? The eye is, in fact, an organ of unprecedented sensitivity, precision, complexity, and beauty. If there is no wonder left in your spirit, perhaps the first clue of that lamentable state can be found in a careless disdain for the eye.

Light first encounters the cornea, the primary focusing structure. It then passes through the iris, which controls how much light is allowed to enter. Once through the cornea and iris/pupil, the light passes through the lens for additional focusing. Finally, the light projects onto the retina, a thin lining in the back of the eye. The retina is comprised of photoreceptor cells that are light sensitive, converting the image into electrical signals that can be interpreted by the brain. The eye takes pictures continuously and develops them instantaneously. Each eye has one million nerve fibers that electrically connect the photoreceptors in the retina to the visual cortex of the brain. In this center, comprising only one percent of the brain cortex, the image is reconstructed in such a way that we "see" it.

Vision functions within a wide spectrum of light availability. The dimmest conditions permitting sight vary from the brightest conditions by a factor of ten billion. On a clear, dark night we can see a small candle flame thirty miles away. The human eye can distinguish millions of shades of color.

The eyes are a window to the soul, and a very elegant window at that. By gazing into our eyes, other people can discern much about us. There is more involved here than cones, rods, and photons, even as life is more than physics.

*R̥ As an act of the will, determine to have eyes that see. We are all born with the same optics but that doesn't mean that we can all "see." Spiritual eyes are an entirely different piece of equipment. When Jesus came and walked among us, some saw Him and some didn't. They all had the same eyes, yet some were spiritually blind "ever seeing but never perceiving."[70] Eyes that see faith and truth provide a prevailing vision even in a dark and troubled world.*

---

A light is still a light — even though
the blind man cannot see it.

AUSTRIAN PROVERB

# DON'T CATASTROPHIZE INSOMNIA

*The best cure for insomnia is to get a lot of sleep.*
W. C. FIELDS

BEING WELL RESTED can augment our energy and facilitate our margin. Insomnia, however, is activity in the opposite direction. This universal and increasing problem complicates our quest for adequate sleep.

If insomnia strikes, don't panic. It happens to everybody from time to time, and one or two nights of sleeplessness does not constitute a crisis. What can become a crisis, however, is your reaction to the experience.

After one or two nights of sleeplessness, a pattern develops. Annoyance turns to fear, then fear turns to panic. And nothing retards sleep like panic. Trying to force yourself asleep is the surest way of preventing somnolence. "Sleep is one of the few things in life that cannot be improved upon by trying harder," explains sleep expert Dr. Peter Hauri.

If insomnia is a problem, don't stay in bed awake. Get up, sit in a comfortable chair or lie on the couch, read, write a letter, have a light snack, drink some milk, take a walk, soak in the bathtub, play relaxing music, watch television. But *don't worry*.

After a night or two of sleeplessness, a common mistake is to go to bed earlier the next night. The thinking is that hopefully nine hours in bed will result in at least seven hours of sleep. But this is the wrong tactic. It is actually more restful to stay in bed seven hours and get six hours of sleep than it is to stay in bed nine hours and get seven hours of sleep. Go to bed later, not earlier. As the problem resolves, you can gradually resume your normal sleep schedule.

Insomnia is sometimes a symptom of depression. The sleeplessness of depression is usually characterized by early awakening, instead of trouble going to sleep. For this condition, antidepressant medications can often be helpful. Such medicines are not sleeping pills, although they can have a beneficial sedative side effect; they are not narcotics, although they can help with chronic pain and its associated sleeplessness; and they are not addicting.

Even though there are occasional indications for sleeping pills, don't grow to depend on them. If you are undergoing a particularly stressful event in your life, sometimes a sleeping aid for a few days will keep sleepless exhaustion from compounding your troubles. But they are only effective for two weeks. After that time, attempting to continue them will result in a rebound insomnia.

℞ *If insomnia strikes, refuse to worry. Instead turn the night into a conversation with God. Pray. Meditate. Read the Word. Begin a spiritual journal. Listen to soothing radio. And don't forget to thank Him for the special opportunity of time together. When tiredness begins to overtake you, retire once again with gratitude for the double blessing of this night: that of fellowship and now that of sleep.*

---

Sleep faster—we need the pillows.

YIDDISH PROVERB

# NOURISHING OUR RELATIONSHIPS

*If we string ourselves out, expending one hundred percent of our time and energy, there is no way in which we can adjust to the unexpected emergency. If we drive ourselves to the point of saturation — and beyond — with professional, community, or social pursuits, we cannot possibly be in a sensitive covenant relationship with another person. . . . We become defensive about our expended energies because there isn't anything left to give. Having nothing in reserve, we tune out the need.*

LOUIS H. EVANS JR., PASTOR AND AUTHOR

---

STUDIES REVEAL THAT healthy relationships result in healthy lives. Having connections with others translates into less physical illness and better mental health. These relational connections, however, must be given room to grow. And in that regard at least, progress has been distinctly uncooperative. Our nanosecond lifestyles make relationships tenuous, and our marginless lifestyles are toxic to relational well-being.

Relationships do not just happen. If you go out into a garden and simply throw seeds on the top of the ground — no tilling, no planting of the seeds, no weeding, no watering, no fertilizing, no nurturing — then you will not have a crop to harvest. Relationships are just like the garden. They require nurturing if they are to grow, and this means the investment of time and energy. It is impossible to develop healthy, nurturing relationships in the absence of time and energy.

We cannot relate a few seconds a day and expect any kind

of quality outcome. It simply is not possible for a husband and wife to become close and to develop any kind of long-term intimacy unless there is some margin given to the relationship. It is not possible for us to be effective loving parents unless we spend time with our children.

Yet today people don't have time for their spouses and they don't have time for their children. And even if they did have time for their children, kids today have so many activities that often they aren't any more available than the parents are.

Likewise, friendships require margin to thrive. Neighborhoods, community, church, work—connections in each setting fare better when breathing the kind of relational oxygen that margin provides. And when we give of our time, energy, and resources for the strengthening of our relationships, they return the favor and give back health, happiness, and longevity.

℞ *Most relationships subsist on a chronic diet of leftovers. Instead adopt a pro-relational philosophy of life, making sure that the integrity of relationships is protected. Create discretionary time in your life for relationships. Create space in your calendar, your schedule, and your heart for the people God has given you.*

—⊂∞⊃—

Friendship is a plant we must often water.
GERMAN PROVERB

# THE PACE OF FAITH

*More mistakes are probably made by speed than by sloth, by
impatience than by dilatoriness. God's purposes often ripen
slowly. If the door is shut, don't put your shoulder to it.
Wait till Christ takes out the key and opens it.*

JOHN STOTT, BRITISH THEOLOGIAN

NOTHING AGAINST JOGGERS, but the Bible doesn't say anything about Jesus running. I know about the cultural context—it is hard to jog in a toga and sandals. But the issue is much more fundamental than a fashion limitation.

Have you ever noticed that Jesus never seemed in a hurry? There is no indication that He worked twenty-four-hour ministry days. Neither does He require it of us. In many ways, God is a demanding God. But what He demands is holiness, not exhaustion. The two are not the same.

The problem is that we are all running, but God is not running after us. He is just waiting, and waiting, and waiting. He knows that speed does not yield devotion. He sees that with all of our running, we are just opening an ever-greater distance between where we are and where He waits for us. I think I would not be far wrong if I were to postulate that our sense of the presence of God is in inverse proportion to the pace of our lives.

Apparently, Jesus believed that very little of lasting spiritual value happens in the presence of speed. Jesus understood that busyness, productivity, and efficiency are speed words, not kingdom words. At times they are appropriate values, but they are never transcendent. Jesus understood that rest is important. Jesus understood that meditation, wisdom, and worship are slow, mellow, and deep.

Jesus understood that loving other people in relationship is the central requirement of all eternity. He wasn't in a speed race: He was in a love race. And it is hard to love people when moving at the speed of light.

When we hurry inordinately through ministry we dishonor God by presuming that He can't adequately manage His own kingdom and thus requires our unsanctified perspiration to balance out His deficiency. With distracted speech, hollow eyes, and exhausted manner, we notch our Bibles with yet one more contact and somehow feel smugness rather than shame. The pace of faith is the pace of love, and that is still the living testimony of the gospel.

*R̸ Stop believing that chronic exhaustion is normal, that a listless spirit is inevitable, and that burnout is piety. In fact, a focused one-person-at-a-time rate of ministry is much more in line with the example of the Savior. It is good news in the extreme that we can return sovereignty back to the Almighty and resume our servant's role of simply loving the person He places in front of us.*

---

God did not create hurry.
FINNISH PROVERB

# TRAVEL IN THE RIGHT DIRECTION

*The sisters are always smiling and happy . . . we are so free. I
think people are so preoccupied with material difficulties. In the
industrial world where people are supposed to have so much, I find
that many people, while dressed up, are really, really poor.
By having nothing we will be able to give everything.*

MOTHER TERESA

MONEY IS UNIVERSAL. I see no way of escaping its touch.
We live in an economic context where earning money and
spending money occupies our daily thoughts. Having said
that, money ought never be in control. Money is a tool and a
servant but should never be in charge.

Yet if we are honest, money *is* in charge. How can we
change this situation? How can we reassert control of our
budget and spending so that financial margin again appears on
the horizon as an achievable destination?

When beginning a journey to a desired destination, it is
important to start on the right road headed in the right direction. In this case, our destination is restored financial margin.
Before beginning our trip, settling the issue of motive and orientation is a mandatory first step. Otherwise we find ourselves
headed off in the wrong direction and mired in a spiritual
morass that I want no part of. So, to clarify, we are not talking
about restoring financial margin for the purposes of pride, of
wealth, or of meeting our security needs in a way that bypasses

the Father. Instead we are talking about the kind of financial margin that is consistent with spiritual authenticity.

Which direction then do we travel? The choice of nearly the entire Western world is to travel in the direction of the economic road. We must realize, however, that the economic road is not and never has been the road Jesus called us to travel.

Economists and politicians of the past fifty years have honestly believed that economic advancement was the solution to the problems of humankind—a view shared nearly universally today. The conveniences I enjoy make me a beneficiary of such thinking. Yet if we are honest, we should admit that the economic road was never suggested to us by Christ. Prosperity might be a secondary consequence of our journey, but it is not to be a primary destination.

The economic answer is not the answer to our problems. Economics will solve some of our suffering but nothing more. Solving our suffering is not the goal of the Christian life; walking in righteousness is our goal.

*℞ To restore margin in finances, first put first things first. Early in life's journey make the fundamental decision that you will use money and you will prevent money from using you. Money makes a good tool but a lousy idol. Making the right choice will make all the difference.*

---

When money is not a servant it is a master.
INDIAN PROVERB

# REST FOR THE WEARY

*Those who are constantly weary are those who think they can always move forward with no pauses, that they can always endlessly achieve with no rests at the safe places.*

GORDON MACDONALD, PASTOR AND AUTHOR

THE PATIENTS WHO came to my office did not seem rested. For that matter, neither do most physicians. The medical residents I taught often were five minutes away from collapse. Many people I meet look haggard and worn out.

Common descriptors of our society include active, busy, driven, fatigued, tired, exhausted, weary, burned out, anxious, overloaded, and stressed. But seldom do you hear our society described as "well rested." We are a tired generation, one for which Matthew Arnold's "hurry sickness" has become a way of life. Our carburetors are running wide open, and our gears are stuck in overdrive. Our lives are nonstop. We have much leisure but little rest. The pace, the noise, the expectations, and the interruptions of modern life have not soothed the soul nor brought refreshment to the burdened spirit.

Having had the opportunity to practice medicine in several developing countries, I have noticed that the pace of life in such places is decidedly slower than ours. The people have much more time to visit with their neighbors, walk to town, or stop and leisurely observe children playing or donkeys braying. No one seems in a hurry. By so commenting, I am not suggesting their way of life is superior or preferable to ours. I am only making the observation that they are not exhausted, neither in body or spirit, whereas we often are. Those who would maintain that progress brings rest are wrong. Education, affluence, and technology have brought us leisure time and conveniences but not rest.

God, however, has commanded us to rest. A biblically authentic and balanced life will include time to be still, to remember, to meditate, to delight in who He is and what He has made. But a large obstacle stands in our way: there is no glory in rest. There is no societal acclaim, and we are never heroes because we rest. We can only be still and better wait upon the Lord. We can only meditate upon the Word more. We can only have more margin with which to serve our neighbor. These things, however, are not societally reimbursable.

"Come to me all you who are weary and burdened," said Jesus, "and I will give you rest."[71] Just because He said it two thousand years ago doesn't mean He didn't say it to you.

R Consider building or dedicating a small, quiet room in the house, a place for rest: a prayer room, chapel, meditation room, or reading room. Perhaps it might have super insulation plus sound-absorptive materials. Also it might have a small bed or comfortable chair and be equipped for quiet music.

⸙

How beautiful it is to do nothing,
and then rest afterward.
SPANISH PROVERB

# THE MARGIN OF A BOOK

*A good life, like a good book, should have a good margin. I hate*
*books whose pages are so crowded that you cannot handle them*
*without putting your thumbs on the type. And, in exactly the*
*same way, there are very few things more repelling than the feeling*
*that a man has no time for you. It may be a most excellent book:*
*but if it has no margin, I shall never grow fond of it. He may*
*be a most excellent man: but if he lacks leisure, restfulness,*
*poise, I shall never be able to love him.*

F. W. BOREHAM, AUSTRALIAN AUTHOR (1919)

---

FEW OF US begrudge a page its margin. If publishers tried to cram the print top-to-bottom and side-to-side, the result would be aesthetically displeasing, hard to comprehend, and probably even chaotic—like some of our lives.

Yet even if we agree that margin is a good idea, for most of us it seems an unaffordable luxury. We don't really desire to be overdrawn on our personal reserves. It's just that we can't seem to keep it from happening. Overbooking overpowers. There is so much to do and so much to buy. Troublingly, each succeeding year the problem only gets worse.

The effects of no margin are familiar to us all: people who are harried, more concerned with personal sanity than with service to the needs of others; people who have no financial margin, painfully uninterested in hearing of yet another "opportunity" to give. Such people are no longer concerned with building a better world. Instead they simply want to survive another day. Such people are no longer motivated to meet the needs of others. Instead they simply want to escape their suffocating schedules. Overworked and overwhelmed victims occupy our no-margined world.

Despite these obvious drawbacks to living without margin, our age consistently deprives us of it. We work hard to gain a foothold of freedom but are quickly pushed back into the quicksand. Overload just happens. Margin, in contrast, requires great effort. Positive margin status is what we call in science an "unstable state," one which spontaneously decays. Margin flows toward overload, but overload does not revert to margin unless forced.

Progress has had many overpriced ideas, but trading us burnout for margin was one of its most uncharitable.

℞ *Nobody can keep running on empty. Begin to develop the necessary theological and psychological underpinnings for margin that will allow you to accept its importance without guilt. For just as you need to eat and sleep, so you also need to breathe.*

———∞∞∞———

If the sailors become too numerous, the ship sinks.
ARABIAN PROVERB

# MUSIC

*I think I should have no other mortal wants, if I could always
have plenty of music. It seems to infuse strength into my limbs
and ideas into my brain. Life seems to go on without effort,
when I am filled with music.*

GEORGE ELIOT, ENGLISH NOVELIST

I SUSPECT GOD knew life was going to be difficult, so He
gave three free gifts to ease our way.

The first is *nature*. No matter where we turn our eyes, the
nature we see will have a lifting effect. And it is free. If we were
required to pay rent for sunsets, I doubt we'd be able to afford
even five minutes. Every sunset is unique. Nature is free, is
equally available to every person, and has a powerful healing
effect on the human spirit.

The second is *laughter*. We can't explain what it is, where it
comes from, or why it works. Yet as a balm for frazzled nerves,
laughter is unique. Laughter is free, is equally available to every
person, and has a powerful healing effect on the human spirit.

The third is *music*. Again we can't explain what it is, where
it comes from, or why it works. One person warbles her vocal
cords while another blows on his pipe—and somehow it
soothes. Music is free, is equally available to every person, and
has a powerful healing effect on the human spirit.

Seventy-five percent of Americans use music to de-stress. In
response to the increasingly wearying conditions of everyday

life, music therapists are emerging all across the nation. Studies reveal that surgeons who can choose their own music in the operating room have improved cardiovascular parameters during stressful surgeries. If, on the other hand, the music was chosen *for* them, there was no such benefit.

When God created music He somehow ordained that it would be able to penetrate through multiple layers of our consciousness and go straight to the depths of our spirit. It has been my own experience during times of significant stress that music has helped me when nothing else could. It sails right past all my defenses and snuggles up next to the pain.

Find the music that matches most precisely your need and play it over and over. Allow it to massage your soul.

*R Try going to bed with music rather than the news. Put a CD player on a bedside table, or perhaps use earphones with a long cord plugged into a table stereo or portable CD player. Send the children to bed with music—one special song upon retiring, after they have been tucked in. Try waking up to music, playing favorite songs during your shower.*

———❧———

Keep a green tree in your heart and the singing bird will come.

CHINESE PROVERB

# EXPONENTIAL E-MAIL

*The high-tech world of clocks and schedules, computers and programs, was supposed to free us from a life of toil and deprivation, yet with each passing day the human race becomes more enslaved, exploited, and victimized.*

JEREMY RIFKIN, AUTHOR ON TECHNOLOGICAL CHANGE

———————————

IN 1996, FOR the first time the volume of e-mail sent exceeded the total amount of regular mail delivered. E-mail is fast and cheap. In many ways, it's a guy's stationery. To write a letter, first we have to find paper, pen, envelope, stamp, and address. E-mail removes all such inconveniences.

Personally, as much as I dislike the phone, I like e-mail. In contrast to the phone, e-mail is not a demanding interruption. I can answer it at my leisure and convenience. Sometimes I do not answer it at all. But recently I was doing a radio interview in Florida. The guest from the previous day receives 1,800 e-mails a day. A man from California, after a week's vacation, had more than a thousand e-mail messages waiting for him. Another editorialist bemoans receiving 250 e-mails per day. Such is the world waiting for us all.

A ninth-grade girl from Mississippi conceived a science project to learn how fast information travels. Sending out an e-mail chain letter to 23 people, by the fourth day she received replies from 23 countries. On the twelfth day alone, she received 8,768 e-mails. Finally, on the twenty-third day she pulled the plug after having received 160,478 replies from 189 countries. For as little as one hundred dollars, a commercial junk-mail spammer can send 50 million e-mail messages.

Americans living abroad love e-mail . . . except when they hate it. "Sometimes I feel that all I do is answer the mail," complains a missionary from Mexico. "When I travel for a few days, it's not uncommon to come back and get as many as one hundred messages that have to be read and answered."

"One thing that bugs me is the short turnaround time churches expect," says another missionary. "I once received a three-page questionnaire to fill out with the request that I send it back within twenty-four hours for their missions conference. I received the e-mail at 5:15 P.M. Friday, and they wanted the information to compile on Saturday afternoon so they could use it on Sunday morning."

This is not to suggest that we should stop e-mailing our friends at home or abroad; mostly this new technology has been a stunning success. But as with everything else, we should be both discerning and sensitive.

> $R$ E-mail can be an efficient, effective tool to connect busy people with divergent schedules in scattered places. However, as with all accessing technology, it must be used with discretion. Once the daily total exceeds a critical volume, e-mail will quickly become onerous. When that volume is reached, intentionally take steps to control the flow so that e-mail remains functional rather than overwhelming.

—∞∞∞—

Words have no wings but they can fly a thousand miles.
KOREAN PROVERB

# THE JOYS OF READING

*I find television very educating. Every time somebody turns on the set I go into the other room and read a book.*

GROUCHO MARX, COMIC ACTOR

SOME PEOPLE ALWAYS seem to be deep into the middle of a book, while others readily admit they haven't read a word since their teachers required it. The vast majority in between, however, would enjoy reading but seldom find the time or opportunity. They are too busy to visit the library, too stressed to explore new titles, too indebted to spend ten or twenty dollars on a new volume. Thus their literary imagination languishes as they miss one of the best-kept secrets of stress relief.

For hectic people desperate to escape the frenzy of a crazy week, there is nothing like burying oneself in a gripping novel while relaxing in bed or soaking in the tub. Such a book is like an engrossing movie you can start and stop when you wish, but the mind's imagination is always superior to any movie set. As a book transports you away, the problems of a demanding day are left behind.

Nationally, over two billion new books are purchased each year. Buying used books is also an option, at used bookstores or library sales. What a thrill to find an out-of-print classic for a dollar or a recent twenty-dollar hardbound best-seller for three dollars. Linda has enjoyed searching for books by the British author Elizabeth Goudge, and we now are working toward completing our collection of her wonderful, otherwise unavailable works.

The library can also be an enjoyable place to visit—even for the entire family, but only if you start young enough. Our local library is nestled on the shores of a beautiful lake, with window seats facing out to the water. It is hard to imagine a better setting to come for a family outing.

Involve the entire family by having a regular or episodic family reading evening. Go through a book or series together, such as C. S. Lewis's *Chronicles of Narnia*. Or have each person read his or her own book but be together while doing it. Make it a special evening, with favorite food, snacks, soda, or juice. Create a warm, quiet, uninterrupted atmosphere. Announce it days in advance; don't spring it on the kids at the last minute.

Our children were "invested" readers—meaning we bribed them. Not paying an allowance, we instead paid a penny a page for reading books. When they wanted to make a special purchase, such as a bicycle, they would "read" for it.

*R Make friends of books. The cost is mere pennies per hour of fascinating fun. Select books and authors that interest you most. Build up your own library, collecting favorite authors. Install a reading light by your bed. Keep a selection of short inspirational readings there, a soothing conclusion to a trying day.*

---

A book holds a house of gold.

CHINESE PROVERB

# THE MYSTERY OF MEMORY

*In the practical use of our intellect, forgetting is as important a function as remembering. If we remembered everything, we should on most occasions be as ill off as if we remembered nothing.*

WILLIAM JAMES, PSYCHOLOGIST AND PHILOSOPHER

THE STUDY OF how memory works is still progressing, but some factors have been clarified:

*Memory is not necessarily a function of study or time.* The amount of effort we put into learning is not necessarily the most important thing. It turns out that meaning is as important to memory as intention.

*Short-term memory and long-term memory are two different commodities.* These two types of memory are apparently located in different places in the brain and etched by different mechanisms. Short-term memory is held for only a matter of minutes and can be maddeningly unreliable. Long-term memory, however, seems to result in a "memory trace" being etched in the brain structure.

*Emotional states and moods can greatly affect memory.* Something that was joyous or tragic seems to etch itself more clearly in the brain. Who doesn't remember what they were doing when JFK was shot?

*Visual images and linguistic memories are stored differently.* When we *hear* something, the memory goes down one pathway and is stored in a certain way. When we *see* something, the brain uses a different pathway and different storage venue. By the time we are thirty, each of us carries around with us a mental videotape containing some three trillion pictures and holograms of ourselves in action. Once those images are stored in the film archives of our brains, there is no delete button.

*Forgetting is as important as remembering.* As important as memory is for our day-to-day functioning, selective forgetting likewise is important for our day-to-day emotional health. Unfortunately, we have no volitional control over forgetting. When the ancient Greek Simonides offered to teach Themistocles the art of memory, he replied, "Teach me not the art of remembering but the art of forgetting, for I remember things I do not wish to remember, but I cannot forget things I wish to forget."

Forgetting is an important component of forgiveness. Would that we had such an ability, or that we even had the inclination toward such an ability. If someone has offended us, do we forgive and forget? "Love," the Scriptures teach, "keeps no record of wrongs."[72]

> $R$ Use the gift of memory for virtuous and eternal purposes, which also entails limiting exposure to sounds and images that might irreversibly imprint damaging memories. Much emotional stress often results from cascading memories we can't shut off. God gave us the gift of memory for many reasons, but chief among them is so that we might remember Him and His great deeds on our behalf. Such memory is the source of gratitude and comfort, even in our darkest hours.

---

God delays but doesn't forget.

# IN DEFENSE OF UNSTRUCTURED TIME

*If your tomorrow is not good it will only be because you have
robbed tomorrow for the sake of today.*

OLD KOREAN GENTLEMAN

TO UNDERSTAND HOW a society experiences time, examine its operative vocabulary. We talk of no time, lack of time,
not enough time, or out of time. Trying to get more time, we
borrow time only to incur a time debt and end up with even
less time. Managers in the workplace are so time conscious
that they practice time management skills and time compres-
sion techniques. They use computerized timepieces to ensure
work efforts are time intensive with no time lost. This sense of
time urgency creates time pressure and time stress.

If God would allow us to delete any of these time phrases
we thought destructive, which would you choose? If you had
the opportunity to set the time agenda for society, which concepts of time would you endorse and which would you
renounce? Many of our most energetic leaders would vote to
keep time linked to speed and productivity. A typical
manager's view of margin? If you can catch it, kill it.

The rest of us, however, would strike these time phrases
from our collective vocabulary as mortifying to the human
spirit. *Of course* work time is important. But so is discretionary
time, that is, margin. Some discretionary time would be used
as leisure time, playtime, free time, rest time, or time off. Some

would be personal time, solitude time, fallow time, and time to think. Hopefully, a good portion of it would be time together: sharing time, family time, couple time, prayer time.

You see, ideally our time should all be God's time, directed by Him and used for His purposes. If God were our appointment secretary, would He schedule us for every minute of every day? Well-meaning people might differ in their answers, but by now it must be obvious that I think the answer would be no. Many arguments could be made in defense of this view, but perhaps the strongest is the lifestyle that Christ Himself chose. Time urgency was not only absent, it was *conspicuously* absent. And I doubt its absence had solely to do with cultural context.

Christ's teaching, His healing, His serving, and His loving were usually spontaneous. The person standing in front of Him was the opportunity He accepted. If He largely chose spontaneous living, isn't that a signal to us? Overloaded and rigid schedules are not the way to walk "in His steps."

> ℞ *Plan for free time. This is not an apologetic for laziness and mediocrity but rather an awareness of the spiritual reality that all of life's meaning cannot be forced into an agenda. Our relationships, in particular, need a combination of scheduled time and unstructured hang-around time together.*

---

When a friend asks, there is no tomorrow.
SPANISH PROVERB

# YOUR BODY AS ALLY

*The real battle over starting to exercise takes place
in your mind, not in your body.*

DON R. POWELL, PH.D., PREVENTIVE MEDICINE AUTHOR

---

THE BODY IS a miracle of complexity and sophistication that exceeds comprehension. Fortunately, most of it runs on automatic pilot: the heart beats, the blood circulates, the glands secrete, the enzymes catalyze, the electrolytes balance, the glucose metabolizes, the liver detoxifies. Even our thinking and breathing are largely automatic and involuntary—functioning not because we tell them to but because God tells it to them.

God gave us an amazing gift, and all we are required to do is feed it, water it, rest it, and move it. Following are a few general suggestions on how to care for the body. Many more are found elsewhere in this book.

*Be realistic.* One of my patients with advanced lung cancer came in wearing a concerned look. "Doctor, I had my cholesterol tested and it is 221. Is that too high?" Three months later, her death had nothing to do with cholesterol. There are enough problems to worry about without adding nonproblems to the list.

*Focus on the important issues.* If you are forty pounds overweight, don't worry about how much vitamin C is in a potato.

*Choose appropriate exercises.* If you are elderly, it is probably best not to choose a running program. If you have arthritis or chronic low back pain, choose nonweightbearing exercises such as swimming or cycling.

*If dieting, aim for only one to two pounds a week.* Don't try to climb twenty stairs in a single bound. Slow changes are more sustainable.

*Be patient and persistent.* "How poor are they who have no patience!" wrote William Shakespeare. "What wound did ever heal but by degrees?"

*Distrust fads.* Fads, scams, and frauds have a therapeutic value "as thin as the homeopathic soup that was made by boiling the shadow of a pigeon that had been starved to death," to borrow from Abraham Lincoln. Remember, *all* diets work short term.

*Expect to have ups and downs.* Even the experts do. Set goals, but let them be reachable. Believe in yourself. I do.

Your body is prepared to be an important ally in the battle against stress and overload. If you treat it well, you will find energy you never knew existed. You will work better, feel better, heal better, and live better.

℞ *Give your body a chance. God has designed remarkable healing and restorative powers. No matter how infirm you are, there are still at least some steps that can be taken to restore function and vitality. Often the battle is won or lost in the mind. Don't waste time considering it. Begin today.*

---

Little by little one walks far.
PERUVIAN PROVERB

# REDEFINING HAPPINESS

*History books are filled with the names of supposedly wealthy*
*people who, upon closer inspection, turn out to have been*
*practically destitute in comparison to me. . . . You would think that*
*simply not having bubonic plague would be enough to put most of*
*us in a cheerful mood — but no, we want a hot tub, too. There is*
*really no such thing as a rising or falling standard of living. As the*
*centuries go by, people simply find different stuff to feel grumpy*
*about. Every improvement in one's own situation is negated by an*
*equal or greater improvement in someone else's. The easiest path to*
*happiness would be time travel. If I took everything I own right*
*now and moved it back 50 years, I would have it made.*

DAVID OWEN, COLUMNIST AND AUTHOR

---

"GRANDMA, I JUST found out what happiness is," said a four-year-old. "It's that feeling you have just after you buy something." Vicki Robin, co-author of *Your Money or Your Life*, overheard these words from a little girl shopping with her grandmother. How many of our children believe that same creed? Indeed, how many of us often share the same feeling?

There is a superficial form of temporary "happiness" that comes from buying and possessing. But true happiness comes from being loved and knowing truth. To convince our children of this reality will require more than preaching. It will require a lifestyle consistent with our definition. Such happiness is available to both the poor and the rich and has nothing to do with possessions.

In my office is a calligraphy Linda commissioned, containing a passage from Dickens' *Bleak House*. The words are the testimony of a virtuous woman who on the last page of the book marries the tenderhearted doctor. "We are not rich in the bank, but we have always prospered and have quite enough," says Esther.

> I never walk out with my husband, but I hear the people bless him. I never go into a house of any degree, but I hear his praises, or see them in grateful eyes. I never lie down at night, but I know that in the course of the day he has alleviated pain, and soothed some fellow-creature in the time of need. I know that from the beds of those who were past recovery, thanks have often, often gone up, in the last hour, for his patient ministration. Is not this to be rich?[73]

Simple words from a simple life. Who could wish for more? If we but valued what Esther valued, she would lead us from a life of envy and clutter into a life of freedom and service.

> ℞ *Anchor your life in the kind of wealth and happiness that survives poverty and prosperity, youth and age, earth and eternity. Such a wealth and happiness indeed exists, but it is not defined by purchasing and possessions.*

---

Happiness is like a field you can harvest every season.
KENYAN PROVERB

# HIGHLY PRODUCTIVE PEOPLE AND LIMITS

*All junior executives should know that if they work hard ten hours
a day, every day, they could be promoted to senior executives so
that they can work hard for fourteen hours a day.*

JOHN CAPOZZI, ENTREPRENEUR AND AUTHOR

---

SOME IN OUR midst are obviously wired for a higher level
of involvement, activity, and achievement than the rest of us.
They get by on less sleep, always seem to have energy to
spare, rise to the tops of organizations, and in general lead the
charge into the future. For purposes of simplification, let's
simply call them highly productive people (HPP)—those in
the top 10 percent of productivity. They have several specific
things to teach us about limits and overload, both positive
and negative.

*HPPs accomplish a great deal.* These extraordinary people
accomplish more before 9 A.M. than the rest of us do all
month. Much of our national success can be attributed to their
efforts.

*HPPs have a remarkable work ethic.* They have a special capacity for putting in long hours, staying focused, and still maintaining energy and passion.

*HPPs often have great vision.* Even in the midst of the smoke
and fire of overload that disable the efforts of others, HPPs can
see where they need to go and are determined to get there.
They have the vision of an eagle and the jaws of a pit bull.

*HPPs often lack good warning signals.* HPPs often find themselves at an even greater disadvantage than the rest of us in discerning the warning signals of overload. While others might be able to tell that something is wrong at 110 percent, HPPs might not realize they are seriously overloaded until they are at 140 percent. By that time, much damage has already been done.

*HPPs sometimes set up unrealistic standards for others.* Because achievement comes so easily to HPPs, they will often set the bar high and then kill themselves trying to live up to it. That may be okay for them, but often they will require this same level of unrealistic commitment from others.

Stoicism is a wonderful character quality. But so are kindness, gentleness, compassion, and humility. Margin will help blend both sides of the character spectrum.

> ℞ *Acknowledge limits not as a personal failure but as a gift from God. Learn to recognize warning signs in early stages. Envision, perhaps, God blowing a whistle in your ear, telling you to take a deep breath and slow down. Both your family and your future will thank you.*

Swallow only as much as will fit down your throat.
HUNGARIAN PROVERB

# HIGHLY SENSITIVE PEOPLE AND LIMITS

*Many of us are used to comparing ourselves with others. We
want someone else's energy level but we are unaware of our
own strengths and weaknesses. It takes time to find our level
of calmness. That level is the state of mind and body at
which we function best for the long haul.*

MIMI WILSON AND MARY BETH LAGERBORG, LIFESTYLE AND COOKING AUTHORS

ON THE OTHER end of the spectrum from the high-energy,
highly productive person (HPP) is the highly sensitive person
(HSP).[74] This is not to imply that they are unproductive, but
just that their personality structure is very different from the
HPP. We could say that HSPs are in the top 10 percent of sensitivity. They often find themselves chronically overwhelmed
by excessive sensory input.

*HSPs have antennae up for social discord or discomfort.* They can
feel the pain in the room. They can read the faces. Even with
subtle indicators they can tell when the social hierarchy is
being unkind. They are also particularly susceptible to the
insults and violence on television and in other media.

*HSPs sometimes seem antisocial.* Because they pay a price for
social interaction, they don't venture out as much. They might
be more socially isolated. It takes longer for them to heal. Their
batteries are discharged by all of this continuous and chronic
sensitivity vigilance. It does not mean that they are truly reclu-
sive but just that they are worn down by the requirement of
excessive sensitivity.

*HSPs often are creative.* They live in a world in their heads. They are good company for themselves on long car trips and don't mind solitude. They dream a lot. They don't try to control others' lives because they intuitively understand how complicated that process is.

*HSPs are more susceptible to overload.* They pay a higher emotional price for almost everything. It is like the world's loudspeaker is always on for them. They wear down more quickly. They must pay special heed to the words of this book.

These interesting people make a special contribution to the world but often at a greater emotional price than others. They give something that no one else can in quite the same way — sensitivity.

> ℞ *If you are an HSP, accept that your sensitivity is a gift but can also be a penalty. Sometimes it is necessary to ignore the sensory overload and keep going — reaching out, communicating, serving. Push past the inappropriate limits high sensitivity imposes, so you do not become a monastic hermit. On the other hand, don't often push beyond the appropriate boundaries you know so well; your reserves can be depleted with alarming suddenness. If you are not an HSP but know one, write that person a note of encouragement. It helps more than you know.*

---

The good are always prone to tears.

GREEK PROVERB

# SET POINTS AND LADDERS

*Those who have nothing, but wish they had, are damned with the rich. For God does not consider what we possess but what we covet.*

SAINT AUGUSTINE, FOURTH-CENTURY THEOLOGIAN

---

THE RELATIVISM OF contentment can be illustrated using the concept of a floating set point. This set point, which is somewhat different for each person, is positioned at that level where you are content. If your circumstances match this set point, you are temporarily satisfied. Once additional possibilities enter your awareness, however, your set point floats to a new level. Then you buy a bigger house, get a better-paying job, move south, or a multitude of other "improvements," and again you are temporarily satisfied.

This contentment set point is free to float upward without limitation. There is no ceiling, and we have not tried to establish one as a matter of public policy, let alone common sense. Instead we have fueled our economy by stimulating the set point to rise even faster than it normally would. While this set point is free-floating, it moves almost always in the upward direction. To see it fall voluntarily in an individual's life is a wondrous thing, almost miraculous; I might even say, suggestive of godliness.

Another erroneous measure of contentment is the prosperity ladder. Most of us look "up the ladder" and notice that the wealthy have more than we do. This, of course, strikes a near-fatal blow at one's contentment. If instead we reversed our gaze and looked down the ladder, our gratitude would thrive and opportunities for sharing would abound.

The pettiness of my own sources of discontent would be amusing were I not so repentant about them. I have been known to grumble when our house temperature drops to sixty degrees, yet there are untold millions in the world who do not have shelter. I have been known to complain if the day is rainy, yet a large segment of the world's land is shriveling up in drought. I have been known to groan if I miss my dinner, yet thousands who went to sleep tonight without food will not awaken tomorrow morning. Christ came to save me from sin— not from sixty degrees, rainy weather, and delayed dinners.

This relativism, where the grass is greener on your neighbor's lawn, can be remedied, but first it must be confessed.

> $R\!\!\!/$ *Quit staring at those who have more than you do. Override the set point by spiritual maturity, look down the ladder rather than up, and fix your contentment on godliness rather than relativism. Surround yourself with a community of like-minded friends rather than a society where envy has been normalized.*

---

What makes us discontented with our condition is the absurdly exaggerated idea we have of the happiness of others.

FRENCH PROVERB

# THE SURRENDERED REST

*Jesus calls us to His rest, and meekness is His method. The meek man cares not at all who is greater than he, for he has long ago decided the esteem of the world is not worth the effort.*

A. W. TOZER, THEOLOGIAN AND AUTHOR

WHEN OUR BODIES find rest, we feel refreshed. When our emotions find rest, our countenance is lifted. Yet relaxed muscles and minds are of little worth unless our souls also find rest in the acceptance of God. Such a rest transcends the problems of our world and shelters us where no injury can follow. His rest is ultimately the only dependable rest.

Sabbath rest is a rest He calls us to, but surrendered rest is a rest He offers to us. Sabbath rest we enter out of obedience; surrendered rest we enter out of our need. Sabbath rest arises from the good and perfect law of God; surrendered rest arises from the good and perfect grace of God. Sabbath rest is remembrance; surrendered rest is meekness.

"Come to me, all you who are weary and burdened, and I will give you rest," offered Jesus. "Take my yoke upon you and learn from me, for I am gentle and humble in heart, and you will find rest for your souls. For my yoke is easy and my burden is light."[75] These are attractive words to weary people everywhere. Yet, as usual, Jesus leaves us scratching our heads: What does He mean, to take His yoke? I'm not sure that sounds so restful.

The answer lies in meekness. In this passage Christ calls Himself meek. He came not to judge but to die. He came not to shout and defend the honor of the Father but to die. He came not to fight but to die. No persecution could disturb Him, for He came to suffer. Yet all the time He was suffering, He knew He was winning. We, too, can suffer and win. We can live with love even when others hate—all the time knowing that Love wins. We can respond with grace when others fight, knowing that Grace wins. When we come to Him and surrender, accepting His yoke, we accept full vulnerability to the onslaught of the world. Yet at the same time we are assured that *nothing* can separate us from the love of Christ. This rest is a self-weakening unto God-strength. It is a self-emptying unto God-fullness. It is the rest of full surrender.

Even when I feel inferior, even when I have been victimized, even when the pace and pressures of life bring me to the point of collapse, Christ brings me to His rest. When my surrender is completed and His yoke is accepted, then my soul will find rest.

*R Discover the rest and strength that come through meekness—a transcending through descending. Hint: You won't learn it at Harvard Business School.*

∞

God is always where we don't look for him.
RUSSIAN PROVERB

# YOUR BREATH IN HIS HAND

*For in the final analysis, our most basic common link is that we all inhabit this small planet, we all breathe the same air, we all cherish our children's futures, and we are all mortal.*

JOHN F. KENNEDY

EVERY BREATH WE take contains 150 million molecules that were breathed by Jesus.[76] The exact same air molecules. It is one of the many ways He shares life with us—intimately. Whenever we inhale, Jesus is there with us sharing Himself minute-by-minute and molecule-by-molecule. Daniel spoke of the God who holds in His hand your breath.[77]

We breathe about 23,000 times per day and 630 million times over an average lifespan. With each inhalation we breathe in $10^{22}$ molecules, more than a billion trillion with each lungful.

Once the air is in the lungs, the next step is to get it into the bloodstream. The lungs first divide the breath into smaller portions and send each down a series of dividing wind tunnels. Finally, the air arrives in different peripheral "rooms" where each molecule of oxygen can receive individual attention.

These rooms, called alveoli, are actually tiny air sacks. Perhaps you can picture them like bubbles, miniature balloons, or clusters of hollow grapes. The average diameter of these alveoli is only twice the thickness of paper. Overall we have about three hundred million such alveoli, greatly increasing the surface area available for the oxygen to come into contact with. If you were to spread out all the alveolar surface and lay it down on the floor, it would equal half the size of a tennis court.

With the inhaled oxygen now closely approximated to the lining of the alveoli, the red blood cells and hemoglobin within the capillaries can attract the oxygen across the thin membrane and begin transporting it to the various cells.

With increased exercise the muscles need more oxygen. Under strenuous conditions, the muscle demand for oxygen may increase as much as ten fold—a demand the pulmonary system can meet because of a huge built-in physiologic margin in our respiratory function.

Once again God has pulled off another display of His creative genius. All He asks in return is "Let everything that has breath praise the Lord."[78]

> ℞ *Inhaling slowly, take a deep breath as you count to eight. Now, hold it for another eight seconds. Then exhale very slowly for the count of eight. This simple breathing exercise is low-tech but highly effective. It forces you to slow the hurry for a brief time and to think about breathing instead of stress. The therapeutic result is a temporary but beneficial melting of tension and mellowing of mood.*

---

He who allows his day to pass by without practicing generosity and enjoying life's pleasures is like a blacksmith's bellows: he breathes but does not live.

INDIAN PROVERB

# MAKING SPACE FOR LOVE

*One word frees us of all the weight and pain of life: That word is love.*
SOPHOCLES, ANCIENT GREEK PLAYWRIGHT

---

PAIN SURROUNDS US all. Much of this pain comes from progress's blatant disregard for our need of margin. And much of this pain—far too much of this pain—is because of neglected and broken relationships. It is difficult to be healthy in a society where relational, emotional, and spiritual sickness is endemic. If you live in a swamp, malaria has a head start.

But do you know what? Malaria can be treated, and so can pain. Margin can be restored. Broken relationships can be healed. It takes work. It takes time. It takes energy. It takes love. It might even take going to the Cross. But healing is worth it. I have never seen a truly healthy person who didn't derive that well-being from the benefits of intact, loving relationships.

As we subjugate progress, we make it subservient to our greater goals and needs, especially relationships. We once again practice economics "as if people mattered." We once again agree that things do not own us and are not even very important. We once again assert that jobs are only jobs, that cars are only organized piles of metal, that houses will one day fall down, but that people are important beyond description. We once again assert that Love stands supreme above *all* other forces, even to the ends of the universe and beyond.

Are you ready to commit to relationships in love? This is

not like asking, "Would you go to the store for some milk?" but more like "Are you ready to lay down your life for your friends?"[79]

If you are, then do everything you can to travel in the health direction. If stress crushes your spirit by poisoning you with despair, then either conquer stress or walk away—but don't stop relating. If overload destroys your relationships, then dispatch overload to the far side. If that malignant, universal enemy of relational health—marginless living—leaves you panting for air and desperate for space, then go and take margin back. Hack it out of your cultural landscape. And guard it for the sake of your God, yourself, your family, and your friends.

Health cannot be far behind.

R℣ *Love one another. Stop right there. Don't go any further until you get that right. If that is not right, nothing else will be either.*

---

A life without love is like a year without summer.
SWEDISH PROVERB

# SHARE, LOAN, AND BORROW

*Man should not consider his outward possessions as his own,*
*but as common to all, so as to share them without*
*hesitation when others are in need.*

THOMAS AQUINAS, THIRTEENTH-CENTURY THEOLOGIAN

---

PART OF THE reason we have the love affair with shopping and consumerism is that we think we need to personally own everything we use. Such an attitude is not only practically untrue but also fiscally unwise and relationally inauthentic.

We need to develop a new *depreciation* of things and a new *appreciation* of people. Things are to be used, and people are to be served. To refuse others access to our possessions places more importance on the thing than on the person. It is a common error in our society, and one that particularly dishonors God. He feels our neighbors are so valuable that He sent His Son to die for them. But we think so little of our neighbors that we won't let them use our lawn mower. These attitudes are literally an eternity apart.

When I brought my chain saw in for repairs several years ago, the attendant offered his philosophy on lending: "Never loan out your chain saw. Other people don't take care of it." While understanding why he made this statement, I beg to differ. I haven't seen my chain saw now for the last twelve months, and I'm not worried a bit. As a matter of fact, I can't think of anything I own that I wouldn't be willing for another person to borrow. Of course I have an advantage in not owning expensive things, making me all the more willing to loan them out. If we are willing to share our possessions, then others will not need to purchase similar items and will therefore have more financial margin.

The idea of owning some things in common is both practical and biblical. Why should each family own its own canoe, Rototiller, and power tools? When we share graciously the things God has given us, the blessing flows to others. It helps contain the clutter, ease the debt burden, and build community.

*R̶ Hold your possessions lightly. Consider developing a borrowing network within your church or neighborhood where you share tents and camping equipment, fishing gear, books, CDs, video cameras, garden tools, ladders, power tools, chain saws, log splitters, heavy-duty kitchen mixers, canning equipment, food dehydrators . . . possibly even a second car, old pickup truck, fishing boat, or riding lawn mower. It goes without saying that we must concurrently develop accountability systems to guarantee responsible behavior by all. Such an approach to sharing will connect us to others and, at the same time, guard our financial margin. "If our goods are not available to the community," said Martin Luther, "they are stolen goods."*

---

When you have given nothing, ask for nothing.
<small>ALBANIAN PROVERB</small>

# PRUNING LIFE

*I view my life as a tree. . . . Even without special care, activity branches multiply. Soon the profusion of branches becomes more prominent than the trunk and limbs. When this happens, I feel trapped, frustrated, and empty. Why? Because my life is shaped and drained by activities that have lost their pertinence to Christ.*

JEAN FLEMING, AUTHOR AND INTERNATIONAL SPEAKER

---

EVERY YEAR THE fruit trees in our front yard sprout new branches without even being asked. It seems logical to think that these branches would increase the yield of the trees. However, such is not the case. Counterintuitively, it is only when I actively prune away unnecessary growth that the trees flourish.

In the same way, every year our lives sprout new "activity branches" without our intending it. There are always new meetings, committees, concerts, lectures, plays, parties, musicals, dinners, and sporting events that add themselves to our lives—sometimes with our permission and awareness, other times without.

Not only do new activity branches appear regularly, but old activity branches are allowed to remain, unexamined. Activities, commitments, duties, obligations—all good things, by the way—often are self-perpetuating. It is much harder to stop something than to start it.

According to time-management author Robert Banks, all

activities "should come up for periodic review and be required to justify their continued existence."[80] It is important to regularly take a critical look at life with the express intention to prune. Mark your calendar, get out the clippers, and prune on schedule.

An important question presents itself: what ought we to prune and what ought to remain? When pruning, be careful to cut only the right things. As activity and commitment overload winds us up and wears us down, often we suffer a temporary loss of interest in long-term values. Impulsively, we start pruning the first things in sight—even when they pertain to our faith and relationships.

> R̸ *Do some surgery. Prune away. Don't cringe—God is a great physician, and it is good to be pruned. Be careful, however, to prune according to eternal priorities rather than temporal pressures.*

───── ⟨⟨⟨⟩ ─────

It is foolhardy to climb two trees at once
just because one has two feet.
ETHIOPIAN PROVERB

# TYPE-A BEHAVIOR AND STRESS

*I don't get ulcers. I give them.*
REAL ESTATE TYCOON

---

SOME IN OUR midst—usually our leaders—grow quickly impatient with all this stress talk and would instead challenge the weak to quit all the whining and get with the program. They love stress and seem to thrive on marginless living. They eat, breathe, and sleep adrenaline. Productivity is the goal, not living. Margin is not a priority to preserve but a gap to be filled.

This type-A personality, usually male, is often characterized as *driven*. Type A's have a drive to control others and an aggressiveness and competitiveness characterized by a need to win. The driven live on the edge and wouldn't have it any other way.

These hardworking, time-pressured individuals have their carburetors wide open and surge into overdrive at the slightest provocation. Their most common traits are a sense of time urgency and free-floating hostility, with the hostility trait causing premature cardiovascular disease. To be fair, every person has a temper; it is only a matter of how deep you have to dig to find it. Because of the way they are wired, the type A's temper is closer to the surface than most other people and thus triggered at a lower threshold.

Most people find a vacation relaxing, but type A's often do not. Relaxing is one of the most stressful things on their agenda, which is why they seldom do it. Progress and type A's feed on each other.

Type A's refuse to rest; to them rest is an enemy. Also, those around them are made to feel weak if they desire a pause. Consequently, life is lived full speed ahead. They work hard, they play hard, and they even Sabbath hard.

Yet even these racehorses have their limits, as they will eventually learn. And when they do, they should not underestimate the stress-reducing value of taking a dose of margin against the pain.

In the New Testament, Paul and Peter were clearly type A—and God used them both mightily. The secret: they bowed the knee. When God saw their humility, He rewarded them with effectiveness.

> ℞ *Stand in line, advises cardiologist Dr. Meyer Friedman, one of the first to describe the type-A personality. Practice smiling. Purposely speak more slowly. Stop in the middle of some sentences, hesitate for three seconds, then continue. Purposely say "I'm wrong" at least twice today, even if you're not sure you're wrong. Listen to at least two persons today without interrupting even once. Seek out the longest line at the bank. Verbalize your affection to your spouse and children. Trash the extraneous. Cut out some of the committees, perhaps all. Give yourself a lunch break—out of the office. Browse in a bookstore, sit in a deserted church, go to a museum.*[81]

---

However early you get up you cannot hasten the dawn.
SPANISH PROVERB

# THE STRANGE IMPROPRIETIES OF SPEED

*The trouble with being punctual is that
nobody's there to appreciate it.*

FRANKLIN P. JONES, AMERICAN BUSINESSMAN

---

SPEED. SOME FIND it exhilarating, others exhausting. Some find it addicting, others aggravating. Whatever your opinion of pace, the effects of speed often lead to bizarre anomalies.

A Purdue engineer who grew tired of waiting for his charcoal briquettes to catch fire decided to add pure oxygen. It worked so well, he next decided to pump in liquid oxygen, the kind they use in booster rockets. It burned up the steaks, the briquettes, and the grill in three seconds. "It was bright," he said. "You didn't want to look at it."

In 2000, renowned Sherpa mountaineer Babu Chhiri climbed Mount Everest in sixteen hours and fifty-six minutes, establishing a new world record. One year later, on the same slopes, he fell into a hundred-foot crevasse and died. Maybe climbing Mount Everest isn't a speed event.

After completing a speed-reading course, Woody Allen read *War and Peace* in twenty minutes. Later, when asked to discuss the plot, he said, "It was about Russia and fighting."

Until 1999, Montana was noted for its daytime speed limit of "Reasonable and Prudent." After the State Patrol clocked one car at 152 miles per hour, however, the speed limit was changed to 70.

Turbo dating services—with names such as SpeedDating, 8minute-Dating, Nanodate, 10-Minute-Match, Hurry Date, and Brief Encounters—have sprung up across the nation and even the world. With SpeedDating, for example, the twenty-five-dollar entrance fee buys you seven dates, each lasting seven minutes. "Hi." "What's your name?" "Are you the love of my life?"

For some the manic level of activity fueled by the speed phenomenon is exactly the goal, reminiscent of Henry Ward Beecher's ideal state of mind in which a person is "so busy that he does not know whether he is or is not happy." Many of us, however, prefer life in a slower lane. After all, we are attempting to follow a different Leader with different values down a different road for a different reason in hopes of a different result.

*R Slow down. Stop hurrying. If you avoid hurry, you will make fewer mistakes and actually finish sooner. Discover the pace of faith, where work is productive, relationships prosper, and your spirit is at peace.*

---

Haste is good only for catching flies.
RUSSIAN PROVERB

# THE STRAW THAT BROKE THE CAMEL'S BACK

*There is a measure in everything. There are fixed limits beyond which and short of which right cannot find a resting place.*

HORACE, ROMAN POET

---

CAMELS MAKE GREAT beasts of burden. In hot weather, a camel can carry 350 pounds on a long journey. On shorter journeys in cooler weather (or in order to avoid customs duties), an animal can be loaded to 1000 pounds. But once a camel is maximally loaded down, a mere straw will break its back. The problem is not with *load*. Camels love to carry loads. The problem is with *over*. As it turns out, camels aren't too crazy about broken backs.

While speaking in Ecuador about overload and margin, I used the straw-that-broke-the-camel's-back illustration, only to discover they did not know about camels. I asked if there was a similar story in their culture. "Use the example of the llama," they said. "When loading a llama, as soon as you put one pound heavier than they can carry, they sit down and refuse to budge. Only when the load is lightened will they agree to continue the journey." Again the problem is not with load but with *over*.

Sled dogs are not afraid of work. They love nothing better than being hitched to the sled and pulling. But it is possible for them to pull so vigorously for so long that they die in the harness. Understanding this, officials for the 1,150-mile Alaskan Iditarod race mandated specific rest periods for the dogs. Still, over one hundred dogs have died.

Belgian workhorses are strong, hardy, and beautiful. These magnificent draft animals love their work, whether plowing a field or pulling a sleigh. Harnessed up with their shoulders to the load is a highlight of their existence. But is it possible to ask such capable horses to pull a load one hundred pounds too heavy on a day ten degrees too hot over a distance one mile too far at a speed that is unsustainable? Of course it is. They would not survive.

Notice, in each instance, load was not to blame. Load is good. Load is normal. Load is God-ordained. Load is essential for a happy life. Load is something to celebrate.

The problem is with *over*.

R Challenge yourself with my blessing—and God's. Just remember that the loathsome straw is not a fairy tale but instead a punishing reminder of our mortality. Mark your boundaries carefully.

———— ∞ ————

"Mr. Camel," asked the nomad, "may I add one more bag of grain to the five already on your back?" "Go ahead," said the camel. "I'm not getting up anyway."

AFGHAN PROVERB

# FOLLOW THE LEADER

*With glorious indifference to position, status, and possession, we can say no to the ridiculous pace that demands we accumulate more. We are committed. We have a focus, and his name is Jesus.*

BARBARA DEGROTE-SORENSEN AND DAVID ALLEN SORENSEN, SIMPLICITY AUTHORS

---

IS SIMPLICITY A fad? Will it fade in significance as did the hippie communes, or is it destined to grow in importance? Our age is ever becoming more complex and diffusely overloaded. For that reason, if for no other, simplicity is a movement whose time has come. Something approximating simple lifestyles will only continue to increase in importance as people downshift and look for the margin off-ramp.

The notion of stepping off the treadmill would sound attractive even if I were not a Christian. Yet for adherents of Christianity, there is even a stronger pull that motivates: to be a follower of Christ means we should *follow* Him. No one lived a simpler, more unencumbered life than He. His birth was in spartan conditions, and His life was free from the ties of possessions or money. He was born with nothing, lived with little, and died with nothing. His simplicity was not an accidental and unavoidable complication of cultural context. Jesus could have chosen any standard, yet He chose to live simply.

The stable was a simple place, Mary was a simple girl, the shepherds were simple witnesses, and the Savior was a simple baby. But don't for a moment believe that *simple* is a synonym for weak, dreary, or unimportant. In fact, God took the simplicity of that day and used it to turn the world around.

In the Sermon on the Mount, Christ told us not to worry even about food and clothing and not to worry about tomorrow. That He did not seek luxury is a statement to us who follow Him. When He demonstrated servitude by washing the feet of His disciples, He explained: "I have set you an example that you should do as I have done for you. . . . No servant is greater than his master."[82]

Peter instructs us to walk after the example of Christ in enduring suffering.[83] Paul teaches us to follow after Jesus' example of humility.[84] "Does the Bible infer that we are to live like a king or like the King?" asks the Reverend Tom Allen. "The simplicity, sacrifice and servanthood of Jesus Christ should be our way of life, too."[85]

*R Wear a WWJD bracelet, and this time take it seriously. Without cultural bias, imagine how Jesus would have conducted Himself in any given situation, and follow that model. Cultural norms will not help.*

—◦◦◦—

You can't claim heaven as your own
if you are just going to sit under it.
CAMBODIAN PROVERB

# FINDING THE PAUSE BUTTON

*Busyness is the enemy of spirituality. It is essentially laziness.
It is doing the easy thing instead of the hard thing. It is filling
our time with our own actions instead of paying attention
to God's actions. It is taking charge.*

EUGENE PETERSON, PASTOR AND AUTHOR

---

WE OFTEN TEND to equate the will of God with busyness. The busier we are, the more (we think) God likes it. But God is actually interested in both sides of the equation: our busyness, yes. But also our rest. Rest is both commended and commanded by God. We might even say that God is a pro-rest God.

The extreme imbalance we live under today is a fairly modern development. Augustine talked of the active life and the contemplative life. While both had an important role to play, the contemplative life—being the domain of reflection, meditation, and prayer—was considered of greater value.

In fact, God created both activity and rest. It is an essential cycle now so distantly lost it seems only historians and archeologists can dig up the memory. From a missionary who served in East Africa decades ago comes a correcting perspective: "I think back to the nine years our family enjoyed on the lower slopes of the Kilimanjaro," reminisces Mildred Tengbom. "There, while our work was sometimes tense, the pace surely resembled more a walk than a run. There were plenty of green trees to sit under and a conscience that allowed us to sit down under them. We weren't constantly being told that our value depended on how 'active' or 'involved' we were."[86]

Busyness itself is not its own reward. There is no direct correlation between busyness and fruit. I am *not* opposed to being busy. But I *am* opposed to being inappropriately busy, just as I am opposed to being chronically overloaded. When we are overly busy and overloaded, our joy, our health, and our relationships pay the price.

*R**x** Repent of the pride of busyness. We are in constant motion, thinking that the busier we appear, the greater the respect afforded us. While the person sitting on a lawn swing is scorned, the speed-of-light jet jockey is venerated. There is a trap here, and pride is its name. Before we can slow down and allow God to set things right in our hearts, we have some confessing to do. It is not busyness that we should honor in our midst, but love.*

---

The devil takes a hand in what is done in haste.
KURDISH PROVERB

# McStay at Home

*Never eat more than you can lift.*
Miss Piggy

---

TECHNOLOGY NOW EXISTS to measure the percentage of body fat in sophisticated ways. One such machine was brought to our clinic for a conference on nutrition and I volunteered to be tested. As they entered data into the computer, I was electronically connected and laid on a special mat. The machine calculated that I weighed twenty thousand pounds and was 99.9999 percent fat. It was funny until I felt myself jiggling when I laughed.

Obesity, or the "rounding of America," is such a ubiquitous problem that one-fourth to one-half of adults are on a diet at any given time. The list of best-sellers always has at least two or three dieting books. One in five Americans is obese, defined as 20 percent above ideal body weight. What can't be dieted off is surgically removed. The incidence of childhood obesity has risen dramatically in the past two decades. All in all, far more Americans die of too much food than too little.

The typical American diet derives 34 percent of its calories from fats. This percentage should drop to 30 percent or below, which means we need to cut a couple hundred calories of fat out of our diet each day. (A hamburger and French fries contain about two hundred calories of fat, while a slice of cherry pie a la mode contains about three hundred calories of fat.)

Of course we all know we should eat less fat, but we eat it anyway. There are three main reasons: it tastes good, it is our habit, and we can afford to. In rebuttal: there are other things that taste good; we can change our bad habits; and we can't afford not to. Pastries, donuts, ice cream, butter, hamburgers, French fries, steak, gravy — they all sound good, but they are all dense in calories. Our margin in physical energy disappears as our waistlines expand.

Good nutrition begins not in the kitchen but at the front door of the grocery store. If it isn't good for you, don't buy it. If it all looks too good, then shop only after a big meal when things don't look nearly as appetizing. If you still can't help yourself, try shopping at a co-op that doesn't carry junk food. If that still doesn't work, send someone else.

℞ McStay at home. Americans spend well over one billion dollars a day eating out. There is often no comparison between the calories, fat, and sodium we consume when we prepare food at home versus eating out. For some, the difference between normal weight and overweight is the difference between eating in and eating out.

---◦◦◦---

How can one start a fast with baklava in one's hand?
ARMENIAN PROVERB

# SOVEREIGNTY AND THE
# REST OF OUR LIVES

*Most of us believe God can move mountains. But how many of us
believe He will? There's a world of difference. We believe God can
work mightily on our behalf, but we really aren't sure He will.*

RUSS JOHNSTON, AUTHOR

---

SCIENCE HAS MUCH to teach us about the power and precision of God. Scripture points in the same direction. Both
reveal that God's strength is impressive, His wisdom is unfathomable, His rule is sovereign.

The discoveries of science and the truths of Scripture
should combine to lift us heavenward. Yet we remain strangely
anxious. Our days are swamped by stress; our nights are swal-
lowed by insomnia. Seldom do we know true restedness. Yet
God would tell us, "Be still before me; wait patiently. Trust in
me, and I will give you rest."

We know that God is out there, that He sees and cares.
But we are still tempted to run our lives independently, often
consulting Him only for crises or trivialities. Yet God would
tell us, "Don't you know that I care more about you than a hundred billion galaxies? That I work in your life on a thousand
levels all at the same time?"

We have heard that God is strong, but perhaps have trouble believing that His strength extends all the way to *our* problems. Yet God would tell us, "I hold together the universe, and

that includes your life as well. If you only knew . . . "

The Almighty has sufficiently demonstrated His creative greatness in both the Scriptures and science. And He has sufficiently demonstrated His caring intimacy in both the life and the sacrifice of Christ. The problem is not a deficiency on God's part but rather a dimness on ours. "Spirit of God descend upon my heart . . . take the dimness of my soul away."[87]

Only when we have been delivered from our dimness will we rest under a full awareness of His dominion. "Now we see but a poor reflection," wrote the apostle Paul. "Then we shall see face to face. Now I know in part; then I shall know fully, even as I am fully known."[88] As we see more clearly, as the "glass darkly" lightens, our understanding of the greatness of God deepens. And with it, our faith.

In the end, sovereignty wins. In the end, glory will be unrestrained. Finally, at long last, God will deliver us from our dimness. And in the shelter of the Most High, we will enter our rest.

*R Study to master the specifics of God's power. Meditate on the particulars of His intimacy. Strive to understand His precision displayed in the created order. And pray that God would reveal Himself on a more profound level and thus deepen your faith. "Oh," said Watchman Nee, "that we might learn the undefeatedness of God!" "Find rest, O my soul, in God alone" said David. "He is my fortress."[89]*

———— ❧ ————

Where God has sown it shall flourish.
ROMANIAN PROVERB

# I CAN DO ALL THINGS?

*We give our family and ourselves an incredible gift when we make the decision to live within God's limits. It opens the door to genuine rest in our lives.*

TIM KIMMEL, FAMILY ADVOCATE AND AUTHOR

ARE SPIRITUALLY MINDED people equipped with a stress exemption? Do they ever burn out? These might sound like heretical questions. Nevertheless, the issue is important to consider, because if we answer the question wrongly—in either direction—there will be significant consequences.

Many people with great faith assume that God gives them a special exemption to stress, overload, and burnout. It therefore comes as a great surprise when they, too, hit the wall. *How could this happen to me? I must not have had enough faith.*

Disillusionment sets in. Then discouragement. They stop ministering. They have no permission to tell others of the pain. What to do? Unfortunately, they sometimes find themselves trapped in a system that provides no comfort—only judgment.

Overload, like influenza, is a nonsectarian pathogen; everyone gets a part of this pain. It strikes indiscriminately. Believers and unbelievers alike experience overload, just as they both experience the flu when it comes to town. Christians have the same limits and susceptibilities as everyone else.

Philippians 4:13 is a wonderful verse, where Paul writes, "I can do all things in [Christ] who strengthens me" (RSV). Can you? Can you fly? Can you go six months without eating . . . or sleeping? Neither can you live a healthy life chronically overloaded. God did not intend this verse to represent a negation of life balance. Jesus did not work twenty-hour ministry days, and He did not fix every problem in Israel. Daily He simply loved the person standing in front of Him.

Philippians 4:13 is completely true. But we need to re-understand it, cleansed from our modern presumptive bias that God is suspending human limits on our behalf. We cannot do "all things," but we can do everything the Father has ordained for us, in the strength that Christ provides.

As it turns out, salvation solves the lostness problem—and that is of incalculable value. But it does little to solve the overload problem. This is not to say we don't have deep spiritual resources that are of immense value. But in some ways we also have a heightened sensitivity to the pain and brokenness of the world around us. And that often hurts unbearably.

God had His reasons for not delivering us from this type of pain. It is best to trust His heart in the matter.

> *R̵ Spend some time reflecting on Philippians 4:13 until you can fully appropriate its riches for your life—not that you have an infinite capacity to do "all things," but instead that in the strength that Christ provides, you can do "all things" handpicked by the will of the Father for your life.*

———⚬⚬⚬———

Every disadvantage has its advantage.
UKRANIAN PROVERB

# COUNTERING CULTURE

*Since we are never entirely free, since we always depend upon someone or something, it is certainly by dependence upon God that we have the means of knowing the greatest possible freedom.*

PAUL TOURNIER, SWISS PSYCHIATRIST

ALTHOUGH FREEDOM IS the cornerstone of our national pride, most of us are not free. Instead we find ourselves chained to scores of societal influences. Culture, as it turns out, has one hand around our throat and the other around our wallet.

The way of the world is not a benign force but instead a dictator that tells us how much education we should have, what kind of job we should seek, what kind of house, car, and clothes we should buy, who is "beautiful" and who isn't. It is rare to meet a person who isn't owned, bound, or trapped by a multitude of such controlling cultural forces. If we remain controlled by such a culture we will have little chance of achieving margin, freedom, or spiritual authenticity. Many cultural expectations wither under the scrutiny of Scripture, yet we willingly subject ourselves to their control.

To counter these dominant cultural values, the church needs to become a counterculture. There is, however, a societal price to be paid for such an action, oftentimes wearing the face of condescension and scorn. But our goal in life is not necessarily respectability. This doesn't mean we seek to be disreputable but only that we willingly accept the disapproval of others if righteous behavior requires it.

God tells us we cannot be conformed to the world and be free at the same time. "Do not conform any longer to the pattern of this world," declared Paul, "but be transformed by the renewing of your mind. Then you will be able to test and approve what God's will is—his good, pleasing, and perfect will."[90]

In other words, Christians who desire freedom must become a "contrast society." This does not mean we drop out but simply that we refuse societal servitude. Our obedience is not to cultural domination but rather to Christ.

Willingly and knowingly we wrestle control from culture and set our orientation in the opposite direction. It is wonderful if a community of believers can support one another in making such countercultural decisions. The more different we are from the ambient culture, the more we need to be surrounded by a group of like-minded people who will support our value structure.

> ℞ *Don't let the expectational norm escalate on your watch. Hold the line. It will not be easy. It helps to have support from like-minded people. Your children will push against it, but in the long run, they will be benefited by a sense of frugality and stability. Control your schedule, your pace, your expectations, and your debt. Stop using the language of the victim. Own your own decisions. Guard your freedom, never relinquishing it except to the kingdom.*

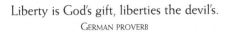

Liberty is God's gift, liberties the devil's.
GERMAN PROVERB

# FEELING GUILTY FEELING BAD

*Some of God's most precious gifts come in boxes that
make your hands bleed when you open them.*

SHEILA WALSH, MUSICIAN, SONGWRITER, AND AUTHOR

---

DESPITE THE IMPORTANCE of emotional margin, our contemporary level of emotional stamina is not high. Those who predicted the human race would evolve out of emotional problems were mistaken. Such troubles, far from being rarities, rage throughout our society. I'm constantly impressed by how drained we seem to be. Broken relationships, financial insecurities, and overburdened schedules rip through us like a chain saw. The wounds we care for in medicine today are more often wounds of the spirit than wounds of the soma.

As a consequence, many people—whether spiritually minded or not—find themselves in an emotional desert. When such pain happens to people of faith, they often don't know what to think or how to respond. Many believe that if they were to admit their unhappiness, they would be disappointing God. To admit emotional exhaustion lets God down.

May I respectfully say—that's theologically groundless. God already knows about your unhappiness. God knows who you are and what you feel. He knows your limits—He created them. He knows your circumstances better than you do. It is impossible to trick God into thinking you are okay when you're not.

God wants honesty, not fiction. He wants intimacy, not pretense. Just because we are honest does not mean we are unfaithful. Half of the Psalms complain to God. Still, God loves the Psalms.

Don't worry. God is not emotionally fragile.

God is not surprised when we hurt, for He knew life on earth would be tough. He knew our emotions would be under continuous assault in a fallen world. Pain is real and God knows all about it. He too was hurt.

God is a compassionate God: "As a father has compassion on his children, so the LORD has compassion on those who fear Him."[91] When Jesus saw the crowds, "he had compassion on them, because they were harassed and helpless."[92] Compassion is one of the things He does best. Don't hide from it—rest in it.

> *R Peace and joy will wax and wane. That's normal. Our moods will dip because the world is a fallen place and pain is real. Traveling through pain to get to our final destination is a valid path to take. But, at the same time, to get stuck in it is a spiritually neurotic thing to do. Even when we hurt, it is good to remember that the banner over our pain is victory. Jesus said, "I have told you these things, so that in me you may have peace. In this world you will have trouble. But take heart! I have overcome the world."[93]*

---

God is closest to those with broken hearts.

JEWISH PROVERB

# TECHNOLOGY, TELEPHONES, AND TYRANNY

*The telephone is one of those miracles one can discuss in terms either sacred or profane. No one has yet devised a pleasant way for a telephone to come to life. The ring is a sudden intrusion, a drill in the ear. . . . The satanic bleats from some new phones are the equivalent of sound lasers. But the ring cannot be subtle. Its mission is disruption. . . . The telephone call is a breaking-and-entering that we invite by having telephones in the first place. Someone unbidden barges in and for an instant or an hour usurps the ears and upsets the mind's prior arrangements.*

LANCE MORROW, COLUMNIST

---

MANY PEOPLE HAVE an ambivalent regard for the telephone. On the one hand it can greatly increase connectivity and convenience. "I got a cell phone for Mother's Day, and it's been great," a young physician said. "Now when I'm on call, I can take my baby for a stroller ride, or I can do an errand at the store." Exactly. If it serves your purposes and you are firmly in control, then use it. But on the other hand, if it is complicating and tyrannizing your already overloaded life, reject it.

I don't recall always hating the telephone, but no ambiguity exists today. How can one ever escape something as prevalent as mosquitoes and as irritating as a chain saw? As a result I find it necessary to often unplug the phone or simply not answer it at all.

One telephone company advertises: "You need a cellular phone. It can save your life!" True. But they can also cause head-on collisions, ring at inopportune times, and result in loud conversations at inappropriate locations.

Call waiting, representing a "last-come, first-served" ethic, is like trying to choke out noxious weeds by planting thistles. But we don't like busy signals either. So this is our choice: to be irritated by call waiting or be irritated by busy signals.

Answering machines and voice mail are services we wish everyone else had but are sometimes glad we do not. The answering machine slickly transforms someone else's desire to contact you into your obligation to return the call.

Unsolicited sales calls are yet another invasion of both privacy and sanity. We once received such a call as we sat down to Sunday dinner.

No discussion of modern telephone frustrations would be complete without mentioning automated menu-driven answering devices. I once tried navigating such a menu for thirty straight days, never able to reach a living human being.

*R Tame the telephone. It can bless you or drive you to the brink. Consider turning off or unplugging the telephone at selected times, getting an answering machine and letting it take calls when you are busy with more important things, or using caller ID. Increasingly, in the face of advancing "unrestrained reachability," we will all develop an affinity for such privacy protections.*

---

Do not throw the arrow which will return against you.

# MARGIN AND THE HEALTHY MARRIAGE

*All good things take time to develop; and marriage, the best gift
to lovers, requires more time for its development and
completion than any other good thing.*

LEWIS MUMFORD, PHILOSOPHY OF MODERN LIFE AUTHOR

---

RELATIONSHIPS REQUIRE TIME. Marriage requires time.
Love requires time. Communication requires time. Shared
experience, romantic dates, reconciliation, errands, play—all
require time.

Husbands and wives, however, have little time for their
marriages, their children, or themselves. One stressed-out
New Jersey couple spends four and one-half hours a day com-
muting and three minutes a day in face-to-face communication. Do the math. It doesn't take a rocket scientist to
understand that this equation will end in tears.

Obviously, for any relationship to function well, there
must be at least a "decent minimum" of time and energy
devoted to that relationship. In marriages, we must budget not
just functional, productive, activity-oriented time but also subjective time: hanging-around time, unstructured leisure time,
walking hand-in-hand time, I'm-sorry time. Time for sharing
deep feelings that don't surface easily, for discussing money
worries or dreams about the future.

Overloaded, overcommitted modern societies are conducting a gigantic sociological experiment to see if people trapped

in a time famine can maintain healthy marriages and families. So far the results are anything but encouraging. Instead of vibrant, stable marriages, we see "serial marriages" and "semi-siblings."[94] Margin is *important* in areas like our work, finances, and physical energy. But margin is *essential* in our marriages.

My father-in-law, Everett Wilson, always seemed to have time for his marriage and family. When at the age of eighty-two he underwent his second brain surgery for meningioma, the post-operative course was difficult. The tumor had been very close to the speech and motor centers. As a result he was disoriented and could not speak more than an occasional word. Yet when Mom came to visit him, despite his disorientation Everett weakly moved himself over in bed and patted beside him, motioning for Mom to climb in. Several of us were in the room to witness this tender gesture. He did not know his name, the year, or the city. But as he neared the end of his life, he knew that the place for his wife of fifty years was at his side.

Is that not what marriage should be—a lifelong journey of ever deepening love, affection, and interdependence? Margin cannot guarantee such a happy destination, but it can at least keep you in the right neighborhood . . . so that even when terminally disoriented, you will still remember that the place at your side is reserved for your spouse.

> ℞ *Make time for your marriage. Schedule time for conversation, walks, shared errands. Have regular dates. Keep short accounts. Don't let conflict simmer. When culture makes home deliveries of stress and overload, don't open the door. Guard the atmosphere of your home and the resilience of your marriage.*

---

What's all the world to a man when his wife is a widow?

IRISH PROVERB

# MARGIN AND HEALTHY PARENTING

*Making an appointment is one way to relate to your child, but it's pretty desiccated. You've got to hang around with your kids.*

PETER HAMMOND, UCLA ANTHROPOLOGIST

---

"PARENTING ON OVERLOAD" is the unfortunate theme song of many weary, well-meaning moms and dads. We all want desperately to parent well. But, on the other hand, there are many tempting competitors for a parent's attention today. This tug of war leaves us in a continuous quandary about how much time and energy we should give to child rearing. Consequently, many studies reveal that parent-to-child quality time runs between one to five minutes a day.

Meanwhile, standing off to the side with their hands stuck deep in their pockets are the kids, waiting for us to make up our minds. The human child is not capable of self-rearing in any healthy sense. So, despite our busyness, we all have a personal and a collective responsibility that will never go away: the responsibility to see that our children are raised in a secure and stable manner.

Life today is more stressful for children. Child development experts warn repeatedly that children are pressed to grow up too soon. They are exposed to issues far faster than in previous eras, and this exposure occurs long before they have the emotional equipment to process what it all means. This constitutes a binding agenda for any parent wishing to raise healthy children.

In our speed-driven lifestyles, parental performance will

not strengthen until we *intentionally* make it happen. Margin is willing to lend a hand, and in practical terms, this is what margin's involvement might look like:

*Show physical affection at all ages.* Cuddle. Hug. Give back rubs. Push the couches together and watch a TV program lying side by side.

*Encourage and praise your children.* Affirm them early and often. Understand and accept that each child is different.

*Have one-on-one time.* Take them to McDonald's once a month. Go fishing with just one child at a time.

*Slow down the entire family.* Take your foot off the family accelerator. Hurry and intimacy are polar opposites. Read to your children.

*Laugh together.* Laughter is a great stress reducer, and one which children are particularly good at. Rent a funny movie. Be goofy.

*Don't expect too much too soon.* Don't talk to children about prowlers when they are three years old or about AIDS when they are in kindergarten.

*Be involved in their lives.* Help them with homework. Subtly guide your child's choice of friends. Encourage "chumships." Insist that competition be kept age-appropriate.

*Establish limits.* Kids actually *like* limits. And it protects them from the temptations of others.

> ℞ *Above all, demonstrate unconditional love. It doesn't make any difference if they drop the fly ball or hit the game-winning home run. "Your best is always good enough." Love them the same in good times and in rough times.*

---

Haste and hurry can only bear children
with many regrets along the way.
SENEGALESE PROVERB

# MARGIN AND AVAILABILITY

*But it is possible that the most important thing God has for me on any given day is not even on my agenda. . . . Am I interruptible? Do I have time for the nonprogrammed things in my life? My response to those interruptions is the real test of my love.*

BRUCE LARSON, PASTOR AND AUTHOR

---

TO DEFEND FULL-throttle progress and its absence of margin is to presume that all which is good in life and all that God wants us to accomplish is only possible in a booked-up, highly efficient, often exhausted way of life. But His asking us to walk the second mile, to carry others' burdens, to witness to the truth at any opportunity, and to teach our children when we sit, walk, lie, and stand—all presuppose we have margin and that we make it available for His purposes. Obedience to these commands is often not schedulable.

Actually, margin is not a spiritual necessity. But availability is. God expects us to be available for the needs of others. And without margin, one has great difficulty guaranteeing availability. Instead, when God calls, He gets the busy signal.

Margin exists not only for the well-being of each individual but also for the service of others. It exists, just as we exist, for the purpose of being available to God.

There are two ways we can be available. The first is for us to make our schedules but then be willing to set aside our agendas whenever God calls. Such willingness, however, seldom happens. Our lives are uninterruptible due to the imperative of staying on task. Maybe tomorrow?

A second way of being available is to make our schedules less full but then offer this extra discretionary time to the Father: "What do you want me to do with this time today?" God's intention might be for us to use the time to pray, to meditate, to rest, to serve, to parent, to tell of the good news, or a thousand other ways of cooperating with His eternal purposes.

Being useful to God and others is a large part of what life is meant to be. And yet "usefulness is nine-tenths availability." When others need help, they don't need it two days from now. "It is part of the discipline of humility, . . . " wrote Dietrich Bonhoeffer, "that we do not assume that our schedule is our own to manage, but allow it to be arranged by God."[95]

> *R* *Make your schedule but then hold it lightly. God might have other use of your time. Learn to differentiate the spiritually illegitimate distractions of the cultural treadmill from the spiritually legitimate calls for kingdom service. A warning: just because a cause is consistent with kingdom priorities does not mean God is assigning you the service. Be sure to consult Him before presuming on His will.*

---

Mañana is often the busiest day of the week.
SPANISH PROVERB

# A FLAWED THEOLOGY

*Doing one thing seems to lead to another.*
*One is never sure when enough is enough.*
GORDON MACDONALD, PASTOR AND AUTHOR

THE DRIVEN NOTION that we must relentlessly pursue activity every waking minute is seriously flawed, both practically and theologically. If we insist that we must be "all things to all people all the time all by ourselves;" that God requires no less than total, all-out, burnout effort; that it would insult Christ's sacrifice for us to rest; that there are too many opportunities for us to slow down, then we will find ourselves backed up against a logical and theological juggernaut. Think about it. If these arguments are valid, then how could we *ever* find permission to stop our work, even to sleep?

For example, if after a productive, busy day you finally quit at midnight, I would go to your house and greet you on the front step. The conversation might go like this:

"Are you done for today?" I would ask.

"Yes. Finally. A long day—seventeen hours. But all important things. It was an exhausting day, but a good one."

"Why are you quitting now?" I would ask.

"Well, because it's midnight."

"So it is. Does that mean that all of your work is done? Isn't there *something* that you could be doing? Isn't there some good that you could still pursue? Isn't there some need you could work on? Some studying . . . or perhaps letters of encouragement to write?"

"Give me a break!" you would say. "What do you expect?"

Exactly my point. Whenever we quit for the day, it is always arbitrary. The world is not yet perfect, but we quit. There is still more to be done, and yet we quit. The fact is, whenever we quit, we are abandoning the job unfinished despite the fact we could still do more.

Life is always a process, and it is the *process* that God is concerned with more than *productivity*. He knows perfectibility is not possible and that all our labors are feeble against the brokenness of the world. When we overemphasize productivity (a typically American thing to do), we often pervert the process: instead of faith, we substitute work; instead of depth, we substitute speed; instead of love, we substitute money; instead of prayer, we substitute busyness. And all the time, we believe we are doing Him a favor.

God doesn't really care how many problems we solve, because tomorrow there will be more. What God wants to know is not "Did you work?" but "Did you love?" Sometimes the two are the same, and sometimes the two are the opposite.

> *Rx Assign God more credit for carrying the world—and assign yourself less. Bow the knee, acknowledge His power, and then humbly do His will by loving the person standing in front of you.*

———❧———

God is bigger than your problems.
MEXICAN PROVERB

# LAYING DOWN THEIR LIVES

*The average American household is in more danger from*
*chemical germ-killers than from germs. I prefer to*
*leave the battle to my own cells.*

PAUL BRAND, M.D., MISSIONARY LEPROSY SPECIALIST

THE RED BLOOD cells are workhorses, but the real heroes swimming through the circulatory system are the white blood cells and platelets. They die for us. They were born ready to die.

Platelets are half the size of red blood cells and survive only a matter of days. This is why we must continually produce five million new platelets every second. They are critical for the clotting of the blood, rushing to the site of injury and heroically throwing their tiny bodies into the hole.

The white blood cells are no less self-sacrificing. They are a vital link in our quest for daily survival. Not to be paranoid about it, but there are billions of microbes continuously seeking to do us harm. This is why the body must have ready fifty billion white blood cells standing guard. These are the active duty forces. But in the reserves, hiding in the bone marrow, we have a backup force one hundred times as large should the need arise. We ought rightfully to be grateful for this profound immunologic margin.

The skin and mucosa of the respiratory track are the first line of defense against microbial attack. Yet should any infectious agents breech this outer defense, the immune system takes over. Here the white blood cell is an important player.

Next time you get a sore throat, swollen lymph nodes, or inflammation, remember that your body is doing battle on your behalf. Don't be irritated by the fever or discomfort. Instead just think about the billions of white blood cells that are dying so that you may live.

These cells have one mission, one purpose: to give their lives in defense of ours. "Greater love has no one than this," Jesus said, "that he lay down his life for his friends."[96] Jesus did it for us; our white blood cells and platelets do it for us. Why do we doubt His vigilance when He so faithfully performs it on the microscopic level every day of our lives? The evidence is overwhelming — He sees, He cares, and He defends.

R̶ *One important reason to guard margin is because of the random, indiscriminate nature of infectious illness. What happens when your three-year-old screams all night with an ear infection and you have ten appointments the next day? Or when you have a maxed-out to-do list and pneumonia at the same time? Build enough margin into life so that illness can be accommodated within a reasonable range of life tolerances.*

---

One who recovers from sickness forgets about God.
<small>ETHIOPIAN PROVERB</small>

# THE TIME DIMENSIONS OF HEAVEN AND PRAYER

*The distinction between past, present, and future is only an illusion, even if a stubborn one.*

ALBERT EINSTEIN

THE ELASTICITY OF time is not a spiritual apparition but rather a proven fact of physics. In physics we know the elasticity of time is related to both velocity and gravity. The faster the velocity or the greater the gravity, the slower time passes. This effect is not simply an observational phenomenon. *It really happens*. It is called time dilation. The time dilation effect maximizes at the speed of light when the passage of time stops altogether.

What does this tell us about God? If time can be influenced by velocity and gravity, imagine how it can be influenced by the Creator of velocity and gravity. In fact God stops time.

When we arrive in heaven we will discover some very liberating ideas regarding the nature and experience of time. We will discover how dramatically we underestimated the true nature of time simply because our earthbound imaginations could never rise that high.

Even more, for the first time we will understand God's own radical power over the time dimension. When His mastery over time is fully displayed, we will wonder what could have been had we not so foolishly limited Him during our short stay on earth.

Try to conceive of the extreme facility with which God operates within time. He lives in the past, the present, and the future all at the same time. "God does not 'foresee' you doing things tomorrow; He simply sees you doing them," wrote C. S. Lewis, "because, though tomorrow is not yet there for you, it is for Him."[97]

Some people balk at prayer because they can't get beyond the time issues involved. They wonder, "How can God listen to a million people praying all at once?" Actually, there are no obstacles in physics that would prevent God from hearing a billion prayers simultaneously. As a matter of fact, God can listen to an infinite number of prayers at the same time and take an infinite amount of time in answering each—all within the bounds of both theological and scientific orthodoxy. A pilot crashing into a mountain can shout a last-minute prayer to God, and God has an infinite amount of time to consider His answer.

Life on planet earth is full of time stress. Life in heaven is devoid of time stress. In His calm power, God patiently waits for His children to look up.

*R Pray. Realizing just how effortlessly and powerfully God moves around within time encourages the habit of prayer. God has no difficulty whatsoever hearing your prayer, considering it, and answering it. If there is any defect in prayer, it is always from the human side related to faith and never from the divine side related to time or power.*

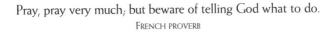

Pray, pray very much; but beware of telling God what to do.
FRENCH PROVERB

# RADICAL VERSUS INCREMENTAL CHANGE

*It's not that some people have willpower and some don't. It's that
some people are ready to change and others are not.*

JAMES GORDON, M.D., PSYCHIATRIST AND AUTHOR

---

DESPERATE FOR SOMETHING other than a daily diet of
stress and overload, many people yearn to regain margin in
their lives. Having contended with the issues over a protracted
course, clearly relief is not forthcoming. They are increasingly
eager to address the problem, but how does one begin? It is
helpful to point out that two roads lead in the margin direction. One road is radical change. The second is incremental
change. Both aim for the same destination, but the first gets
you there more quickly.

*Radical change*—A small but growing percentage of
stressed-out Americans are ready for sweeping change. They
have coexisted with overload for years and have tired of the
struggle. When they see a restructuring that makes sense emotionally and spiritually, they want nothing more than to sweep
away the old and replace it with something better.

Such a decision might entail cutting work hours, starting
over in a different job, having one spouse drop out of the
workforce, buying a smaller house, relocating in another state
or country, or selling expensive cars, boats, or planes. Most of
these changes require considerable simplification.

This approach can be very helpful in reestablishing margin.

The caution, however, is not to make such an important restructuring on impulse. The more important the decision, the longer we should take to deliberate.

*Incremental change*—Most people are not able or willing to consider radical solutions to life's problems. These people are weary, to be sure. But, fearing the disruption and even chaos of sudden change, they prefer to ease their way out of the torment one step at a time.

This group, therefore, is more inclined toward the "baby steps" approach to establishing margin. The caution in this scenario, however, is that many of our lives are so marginless that incremental revisions might not accomplish enough substantive change to decompress the pain. In this case my advice is to do something bolder.

> ℞ *Consider carefully which approach to adopt. Much is riding on the course of action you choose. Seek the counsel of wise and trusted friends. Pray. Use faith, but also use sanctified common sense.*

---

If we do not change our direction, we are likely
to end up where we are headed.

CHINESE PROVERB

# EATING JELLYBEANS

*You can tell a lot about a fellow's character
by his way of eating jellybeans.*
RONALD REAGAN

FOOD IS A major part of life and also of margin. Proper nutrition is necessary for margin in physical energy, but as with all things, too much nutrition destroys that same margin. A reasoned approach to reestablishing balance in diet requires attention on multiple fronts.

*Decrease intake of sugars.* Two hundred years ago we ate two pounds of sugar a year per person; now the figure is closer to 150 pounds a year. Actually, the use of table sugar has been declining. The real problem comes in the "invisible" or "hidden" sugar added during food processing.

*Replace processed snacks with fruit.* Fruit can be a good substitute for fats and "hidden" sugars. Often we bypass fruit, thinking it is too expensive. Then we travel down the aisle and pick out cookies, chips, and candy instead. Yet the argument that fruit is more expensive just disappeared, for compared to other types of snack foods, fruit is actually cheaper. It is tasty. It is liked by both children and adults. It is a good source of fiber. My advice: spend less money on processed snacks and more on fruit.

*Garden or buy direct.* There are two ways to process food: God's way and the factory way. God knows what He is doing; the factory often doesn't. The ground, taking its orders from

God, fortunately doesn't process food the way factories do. And the less factory processing, the better the food. Always protect the most direct connection from the Father's hand to your table.

*Drink lots of water.* Drinking a large glass of water before sitting down for a meal can help suppress the appetite. The universal recommendation is six to eight glasses of water a day. A simple rule: never pass a drinking fountain.

*Use exercise as both appetite and weight reducer.* In many cases, vigorous exercise diminishes appetite. Also, if the goal is weight reduction, adding exercise is a more balanced approach than is dieting alone. Dieting alone will result in the loss of not only fat but also muscle. On the other hand, exercise alone requires a huge amount of effort for a small amount of weight loss. For example, three hours of running is required to work off one pound (3,500 calories). The balanced approach, therefore, combines both calorie restriction and calorie incineration in a weight-reduction program.

> ℞ *Avoid overeating. Put smaller portions on the table. Use a small plate. Chew food longer. Set your fork down between every bite. Don't prepare the next bite until you have finished chewing and swallowing the one in your mouth. Consciously taste your food. Don't take seconds. Always sit down to eat. Eat at only one place in the house. Don't eat in front of the television. Don't snack. Bite your tongue.*

---

Even food can attack.
NEW ZEALANDER PROVERB

# CONTENTMENT AND MONEY

*To Americans, usually tragedy is wanting something very badly
and not getting it. Many people have had to learn in their private
lives, and nations have had to learn in their historical experience,
that perhaps the worst form of tragedy is wanting something
badly, getting it, and finding it empty.*

HENRY KISSINGER

---

OUR RELATIONSHIP TO money is an area where contentment is essential. The poor envy the rich while the rich envy
the richer. Money gives a thrill but no satiety. The rich soon
sense this and are perhaps surprised by it, but then go back to
making more money anyway. Satisfaction will come later, they
speculate, and if it never comes, at least there is the thrill.

Money does seem to meet our needs short term. It buys us
food, shelter, vehicles, and experiences. It does not, however,
meet any of our long-term needs: love, truth, relationship,
redemption. This short-term deception is a tricky obstacle for
us to understand and is one of the reasons God spent so much
time instructing us concerning money and wealth. Money is
treacherous, we are told, and riches are deceitful. It is not a sin
to be wealthy, but it can be dangerous.

As Kissinger hints, millions have had to discover that you
can't find true contentment in wealth and that the advertised
contentment brought by cars, houses, and wardrobes is but a
short-term hoax. The things one can buy with money are

never the things that last. "Keep your lives free from the love of money and be content with what you have," we read in Hebrews, "because God has said, 'Never will I leave you; never will I forsake you.'"[98] Did your car, your house, or your wardrobe ever say, "Never will I leave you."?

While, at some level, earning money is necessary, the apostle Paul taught that seeking wealth would threaten us with devastation:

> People who want to get rich . . .
>> . . . fall into temptation
>> . . . fall into a trap
>> . . . fall into foolish and harmful desires
>> . . . are plunged into ruin and destruction.
>
> Some people eager for money . . .
>> . . . have wandered from the faith
>> . . . have pierced themselves with many griefs.[99]

Do you want to be plunged and pierced? Nor do I. But that doesn't seem to stop us from wanting to get rich. Were Paul's message not included in the biblical text, it would be out of print. No readership remains.

*R̸ Develop a studied distrust of riches. Be sure to continually expose your heart before God. Concentrate on contentment rather than riches and don't allow your affections to wander.*

―◦◦◦―

When death comes, the rich man has no money
and the poor man no debt.
ESTONIAN PROVERB

# PETS

*I have found that when you are deeply troubled there are
things you get from the silent devoted companionship
of a dog that you can get from no other source.*

DORIS DAY, MOVIE STAR

---

A FEW YEARS back, when I was speaking in the Seattle area,
the seminar took a break immediately after my presentation
about emotional well-being and margin. Five minutes into the
break, from where I was standing in the lobby I overheard an
older couple talking to each other while shuffling slowly
across the foyer.

"Well," the man asked, "what do you think?"

"I don't know. What about you?" she replied.

"I think we should," he said.

"Okay," she said. "We'll go pick out a cat tomorrow at the
pet shop."

For some reason not completely clear to me, people who
are pet owners tend to be healthier and happier. This does not
rise to the level of scriptural truth—just empiric fact. Research
has shown that they live longer and visit the doctor less often.
One life insurance company offers an 8-percent discount on
your premium if you are a pet owner.

We all need interaction, affection, contact. Sometimes,
because of social conventions, we are inhibited from touching
one another. For those caught in such a void and left with a

dearth of physical closeness, I would strongly suggest considering surrogates: pets.

When God wrote the inviolable law that requires living things to need one another, He included the animal world. And it is remarkable how closely we can approximate human-human warmth and devotion by substituting human-animal contact. Pets are capable of bonding, are extremely loyal, and often exhibit deep appreciation for our attentions—exactly the kind of responses needed to increase our emotional reserves.

If, for example, you are single or lonely or bereaved or adolescent and you come home to a dark place, a cat or dog will show obvious delight in welcoming you home. They will sit on your lap, give affection and receive affection, and they don't bite the way humans do. "A dog," wrote Josh Billings, "is the only thing on earth that loves you more than he loves himself."

℞ *Consider the benefits of pet ownership. Dogs and cats are of course the most popular choices because they are the most interactive and tend to bond better. But other species can substitute as well. An additional benefit of having a dog is the increased incentive and opportunity for taking a daily walk.*

---

A dog shows affection even to a poor family.
CHINESE PROVERB

# MARGIN AND THE PERFECT LIFE

*Perfection is achieved not when there is nothing more to add,*
*but when there is nothing left to take away.*
ANTOINE DE SAINT-EXUPERY, FRENCH POET

---

PRIOR TO BEGINNING medical school in 1970, if I had written my assumed formula for the perfect life, it would have been straightforward:

> Great Job + Great Income + Great Patients + Great Colleagues + Great Clinic + Great Hospital + Great Town + Great Church + Great Family + Great Faith = Utopia

Ten years later, I had achieved everything in the formula. . . except the utopia. Surprisingly, my life was anything but perfect. True, I had a nice house, a comfortable income, a wonderful wife, and delightful children. But something was seriously wrong.

Somehow, unexpectedly, everything had become a burden: medicine and patients and caring. How could so many good things bring such pain? We were not involved in anything that was bad—nothing unsuccessful, nothing evil, nothing that did not honor God. It was all serving, caring, ministering, doctoring, teaching. Linda and I were meeting needs everywhere we turned.

Yet life was obviously out of control. My buoyancy had

sunk. Rest had become a theoretical concept. My passion for medical practice and for ministry had disappeared. Frankly, I was mystified. No one had taught me about this in medical school. Nor had anyone taught me about this in the church. What went wrong? If I had achieved everything in the formula for the perfect life, why was it so hard to get out of bed?

*Diagnosis*: Overload. Linda and I were not only committed: we were overcommitted. We were not only conscientious: we were overly conscientious. We were not only ministering: we were overministering. We were not only tired: we were exhausted.

What I should have known intuitively, I had neglected to acknowledge: I had limits. I was finite. As it turns out, I am not alone in this. There are only so many details in *anyone's* life that can be successfully managed. Exceeding this threshold will result in frustration, disorganization, and exhaustion.

*Prescription*: Margin. When I finally understood about margin and freedom and balance and rest, life changed. We replaced overload with margin. We put some space between our load and our limits. When we did, life came alive again. My passion for life and medicine and ministry returned in full force. It was a miracle cure. Margin was indeed the missing ingredient in the formula for the perfect life.

> *R͜ Write your own formula for a "perfect life." In what ways is this formula influenced by the culture and in what ways is it determined by the kingdom? Rather than spending forty years striving after a flawed formula, make the needed correctives preemptively. Judge your values and goals with spiritual wisdom.*

---

Having just enough is better than having too much.
BASQUE PROVERB

# THE BRAIN AND TRUTH

*We need to discredit the belief held by many scientists that science*
*will ultimately deliver the final truth. . . . They argue that someday*
*science will explain values, beauty, love, friendship, aesthetics and*
*literary quality. They say: "All of these will eventually be*
*explicable in terms of brain performance. We only have to know*
*more about the brain." That view is nothing more than a*
*superstition that confuses both the public and many scientists.*

SIR JOHN ECCLES, NOBLE LAUREATE IN MEDICINE AND PHYSIOLOGY

ANY DISCUSSION OF the brain in the context of faith would
be incomplete if it did not at least attempt to clarify the limits
of what the brain can do, that is, the spiritual limits of knowledge. The brain is a proven expert in the gathering and processing of data and information. But can we trust it to bring us
all the way Home?

There is no clear correlation between filling the mind with
facts and discovering truth; between advancing in educational
attainment and advancing in the things of God; between IQ
and righteousness. Should we then forsake education and go in
the other direction? On the contrary, we *should* instruct and
discipline the brain. But if at the beginning of every day the
brain will not humbly bow to truth, then our synapses are
pointed in the wrong direction.

The brain is the realm of data, information, and knowledge. The spirit, however, is the realm of understanding, wisdom, and truth. The brain ought not assume that it rules over

the spirit, for such a course leads only to enormous existential strife. "In His will is our peace," wrote Dante.

The brain must act humbly or it will sabotage its own search. God resists the proud, and He surely will resist the brain when it defies Him. This is why, sadly, many brilliant thinkers stumble in the darkness their entire lives. "The uncomprehending mind," observed A. W. Tozer, "is unaffected by truth."[100]

God has ordained from the beginning that worldly learning will never be sufficient to reveal Christ.[101] This does not mean that the message of Christ is irrational but only that it is extra-rational. Its meaning is not accessible through neurons and synapses, no matter how exceptional.

The brain is quite spectacular in its own right, and it does not need inflated claims about its potential. Let's challenge it diligently to learn, but then let's accept the borders it cannot cross. Even given its limitations, the brain's amazing capacity speaks to the genius of the God who endowed it.

R Don't expect truth from information. A prideful brain might fill itself with information, but if the human spirit is not acquainted with truth, anguish is inevitable. Peace comes to restless lives only when the spirit and brain together have made their peace with God.

---

A handful of patience is worth more than a bushel of brains.
DUTCH PROVERB

# THE FINE ART OF NAPPING

*Naps are nature's way of reminding you that life is nice —
like a beautiful, softly swinging hammock strung
between birth and infinity.*

PEGGY NOONAN, PRESIDENTIAL SPEECHWRITER AND JOURNALIST

EVERY PHYSIOLOGIC FUNCTION of the human body undergoes a diurnal variation, meaning that it phases and fluctuates throughout the day. This is true for the sleep/wake cycle — not only at bedtime but at midday as well. After lunch our biorhythms experience a natural slump, as a mild somnolence intrudes on our wakefulness.

These slumping biorhythms can be resisted with caffeine and stimulation. But throughout history, many cultures have instead treated this natural somnolence as a nonthreatening occurrence. Rather than kicking against it, they have accommodated this dip by developing the culturally accepted habit of napping, the idea of taking a siesta.

Many of the world's greatest leaders were nappers. Thomas Edison is said to have catnapped up to eight times a day. John F. Kennedy napped in the White House, and Winston Churchill took daily naps even during World War II. No doubt Jesus Himself napped. For example, when the boat was being buffeted by the wind and the waves, Jesus was sleeping in the bow. The disciples first had to awaken Him before begging for a miracle.

Naps can be revitalizing, adding energy and productivity for later in the day. If you have the opportunity and need to nap, it is best to follow certain guidelines. Don't nap for more than one hour. If you do, understand that a longer nap is not necessarily more restful. Even a nap of fifteen minutes can help to improve alertness and concentration and, to some extent, make up for a disturbed or shortened night of sleep. Mothers of babies and young children may freely nap whenever they get the opportunity, as they usually need it the most.

The most helpful naps are in the afternoon, taking advantage of the mild drop in body temperature that induces somnolence. A short nap in the early evening can give added stamina for the hours ahead. A longer evening nap, however, will often hinder the initiation of sleep that night.

R *Learn to enjoy a nap without feeling guilty. Especially cultivate the pleasure of a Sabbath nap.*

---

Only mad dogs and the British go out in the noonday sun.
INDIAN PROVERB

# THE THEOLOGY OF ENOUGH

*Faith in God will not get for you everything you may want,*
*but it will get for you what God wants you to have.*
*The unbeliever does not need what he wants: the*
*Christian should want only what he needs.*

VANCE HAVNER, PASTOR AND AUTHOR

---

CONTENTMENT IS NECESSARY for us to correctly relate to both money and possessions. The rules here are simple:

1. God comes first and possessions come second.
2. Possessions are to be used, not loved.

One of Jesus' most frightening warnings to affluent modernity is His rebuke of the rich landowner in Luke 12. When the fields yielded a great harvest, the landowner proudly built huge barns and stored up his treasure for the years to come. Now, he thought, life will be easy and secure.

God's judgment was quick: "You fool!" That night the man's life was taken from him.

"Watch out!" warns Jesus. "Be on your guard against all kinds of greed; a man's life does not consist in the abundance of his possessions."[102] Tragically, for many today, their lives do indeed consist in the abundance of their possessions.

"Within the human heart 'things' have taken over," asserts A. W. Tozer. "God's gifts now take the place of God, and the whole course of nature is upset by the monstrous substitution."[103]

Why hasn't the church stood against this popular error? Why hasn't there been a clear expression of a "theology of enough"? Perhaps it is because *things* are not evil, as stealing and adultery are: only the *love* of things, like the *love* of money, is evil. It is easy for us to say, "I don't love this thing; it's just that I *need* it." God is what we need; things are what we use. In the words of one Christian journalist: "Contentment lies not in what is yours, but in whose you are."[104]

> *R̶ Subtract from your needs. Make a list of all the things you "need" and then start crossing things off. It might at first be painful, but after a while it becomes fun. "There are two ways to get enough," G. K. Chesterton pointed out. "One is to continue to accumulate more and more. The other is to desire less."*

---

The richest man, whate'er his lot,
is the one content with what he's got.
DUTCH PROVERB

# ABOVE ALL, LOVE

*Love is the medicine for the sickness of the world.*
KARL MENNINGER, M.D., PSYCHIATRIST

---

GOD HAS SHOWN us the road to health, the path to blessing: It is the way of relationship. Do you see now why careers, degrees, and estates can never quite get the job done? Somehow we just keep taking our expensive automobiles to our posh offices to make another $100,000, while all the time our relationships vaporize before our eyes and our loneliness deepens.

But we are not helpless. Progress does not own us. We do not have to let history "happen to us." We are free to change. And God is still interested in lending a hand.

We can focus on relationship and create a margin for it. We can simplify and balance our lives so that relationships have some space. We can invest ourselves in other people. When we don't feel like it, we can still do it. Even when we can't find anyone else interested in friendship, we can always start spreading around quiet kindnesses, expecting none in return.

Soon love will begin to flow out from us, and with the flow there will also come a flowing back. For love, you see, is the most excellent way.[105] All the commandments in Scripture reduce to Christ's Great Commandment, and the Great Commandment reduces to one concept: love.

God is in love with His creation. The creature has something of the Creator in him, and God has loved us from the beginning. Even when the creature turned his back on heaven, yet God loved him: "I made you, and I will carry you. I don't hold anything against you. Let me rescue you."

The history of the world reduces to this: you being pursued by love. He courted you; He followed you; He loved you. If you go to work or school or church, He is there. If you go to the edge of the universe or if you go to the borders of hell, He is there. If you go deep inside yourself, He is there. In the dark of the night, in your depression, He is there. On your deathbed, when you don't want anybody to leave you, He is there. If you look behind you or before you, He is there, waiting to be allowed entrance into your life.

In the economics of eternity, God paid a great price. If we only better understood the cost, we would also better understand our worth.

> $R$ *Love is an action rather than an emotion. It is a matter of the will, an act of obedience.* [106] *Don't sit around waiting for flowery feelings to bubble up. Make yourself useful. Spread around quiet kindnesses, expecting none in return. Expend yourself for the sake of others. Every expenditure will be repaid, in this world or the next.*

---

It is easy to halve the potato where there is love.

IRISH PROVERB

# WHEN WAITING IS BEST

*We must wait for God, long, meekly, in the wind and wet, in the*
*thunder and lightning, in the cold and dark. Wait, and he will*
*come. He never comes to those who do not wait.*

FREDERICK WILLIAM FABER, ENGLISH THEOLOGIAN

---

WHATEVER HAPPENED TO waiting? "Once a man would
spend a week patiently waiting if he missed a stage coach,"
observed one critic, "but now he rages if he misses the first section of a revolving door." Moderns don't have the slightest idea
how to begin the process, and furthermore are not much interested in exploring the concept. We have come to believe that
waiting is instead a negative activity rather than a virtue to
desire, pursue, and nourish.

From the spiritual perspective, waiting on God has been a
mainstay of theology for at least three millennia. Yet over the
last thirty years, we have sacrificed this important truth and
don't even have the wisdom to realize it's been a serious loss.
Did the word all of a sudden disappear from the Scripture as it
has disappeared from our vernacular? To the contrary, waiting
is a well-established concept throughout the Bible, mentioned
twenty-two times in the book of Psalms alone.

Waiting is a dimension of faith—an anchor of the spiritual experience—that modern people know little about. If we
are fatigued, exhausted, and hurrying to and fro with no rest in
sight, is it possible that "waiting upon the Lord" is the answer

to our problem? "They that wait upon the LORD shall renew their strength," wrote the prophet Isaiah.[107]

When David penned, "Be still before the LORD and wait patiently for him," did he have the Father's permission to offer such counsel?[108] If so, what implications does this have for our daily behavior? What does *be still* or *wait patiently* mean in the twenty-first century? "I wait for the LORD," wrote the psalmist, "my soul waits, and in his word I put my hope."[109]

*R Determine to once again take the concept of waiting seriously—not the laziness part, the wisdom part. "When you don't know what to do, wait!" wrote Roy Lessin. "God never panics and is never under pressure."[110] If we will not recover the discipline of waiting, God is under no moral obligation to speed up His timetable to accommodate our urgency. In waiting is strength. And if the waiting is godly, it will lead to walking confidently in the light rather than stumbling blindly in the night.*

---

There is no bad patience.
SWAHILI PROVERB

# COMPOUNDING THE PAIN OF DEPRESSION

*Of course it is more than possible that most of my readers will never experience this particular Hell which life can inflict upon human beings. In that case, I beg you not to be unmindful of the unseen and often inexpressible sufferings of others. At least do not look down on those who are undergoing what seem to you to be purely imaginary terrors. And please have the charity to remember that most of them are fighting a battle of almost unbelievable ferocity just to keep going at all.*

J. B. PHILLIPS, BIBLE TRANSLATOR AND AUTHOR

---

DEPRESSION IS EXCEEDINGLY common. So common that it is called the common cold of psychiatry. To medical researchers this was unexpected—that more affluence, education, and technology would be accompanied by more depression.

Christians, perhaps surprisingly, also have a fairly high incidence of depression, yet little permission to talk about it. Depression isn't supposed to happen to spiritually stable people.

For example, one prominent pastor said, "I, for the life of me, can't understand these Christians with the long faces. How is it possible for Christians to believe in a God who is good and gracious and powerful, and yet to have such sadness in their lives!"

What would he say to the famous preacher Charles Spurgeon, who suffered from repeated prolonged bouts of depression? Or to William Cowper, composer of such hymns as "There Is a Fountain," who was severely depressed and even suicidal most of his life? Or to Sheila Walsh, who emerged from her depression with perhaps the most vibrant testimony in the land?

Actually, there are times when depression can be a normal Christian response to the pain of life. Depression is caused by a deep hurt in the heart and results in a profound sadness. It is indeed spiritually possible to feel such a deep pain and still have God be God.

Think about it: If a person looks around with sensitivity, pain is everywhere: family pain, physical and emotional illness, tragedies, violence in the streets and on television, sexual struggles, loneliness, political bickering, ethnic strife. It is a very broken world. To a sensitive person, seeing such pain is painful. If you open yourself with vulnerability to the hurt of the world, depression is sometimes a biblically valid result.

How wonderful it would be if depressed people coming to the community of faith were healed rather than hurt. Instead they often receive a scorn that compounds their woundedness.

*R Stop stigmatizing the pain of depression, and stop pretending it away. Allow people to be honest. Be a hospital rather than a courtroom. If you are depressed, be patient and seek help—both spiritual and medical. Almost certainly you will one day feel better. If you know people who are depressed, compassionately walk with them until they are again whole.*

---

Shared sorrow is half sorrow.
<small>DANISH PROVERB</small>

# FOCUSING MEANS SAYING NO

*Time is the coin of your life. It is the only coin you have,*
*and only you can determine how it will be spent.*
*Be careful lest you let other people spend it for you.*

CARL SANDBURG, POET AND BIOGRAPHER

NO IS AN uncomfortable word. It is often a difficult word to utter, for many reasons: we are afraid of disappointing our friends, of missing interesting opportunities, of not getting promoted. Nevertheless we are all human and bound by the same human limits, including the twenty-four-hour day. When demands on our time exceed the time available, then *no* is the operative word.

Saying no is not an excuse for noninvolvement, laziness, or insensitivity. Instead, when used correctly, it is purely a mechanism for living by our priorities, allowing God to direct our lives rather than a tyrannizing culture. It is a way of preserving our margin for the things that matter most.

*No* is a focusing word. When Steve Jobs took over Apple Computer again for the second time, he decided the company needed focusing. "Focus does not mean saying yes," Jobs decided, "it means saying no."

That same focusing is often needed in our spiritual lives. One pastor told me that in his church, *no* is a holy word. If we wish to focus on things of the kingdom, it will require saying *no* to things of this world. "For the grace of God that brings salvation has appeared to all men," wrote Paul. "It teaches us to say 'No' to ungodliness and worldly passions, and to live self-controlled, upright and godly lives in this present age."[111]

To live "self-controlled" lives will require introspection and insight. Why do we say yes when we do and no when we do? "Much of our acceptance of multitudes of obligations is due to our inability to say No," writes Thomas Kelly.

> We calculated that that task had to be done, and we saw no one ready to undertake it. We calculated the need, and then calculated our time, and decided maybe we could squeeze it in somewhere. But the decision was a heady decision, not made within the sanctuary of the soul. When we say Yes or No to calls for service on the basis of heady decision, we have to give reasons, to ourselves and to others. But when we say Yes or No to calls, on the basis of inner guidance . . . then we have begun to live in guidance. And I find He never guides us into an intolerable scramble of panting feverishness.[112]

*R Practice saying no even to good things, so you can say yes to the right things. Be extraordinarily cautious that you understand which priorities you are embracing with your yes and which you are denying with your no. To get this right will make all the difference.*

---

To ask is no sin, and to be refused is no calamity.
Russian proverb

# WHAT CONTENTMENT IS NOT

*I am not saying this because I am in need, for I have learned to be
content whatever the circumstances. I know what it is to be in need,
and I know what it is to have plenty. I have learned the secret of
being content in any and every situation, whether well fed or
hungry, whether living in plenty or in want.*[113]

APOSTLE PAUL

---

ONCE CULTIVATED, MARGIN needs help to survive.
Contentment can be a wonderful ally in this cause, as long as
the contentment we are talking about is authentic. If, on the
other hand, the "contentment" is a misrepresented counterfeit,
it will turn the pursuit of freedom into a drudging burden.

In our propensity to get things wrong, we have credited a
number of attitudes and feelings as contentment that have
nothing to do with it. Contentment isn't denying one's feelings
about unhappiness, but instead a freedom from being controlled by those feelings. It isn't pretending things are right
when they are not, but instead the peace that comes from
knowing God is bigger than any problem and He works them
all out for our good.

Contentment isn't the complacency that defeats any
attempt to make things better, but instead the willingness to
work tirelessly for improvement, clinging to God rather than
results. It isn't a feeling of well-being contingent on circumstances under control, but instead a joy that exists in spite of

circumstances and looks to the God who never varies. It isn't the comfortable feeling we get when all our needs and desires are met, but instead the security in knowing, as A. W. Tozer reminds us, "The man who has God for his treasure has all things in One."[114]

Finally, contentment isn't that pseudo-virtue of the American Dream, where we claim solidarity with Paul from the easy chair of middle-class America. We profess to having learned the secret of contentment in all circumstances, yet never having experienced forty lashes, stoning, shipwreck, hunger, thirst, homelessness, or imprisonment. Perhaps none of us should presume maturity until the truer tests have been endured. To snuggle up alongside Paul and profess contentment without having known want seems a bit impudent on our part. Paul's contentment in need and plenty is mostly of interest because of the need. Until we know true need and survive the test, we must not presume to be his companion.

> *R Don't fake being OK when you're not. Instead, transcend it. Admit to yourself and to God when you're envious and discontent. Travel directly through the discontent into the 'secret' of contentment that Paul describes. Only God Himself can reveal this secret, taking your unhappiness and turning it into freedom.*

∞∞

Abundance doesn't know contentment,<br>but contentment is abundance.<br>Turkish proverb

# THE SPIRITUAL COST OF OVERLOAD

*Why on the one Sunday in five years when a New England
snowstorm forced us to close down our church was it universally
recognized by the congregation as the most wonderful Lord's
day they had ever had? What was being said?*

GORDON MacDONALD, PASTOR AND AUTHOR

---

SOMETHING IS HAPPENING on our generational shift that
the world has never seen before. There is a ubiquitous overloading in every quadrant of personal and societal experience
that threatens to overwhelm even the most stoic. This creates
a special agenda for the church. As overload sucks the oxygen
out of our life together, our testimony becomes joyless, our
devotions distracted, and our prayers blighted. We tend to be
less interested in serving the needs of others when we can't
even make it through the day ourselves.

Are Christians immune from the toxic effects of overload?
Has not God surrounded us with an invisible stress-resistant
firewall that constitutes a functional exemption from the rav-
aging effects of overload? To the contrary. The most spiritually
sensitive among us are frequently the greatest victims. As fol-
lowers of Christ we are often painfully sincere. We want to
serve the Savior, and seeing the many needs, we ratchet up our
efforts yet another notch. Then we hit the wall, collapse in
exhaustion, and wonder what happened. Interestingly, the
same conversion experience that takes care of the sin problem

seems to have little effect on the problem of human limits. Accepting the finished work of Christ makes us clean, but it doesn't make us God.

Christians today are as overloaded, indebted, and unfocused as the rest of our worn-out, fast-paced, secularized culture. What effect does this overly congested life have on the people of God? Once our limits are exceeded, we become too busy to pray and to serve. We become too exhausted to nourish our relationships. Irritability poisons our attitude, as burnout lurks around every corner. Even God has trouble getting our attention, receiving instead a busy signal.

Recent studies reveal that it takes twenty to thirty phone calls in the average church to get the same number of volunteers it used to take two or three phone calls to get; 85 percent of Christians admit they do their main praying or their only praying "on the run;" 70 percent of pastors have a lower self-image now than when they entered the ministry. A denominational leader told me: "The pastorate used to be a low-stress, high-reward job. Now it is a high-stress, low-reward job."

Surely, this is not the way to live our faith, nor is it the best way to advertise it before a watching world. It is time to conform our pace and lifestyle to the God of the Scriptures.

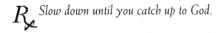 *Slow down until you catch up to God.*

———∞∞∞———

Take what you want, God said to man, and pay for it.
SPANISH PROVERB

# CONTENTMENT AND RELATIONSHIPS

*Simple people with less education, sophistication, social ties, and
professional obligations seem in general to have somewhat less
difficulty in facing this final crisis than people of affluence who
lose a great deal more in terms of material luxuries, comfort, and
number of interpersonal relationships. It appears that people who
have gone through a life of suffering, hard work, and labor, who
have raised their children and been gratified in their work, have
shown greater ease in accepting death with peace and dignity
compared to those who have been ambitiously controlling their
environment, accumulating material goods, and a great number of
social relationships but few meaningful interpersonal relationships
which would have been available at the end of life.*

ELISABETH KÜBLER-ROSS, M.D., PSYCHIATRIST

---

PERHAPS ONE REASON God commanded contentment is
because He knew we would need it to anchor right relationships.

*We relate better to God* when we are satisfied with what He
gives. We might say words of worship, but if our heart is not
resting in the contentment of His presence, He is not fooled.
We are contented in God's presence, not because of the money
and possessions that He gives us, but because we know He
accepts us despite ourselves and He loves us more than life.

*We relate better to self* when contented with our circumstances. If allowed to write a prescription redesigning our
body, personality, or station in life, most of us would grab at
the chance: smarter, funnier, richer, better looking, taller,

thinner, more athletic. Yet none of these requests would be an issue were it not for our comparisons with others.

If we were all alone with God—which, in regard to contentment, we are—we would have a different set of values than the one society offers.

*We relate better to others* when the relationship is stabilized by contentment. If every encounter with my neighbor reminds me of something I covet, that relationship becomes tenuous. Envy makes it hard to have friends: everyone I know has something I do not.

*We relate better to family* when contentment anchors the bond. How often have we seen the devastation visited upon families through the "if only" syndrome. Emotional margin is an early casualty with such discontent as: "If only my wife were more appealing or more sexually interested"; or "If only my husband made more money or had more hair"; or "If only my children had that kind of talent." Infidelity, even in thought, is greener grass only because it's been spray painted by the Deceiver himself. Contentment keeps our eyes on the right side of the fence.

 *R* *Defer to God's opinion concerning your relationships, especially the family. Show an easy acceptance of people, a warmth that attracts. If you wish grace for yourself, grant it to others. Determine to be content as an act of the will. Right feelings will follow.*

⸺⟊⸺

One who looks for a friend without faults will have none.
<small>HASIDIC PROVERB</small>

# LIVING OUR VISION

*I don't know where we are going or how we will get there, but when we get there, we'll be there. And that's something even if it's nothing.*

S. J. PERELMAN, HUMOROUS ESSAYIST

VISION HAS LANGUISHED under the stressful and over-loaded demands of our modern age. When dodging bullets on a nanosecond basis it is hard to feel in a visionary mood about the long haul. But vision is important for both direction and hope. Can we articulate a vision of authentic kingdom living that can transcend our free-floating chronic randomness?

A vision is not an arbitrary string of verbiage constructed to fill a vacant morning at the corporate board retreat. It is the foundation for our thoughts, actions, and values. Therefore it is not enough to have a vision—we must also *live* it.

As a part of this vision, we will see God clearly, and understand that He is good and that He is love. We will understand that He is a God who cares, who changes hearts, who redeems pain, and who works in history. We will understand that He is drawing all people; He is reconciling the world to Himself; He is building His church. We will understand that He holds both our present and our future; He has given us a foundation on which to stand that is unmovable and unshakable.

As a part of our vision, we will understand that we are broken, empty, and vulnerable, yet hopeful, redeemed, and thoroughly forgiven. We are ambassadors of reconciliation and witnesses, equipped with truth and love, gifted with the Word, the Spirit, and the mind of Christ.

As a part of our vision, we will commit to love the Lord, ourselves, and one another. We will seek first His kingdom. We will seek to guard our unity and to resolve conflicts. We will seek to nourish and protect relationships. We will seek to build the kingdom, telling others the good news with "gentleness and respect."[115]

God's ways are vindicated in every social experiment ever conducted. His advice always turns out to be the healthy option. We have assurance that our biggest problem — larger than all our other problems added together and multiplied by infinity — has been solved. We know forgiveness, we know grace, we know hope. We know love, we know truth, we know the Cross, and we know the Savior of the Cross.

Such a vision is staggeringly comprehensive, and the only vision capable of carrying us all the way Home.

*R* *Reach higher than tomorrow, higher than the basement, higher than your moods, and higher than your appetites. Find transcendence in the kingdom of God and determine to live there — even when it is lonely and even when culture isn't helping. It will be the right decision.*

———⊗⊗⊗———

Men see only the present; heaven sees the future.
CHINESE PROVERB

# CONTINUE EXERCISE UNTIL THE HEARSE ARRIVES

*A bear, however hard he tries, grows tubby without exercise.*

WINNIE THE POOH

---

IN THE CONTINUOUS battle to gain margin, your body can be an asset or a liability. Once you embark on an exercise program, a myriad of temptations and excuses will arise to bump you off course. Don't quit.

*Fatigue*—Many complain of being too tired. But when you feel too tired to exercise is actually a good time to do it. Paradoxically, you often will feel *less* tired after the workout than before. Several nurses at one of the hospitals where I work go to the exercise lab after a long day on the wards. Are they tired? Of course they are. But do they feel better after working out for a while? Do they have a more energized, productive, and enjoyable evening? Yes.

Have you ever noticed how you can come home fatigued, only to see the exhaustion disappear soon thereafter when doing something enjoyable? I specifically remember one evening being very tired but needing to mow the lawn anyway (something I normally enjoy doing). After fifteen minutes I was surprised to notice that the tiredness had disappeared. Studies suggest that often fatigue has its source in emotional rather than muscular or cardiovascular exhaustion—although this is not to deny the validity of muscular tiredness as well.

*Waning enthusiasm*—Another reason for wanting to quit is decreasing enthusiasm. You begin to wonder why you ever started this training program. Don't worry—it happens to everybody. Just keep going. Eventually your enthusiasm will return.

*Discouragement*—The feeling arises that all this effort isn't doing any good. What you don't realize is that it *is* doing good—you just can't fully sense it yet. Approach exercise as an investment. If you don't begin to receive dividends within two months, you have my permission to quit.

> ℞ *Commit to the long haul. You can't store up energy or the benefit of exercise for the future. If you exercise six months for cardiorespiratory fitness but then stop, within two weeks the benefits will begin to fade. Once you begin a program, plan to maintain it in at least some form for the rest of your life. Continue it until the hearse arrives. If that sounds like a big commitment, maybe that's because it's a big commitment. The majority of recommendations in this book for restoring margin have to do with sustainable lifestyle changes rather than "momentary compliance."*

———※———

If you go slowly you will go far, if you never stop.
BASQUE PROVERB

# LOOKING UP

*The universe is but one vast symbol of God.*
THOMAS CARLYLE, SCOTTISH HISTORIAN

———————————

SOMETHING ABOUT THE heavens leads to thoughts of heaven. There is one sense in which the night sky is God's response to our questions and fears. "Lift your eyes and look to the heavens," wrote Isaiah. "Who created all these? He who brings out the starry host one by one, and calls them each by name. Because of his great power and mighty strength, not one of them is missing."[116]

The universe is a vast, rich, and beautiful place. It is both comforting and fear-inspiring. Every molecule and every magnetar speak of God. All throughout Scripture we read how God forged His creation and then indelibly stamped it with His glory.

Partly, the hand of God is seen through beauty. Aesthetic sensitivity and harmony were not necessarily a given. God *decided* on beauty. Sunsets and stars, northern lights and meteor showers, blue oceans and green forests . . . we should rightly be grateful that God ordained such elegance.

Partly, the hand of God is seen through power. In the beginning, God spoke and the universe showed up. Out of nothing—*ex nihilo*—He made something, a combined mass of a trillion trillion trillion trillion tons of matter. The extensive power of gravity that holds it all together, the concentrated power of nuclear fusion that fuels the stars, the awesome power of supernovas, quasars, and gamma ray bursts—His might is on lavish display.

Partly, the hand of God is seen through precision. There can be little doubt to any objective observer that the universe was indeed a behind-the-scenes, fully manipulated effort by a detail-oriented genius. Our planet's requirements for sustainable life were impossibly and narrowly defined from the beginning: not too much mass or not too little mass; not too far from the sun or not too close to the sun; not too far from Jupiter or not too close to Jupiter. The gravitational force had to be precise. The number of stars in the universe had to be precise. The exquisite fine-tuning of the entire created order reveals God's immeasurable attention to detail.

If He has displayed such beauty, power, and precision, why do we have such difficulty resting in His sovereignty? The abundant witness of a created universe leaves no rational excuse for existential insecurity. If we have a problem with spiritual confidence, it is not from God's lack of revelation. Let the record show: God is impressive.

*R Do not fret your weakness, for His strength is perfected in weakness. Do not bemoan your lowly estate, for He dwells with the contrite, gives strength to the weary, and lifts the humble. If your only hope is God, He will not fail to hear.*

❧

God hears things upside down.
<small>LEBANESE PROVERB</small>

# GOD HAS COME TO HELP

*If Jesus is coming again—which He is—perhaps we should
cancel a few more of our earthly involvements in order to
hear what He has to say about our times.*

DAVID BREESE, AUTHOR AND RADIO PERSONALITY

---

LET'S REWIND THE videotape four thousand years, back to
a time when people knew little about God. The Almighty,
shrouded in mystery, called Abram's name and led him to a
new land. As a result, he knew more about God than those
before him. Moses heard God speak in a burning bush, witnessed the miracles of the plagues, received the commandments, felt the mountain tremble, and saw God's glory. Then
he wrote it all down, and we began to understand God better:
that He was awesome and righteous, that He was concerned
with justice, and that He loved us.

Four hundred years later, God promised David an eternal
kingdom, and the plan of a messiah began to emerge out of the
mystery surrounding God. A millennium passed. Then, in the
greatest unveiling of mystery since creation, a baby was born.
That event changed everything.

With the birth of Christ, God now lived and breathed in
our midst, walked and worked at our side. But even this Jesus
was often mysterious, speaking in cryptic parables. Yet it was
impossible to conceal that there was something different about
this Man.

By allowing the world to see Jesus directly, God opened

wide a window. Now we could glimpse all the way into the eternal. Those who surrounded Christ experienced His words and power firsthand: seeing His miracles, hearing His wisdom, feeling His compassion.

Those who walked with Christ were consistently amazed and overwhelmed. Their hearts burned. It was surely an incomparable experience. Here was powerful, almost irresistible, evidence of the nature of God—a deity who could cure illness, conquer death, and rule time, space, and matter. He was unjustly accused, wrongly condemned, and brutally crucified. Yet when He climbed back out of the grave, He wasn't even mad! What kind of messiah was this? He was, said Malcolm Muggeridge, the kind of messiah who ruled from the cross.[117]

We were not there, of course. But God made provision for us to listen in. Through the Gospels we read that the people were filled with awe: "A great prophet has appeared among us," they said. "God has come to help his people."[118]

Is there not a message here for our anxious age? Just because He visited villages two thousand years ago doesn't mean He won't visit your living room today. Just because He had compassion on the ancient oppressed doesn't mean He neglects the modern oppressed. Just because He healed then doesn't mean He healed *only* then. The same Jesus who stopped for the blind beggar will stop for you. Anytime, anywhere.

*R Stop depending so much on careers, cash, and cars. Depend instead on "Never will I leave you; never will I forsake you."[119] If you ask "Why?" ask again in a thousand years.*

⊷⊶

If God were not forgiving, heaven would be empty.
BERBER PROVERB

# PRIORITIES FROM OUR DEATHBED

*To know you're going to die, and to be prepared for it at any time.*
*That's better. That way you can actually be more*
*involved in your life while you're living.*

MORRIE SCHWARTZ, *TUESDAYS WITH MORRIE* BY MITCH ALBOM

---

THE DEATHBED HAS a way of focusing our attention as nothing else. Our relational failures and successes are suddenly magnified, and we wonder how all the distractions of busyness could have obscured what has now become so obvious.

While still in my training, I was called to the Intensive Care Unit bed of a dying man. He was perhaps sixty-five years old and bleeding from the neck. My job, at midnight, was to stop the hemorrhage. I talked with the nurse and glanced quickly at the chart. He was terminal, a neck tumor having eroded his carotid artery.

The scene was extraordinary. Surrounding this remarkable patriarch was his family: wife, children, and their spouses. Despite the blood, there was no hysteria. The patient was calm and alert. An oxygen mask in place, his eyes glanced lovingly from person to person around the bed. The family was gathered close, holding his hand, sober but not crying. Their eyes glistened; their mouths wore sad, affectionate smiles. They knew he was going to die and that it would probably be soon.

I put pressure on the neck wound. Not surprisingly, this caused stroke-like symptoms, which seemed to reverse within a short time after I relaxed the pressure. Eventually, the bleeding slowed. I was in the room for about an hour and then left, knowing I would be back.

Later that night, they paged me STAT. The scene was similar. The patient, waning yet alert; the family still in a tender vigil. But this time, the hemorrhage couldn't be stopped. His blood pressure dropped. He looked again lovingly at his family and died.

There was something unforgettable and deeply moving about this experience. It was, of course, medically dramatic. But beyond that, I felt an awesome privilege to be in attendance as this man said good-bye. I knew few details of his life, yet it was apparent he had lived without relational regrets.

When I lie on my deathbed, I don't want to hide behind the excuse of overload. I want to be able to look my family in the eye, each one, and say, "I love you." And I want the experience of my life to confirm those words.

Overload distracts us from the true meaning of life. Overload distracts us from love. And in the end, excuses don't hold up. The choice, it turns out, has always been ours.

$R$ *Write down your priorities, but do it as if from your deathbed. Keep short accounts, including no record of wrongs. Reconcile quickly. While you yet have time, budget time and energy for the people who matter most. Say what you have to say without delay.*

---

Death is God's broom.
<small>SWEDISH PROVERB</small>

# FLOWERS FROM THE GRAVE

*If I can put one touch of rosy sunset into the life of any man*
*or woman, I shall feel that I have worked with God.*

GEORGE MACDONALD, NINETEENTH-CENTURY SCOTTISH AUTHOR

---

EILEEN WAS SIXTY-THREE years old and already had advanced cancer when I first met her. After surgery there was little that could be done. She healed nicely from her operation but then developed a persistent cough. "It is probably the tumor, Eileen," I said. "We should get a chest X-ray."

"No, doctor," she replied. "I don't want to know." Soon, however, her shortness of breath left us no choice but to investigate.

"Eileen," I said. "Your X-ray shows fluid. We can make you more comfortable by draining some of the fluid off. It doesn't hurt much, and you should be able to breathe easier."

Under normal circumstances, tapping the lung is followed by an X-ray to make sure the lung has not been punctured. But after three uneventful taps in the clinic, I decided to deviate from protocol and do the procedure in Eileen's home. By now she was having difficulty getting around.

Each time I entered the room, I would sit on the bed and we would talk. Then I would examine her lungs, prepare her for the procedure, and introduce the needle into her chest.

On the third visit I held her hand and together we looked out the open window. Each sensed the end was near. "Those are beautiful lilacs," I said, noticing for the first time the flowers hardly a foot outside her open window. The room was full of their fragrance.

"Lilacs are my favorite," she replied. "That is why I wanted to be down here, close to them." After draining another quart of fluid off her lung, I left the house for the last time. A week later she died.

After her death Eileen's daughter brought a huge bouquet of purple lilacs to the clinic. She asked the receptionist to bring the flowers to my office, explaining that it would be too hard for her to see me just then. This was the note: "Words seem inadequate to express our thanks for all you have done for our family. Because of your kind, caring ways Mom was able to stay in her home and be as comfortable as possible. Mom wanted the 'Best Doctor in the World' to enjoy her special lilacs. God Bless You!"

I have received many expressions of thanks from the relatives of deceased patients. But this was the first time I had been given flowers from the other side of the grave.

I certainly am not the "Best Doctor in the World." But for a moment I felt like it. Medicine can be a grinding profession when money is the only reward. But when love is the currency of exchange, gratitude alone can pay the debt in full.

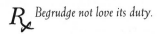 *Begrudge not love its duty.*

---

Love is returned where love is given.
KOREAN PROVERB

# NOTES

1. Hebrews 13:5.
2. Slogan in a MasterCard ad.
3. Acts 20:35.
4. Quoted in Daniel J. Boorstin, *The Discoverers* (New York: Random House, 1983), p. 25.
5. Boorstin, p. 39.
6. Harper Lee, *To Kill a Mockingbird* (New York: Little, Brown, 1961), p. 10.
7. Leo Tolstoy, *War and Peace* (1869; New York: Washington Square Press, 1963), pp. 430-431.
8. Quoted in Cynthia Crossen, "Americans Have It All (But All Isn't Enough)," *The Wall Street Journal*, 20 September 1996, R1, R4.
9. See Colossians 3:14.
10. Advertisement of Digital Alliance for Enterprise Computing, *The Wall Street Journal*, 26 April 1996, B7.
11. Advertisement of Lucent Technologies, *The Wall Street Journal*, 17 March 1997, A9.
12. Peggy Noonan, "There Is No Time, There Will Be Time," *The Wall Street Journal*, 18 September 2001, www.WSJ.com.
13. J. I. Packer, "The Secret of Contentment." Address given 27 February 1984 at Wheaton College, Wheaton, Illinois.
14. Jeremiah Burroughs, *The Rare Jewel of Contentment* (1648; Aylesbury, Great Britain: Hazell Watson & Viney Limited, 1987), p. 19.
15. Bob Benson, *"See You at the House," The Very Best of the Stories He Used to Tell* (Nashville, Tenn.: Generoux Nelson, 1989), p. 211.
16. Psalm 127:2.
17. Alan Lightman, "A Cataclysm of Thought," *Atlantic Monthly*, January 1999, pp. 89-96.
18. Anthony Smith, *Intimate Universe: The Human Body* (London: BBC Books, 1998), p. 152.
19. Darold A. Treffert, M.D., *Extraordinary People: Understanding Savant Syndrome* (New York: Ballantine, 1989), pp. 1, 59.
20. Genesis 2:3.

21. Deuteronomy 5:15.
22. Edna Hong, *The Nostalgic Almanac* (Minneapolis: Augsburg, 1980), p. 106.
23. E. F. Schumacher, *Small is Beautiful: Economics as if People Mattered* (New York: Harper & Row, 1973), p. 154.
24. Schumacher, p. 33.
25. Hebrews 13:5: "Keep your lives free from the love of money and be content with what you have, because God has said, 'Never will I leave you; never will I forsake you.'" Here contentment is commanded, and discontent is thus a sin.
26. Mark 12:29-31.
27. Matthew 6:34.
28. Psalm 37:1-8.
29. Philippians 4:6.
30. Psalm 37:1-8.
31. Philippians 4:6.
32. Matthew 6:34, from the Sermon on the Mount.
33. John Charles Cooper, *The Joy of the Plain Life* (Nashville: Impact Books, 1981), pp. 27-28.
34. An interview with Dr. James Dobson, "The Family in Crisis," *Focus on the Family*, August 2001, p. 4.
35. Galatians 5:22-23.
36. Joseph Katz, ed., *The Poems of Stephen Crane* (New York: Cooper Square Publishers, 1966), p. 102. Originally published in Stephen Crane's book of poetry *War Is Kind*, 1899.
37. John and Mary Schramm, *Things That Make for Peace: A Personal Search for a New Way of Life* (Minneapolis: Augsburg, 1976), p. 87.
38. Philippians 4:4.
39. "Wise Woman," *Physician*, September/October 1996, p. 22.
40. Arthur G. Gish, *Beyond the Rat Race* (New Canaan, Conn.: Keats, 1973), pp. 73-74.
41. Psalm 8:5 and Hebrews 2:7.
42. Colossians 1:17.
43. Larry Crabb, *Understanding People: Deep Longings for Relationship* (Grand Rapids, Mich.: Zondervan, 1987), p. 163.
44. James 4:14.
45. Psalm 39:5.

46. 2 Corinthians 4:17.

47. A. W. Tozer, ed., *The Christian Book of Mystical Verse* (Harrisburg, Penn.: Christian Publications, 1963), p. 14. This poem, "The Thought of God," is composed of fourteen stanzas, of which only two are quoted here.

48. Anna Quindlen, "Playing God on No Sleep," *Newsweek*, 2 July, 2001, p. 64.

49. Brigid Schulte, "Living Large," *Saint Paul Pioneer Press*, 19 October 1997, p. 4A.

50. Annie Dillard, *Teaching a Stone to Talk: Expeditions and Encounters* (New York: HarperPerennial, 1982), p. 52.

51. 1 Timothy 6:6.

52. Hebrews 13:5.

53. Philippians 4:12.

54. J. I. Packer, "The Secret of Contentment." Address given 27 February 1984 at Wheaton College, Wheaton, Illinois.

55. Richard Blackaby and Henry T. Blackaby, *Spiritual Leadership: Moving People to God's Agenda* (Nashville, Tenn.: Broadman & Holman Publishers, 2001), p. 205.

56. See Psalm 34:18.

57. See James 4:6.

58. See 1 Corinthians 13:5.

59. Isaac Asimov, "In the Game of Energy & Thermodynamics: You Can't Even Break Even," *Smithsonian*, June 1970, p. 10.

60. 2 Corinthians 10:5.

61. Philippians 4:8.

62. Barbara Reynolds, *Dorothy L. Sayers: Her Life and Soul* (New York: St. Martin's Press, 1993), p. 369.

63. John R. Cameron, James G. Skofronick, and Roderick M. Grant, *Physics of the Body* (Madison, Wis.: Medical Physics Publishing, 1999), p. 276.

64. Gordon MacDonald, *Ordering Your Private World* (Nashville, Tenn.: Oliver-Nelson, 1985), p. 126.

65. Dietrich Bonhoeffer, *Life Together* (New York: Harper & Brothers, 1954), pp. 79-80.

66. Roy McCloughry, "Basic Stott: Candid Comments on Justice, Gender, and Judgment," *Christianity Today*, 8 January 1996, p. 25.

67. A. W. Tozer, *The Pursuit of God* (Harrisburg, Penn.: Christian Publications, 1948), p. 17.

68. See Isaiah 25:4.

69. Nguyen Thi An, "A Letter Written to Vietnamese Friends in Canada," *Alliance Witness*, 10 December 1986, p. 17. (A fictitious name has been used to prevent any additional hardship to the family.)

70. Matthew 13:14; see verses 13-17.

71. Matthew 11:28.

72. 1 Corinthians 13:5.

73. Charles Dickens, *Bleak House* (1853; Boston: Houghton Mifflin, 1956), p. 665.

74. Elaine N. Aron, *The Highly Sensitive Person: How to Thrive When the World Overwhelms You* (Secaucus, N.J.: Birch Lane Press, 1996). The highly sensitive person has been well described by psychologist Aron in this book. For purposes of symmetry I write that both highly productive people and highly sensitive people are 10 percent of the population, on different ends of the personality spectrum. Aron, however, concludes that HSPs are 15 to 20 percent of the population.

75. Matthew 11:28-30.

76. Cameron, Skofronick, and Grant, p. 146.

77. See Daniel 5:23, RSV.

78. Psalm 150:6.

79. See John 15:13.

80. Robert Banks, *The Tyranny of Time: When 24 Hours Is Not Enough* (Downers Grove, Ill.: InterVarsity, 1983), p. 247.

81. Nancy Yanes Hoffman, "Meyer Friedman: Type A Behavior Cardiovascular Research Continues," *Journal of the American Medical Association* 252 (1984), pp. 1392-1393.

82. John 13:15-16.

83. 1 Peter 2:21.

84. Philippians 2:5-7.

85. Tom Allen, "Living Like the King," *The Alliance Witness*, 10 June 1981, pp. 4-6.

86. Mildred Tengbom, "Harried Lives," *Focus on the Family*, October 1985, pp. 10-12.

87. George Croly (1780–1860), "Spirit of God, Descend upon My Heart."

88. 1 Corinthians 13:12.

89. Psalm 62:5-6.

90. Romans 12:2.

91. Psalm 103:13.

92. Matthew 9:36.

93. John 16:33.

94. Alvin Toffler, *Future Shock* (New York: Bantam, 1981), pp. 252, 257.

95. Bonhoeffer, p. 99.

96. John 15:13.

97. C. S. Lewis, *Mere Christianity* (New York: Macmillan, 1952), pp. 148-149.

98. Hebrews 13:5.

99. See 1 Timothy 6:9-10.

100. A. W. Tozer, *Born After Midnight* (Camp Hill, Penn.: Christian Publications, 1992), p. 62.

101. 1 Corinthians 1:21.

102. Luke 12:15,20.

103. A. W. Tozer, *The Pursuit of God*, p. 22.

104. Doug Trouten, "Discontent Is the New Spirit of the Age," *Twin Cities Christian*, 13 September 1984, p. 6.

105. See 1 Corinthians 12:31.

106. See John 14:15.

107. Isaiah 40:31, KJV.

108. Psalm 37:7.

109. Psalm 130:5.

110. Gordon S. Jackson, ed., *Quotes for the Journey* (Colorado Springs, Colo.: NavPress, 2000), p. 174.

111. Titus 2:11-12.

112. Thomas R. Kelly, *A Testament of Devotion* (New York: Harper & Brothers, 1941), pp. 123-124.

113. Philippians 4:11-12.

114. A. W. Tozer, *The Pursuit of God*, p. 20.

115. 1 Peter 3:15.

116. Isaiah 40:26.

117. Malcolm Muggeridge, *Jesus: The Man Who Lives* (New York: Harper & Row, 1975), p. 74.

118. Luke 7:16.

119. Hebrews 13:5.

# INDEX

(These numbers refer to the reflection number)

# AUTHOR

RICHARD A. SWENSON, M.D., is a physician and futurist with a B.S. in physics Phi Beta Kappa from Denison University. After having taught at the University of Wisconsin Medical School for fifteen years, he currently conducts research and writes full-time about the intersection of culture, health, faith, and the future. He is the author of *Margin, The Overload Syndrome, Hurtling Toward Oblivion,* and *More Than Meets the Eye.* Dr. Swenson and his wife, Linda, live in Menomonie, Wisconsin. They are the parents of two sons, Adam and Matthew.